CARON

COMEBACK FROM TBI

C. J. TEAHAN

Gotham Books
30 N Gould St.
Ste. 20820, Sheridan, WY 82801
https://gothambooksinc.com/
Phone: 1 (307) 464-7800

Published by Gotham Books (September 1, 2022)

ISBN: 979-8-88775-041-5 (h)
ISBN: 978-1-956349-54-2 (sc)
ISBN: 978-1-956349-55-9 (e)

To all of my students who loved my stories and to Caron, who *lived* this story and is willing to share it with families who may be living it now—to whom we *both* dedicate this one.

To protect their privacy, all patient names and their family's names have been changed.

The names of a few hospital staff members have been changed, and some are mentioned by position only, not by name; but most have been retained in respect for the high quality of care my daughter received at the hospital and from these professionals in particular.

The names of our family members, friends, neighbors, colleagues, etc., have been retained in appreciation to them for their support and help.

"Far better it is to dare mighty things . . . even though checkered by failure, than to rank with those spirits who neither enjoy much nor suffer much, because they live in the grey twilight that knows neither victory nor defeat."

—Theodore Roosevelt

CONTENTS

PREFACE

A teacher by profession, I learned quickly that no two students are alike; nor are any two families. Each individual and every family has needs and problem solving strategies, as well as a multitude of other distinctions, that differ from those of every other individual and family. Therefore, State Boards of Education can mandate that every student learn certain curricular material at an identified percentage of accuracy, but no two students will learn it to the same depth of understanding, and no two families will view and put to use the results with equal appreciation. *Our nature, as human beings, is to be unique.* Yet we continue to establish norms to be expected of people in every conceivable situation.

My daughter suffered a traumatic brain injury in an automobile accident and while she lay comatose, seemingly without a care in the world, her family was thrust into the abrupt nightmare of a head injury's effect on a family. In addition to our grief, disorientation, and feelings of inadequacy, we would feel the burden of medical personnel and perhaps others in general expecting us to manifest a preordained series of emotions in reaction to Caron's tragedy. Yes, we would exhibit many if not all of those emotions, but perhaps not in the expected sequence and sometimes to lesser or greater degrees than the norm, or average. Didn't anybody tell *them* that I am a unique human being and that my family too is like no other?

One of the characteristics setting me apart from the majority of people is that I am not an auditory learner, and while I learn things better when I see them, I'm not especially a visual learner, either. I learn tactilely, kinesthetically: messages traveling to my brain are most likely to take up residence there if they enter by way of my fingers, rather than solely my eyes or ears. In other words, if I want to retain what I see or hear, I must write it down—so I'm most often seen with a pad of paper and a writing utensil in hand.

For almost two years beginning the day of my daughter's accident, I was never without a couple of pens and a thick college-ruled notebook. In the years that followed, my notes unfolded into a manuscript. Because I'm tactile kinesthetic, just writing the story was therapeutic for me and I was able to set it aside and move on. But over the years a number of friends have read it and have urged me to get it published because "it would help so many other people going through this . . ."

Now it is a considerable number of years after this story played out within our family and our community. You'll find evidence of this in my mention of coin phones, privately owned pharmacies, tape recorders and tapes . . . and people actually using the yellow pages of their phone books rather than tapping into the Internet. I've intentionally included these references to keep reminding you that this story is someone else's, not yours. I hope you will never experience a head injury in your family. If you do, however, I want you to be sure to realize that your ordeal will not be the same as ours. Just as no two students are alike, no head injury looks or acts like any other, and no family will respond to it in like manner or with cookie cutter results.

For most people, notification of a family member's head injury may as well launch them into another galaxy, for all they know about head injuries. This was the situation in which I found myself on the day my daughter sustained a closed head injury, slipped into a comatose state, and became a patient in SICU, where words like angiogram, laparotomy, and disseminated intravascular coagulation were being hurled into my auditory space and I was visually bombarded with sights of numerous unfamiliar apparatuses, all of which were somehow connected to various parts of my daughter. The scenery was frightening, the local lingo was indecipherable, and the white-gowned aliens speaking it from behind their masks didn't seem to be able to communicate in any other way. How was I to find out what I needed to know? and what *did* I need to know?

I was not afraid to ask questions, even "dumb" ones, although I was boggled by a cacophony of divergent responses from the various medical personnel, and this often led to more questions rather than definitive answers. Then I spent hours in the medical library of the hospital, looking up the terminology that had been applied to my Caron. In this book, as I tell my daughter's story, I reduce to simpler terms the medical jargon I encountered. Often, when a loved one has suffered a head injury, such ingenuous explanations are all that one can comprehend. Later, as needed, one can delve deeper into the more thorough meaning and the finer nuances.

I owe a tremendous amount of credit and thanks to David M. Gamm, MD, PhD, now a doctor and researcher at University Clinic and Waisman Center in Madison, Wisconsin, and a professor at the University of Wisconsin. When I had completed the first draft of my manuscript, I appealed to him to evaluate the second through ninth chapters for medical inaccuracies. While I wanted the text to be a comfortable read for people not in medical fields, I did not want to disseminate ideas that were not correct! He was very thorough in his written notes, vastly expanding my comprehension of the instruments, procedures, and outcomes pertinent to Caron's care in the SICU. If any errors remain in the text of this book, those would be attributable to my inaccuracy in re-wording Dr. Gamm's enriching lessons, not to Dr. Gamm's explanations themselves.

But this book is not *about* medical terminology, which is merely included in small doses in just seven of the first nine chapters. Rather, this book is about is a young girl's journey from the confusion of awakening from unconsciousness to understanding the ramifications of an insult to her brain and, finally, to her struggle to emerge from this nightmare and piece her life back together again. It would never be the same, but it is possible for someone with strong motivation and an equally determined supportive family to pull a triumph out of a tragedy.

Every year, in our county, often around commencement time in late May and early June, there are accidents involving young people in our local high schools. Medical technology has advanced to such sophistication that many youth who may have died some years ago are now being saved and families are now caring for family members who have suffered traumatic brain injuries. I would suspect that, across the United States, there are probably few high school graduates who have not been touched by the trauma of a classmate involved in an accident. This book will be helpful to such families and to high school students, for several reasons: 1. While it is a true story, most of it reads like a novel, so it is a gentle introduction to the world of head injuries. 2. It shows that, despite the initial trauma, there are sometimes happy endings to stories about friends' and family members' head injuries. 3. The story can be adapted to include all head injuries—whether from vehicular accidents, on-the-job accidents, gunshot wounds, falls, cardiac arrests, physical abuse, near drownings—and whether the loved one is a daughter or son, a spouse, a parent, or any relative or friend with whom one is closely bonded.

I made some mistakes as the main family caregiver in my daughter's TBI rehabilitation, only through love for her and to further her interests as best I understood them. I also did many things in a way that was right for Caron (but may not be the correct methodology for all persons with head injuries). I hope that you will learn from my mistakes and also from the things that worked to Caron's advantage as she wended her way back to a life of her choosing. What is most important, I believe, is to give voice and action to your thoughts about your loved one's care. When it works, keep at it! When not, move on to something else.

I also pray that you will glean from these pages ways that you can help others who may suffer a head injury, either now or in the future, and their families, who especially need your support at such a time.

Above all, enjoy the story! Laugh and cry with the Schreer and Teahan families as we muddle through adversity and emerge, eventually, still united, with our sanity mostly intact, and continuing to laugh as often as possible.

CHAPTER 1

"YOUR DAUGHTER HAS BEEN HURT IN AN AUTO ACCIDENT."

Unseasonably warm for January in Michigan, the sun peeking invitingly between the heavy drapes, the day prematurely beckoned me to arise. After all, I argued back from that comfortable place between the sheets, it's Saturday, and the time-consuming task of completing report cards at the end of the first semester is behind me, so I deserve the luxury of sleeping in—but the sun was just too inspiring and settled the argument. I've always been envious of people who could sleep in, but my lot had been cast early as a morning person, and a morning so bright as this one was not to be denied.

Larry had been up much earlier, not by physical choice, for he is one of those blessed with the disposition and ability to sleep in. Rather, his early arising was due to a love of swimming and a joy in imparting this passion to others. In addition to his duties as a social studies teacher, he coaches swimming at his high school. This morning there was a swim meet in a town thirty-some miles southwest of us, but Larry had had to make the half-hour drive to his high school east of us first to accompany the team on the school bus.

As I trekked to the bathroom, I stopped at the front living room window and pulled open the drapes, quickly surveying the street. It was free of snow, and cars were passing by at the speed limit, so I continued on, past the staircase, through the foyer, and into the half bath on this main level of our two-story home. Because ours is the first house inside the city limits, the bathroom window offers a vantage point for viewing two other types of road conditions: county roads, which begin at our driveway, and an expressway, which the county road crosses just beyond. For nineteen winters in this house, checking road conditions had been my first official act each morning, but never had my assessment been so intense as it was this winter, for this was my daughter's first year behind the wheel of a car. I was relieved this morning to see that the county road, which was usually not cleared so quickly as the city street, was in good condition, no snow having fallen the night before, and the expressway traffic beyond was moving smoothly.

I could hear the click of makeup containers and the *pshhhht* of an aerosol spray can upstairs, the finishing touches on a teenager's face and hairdo. Caron, always the early riser, had already showered and was nearly presentable. Earlier, she had been down to iron her new plaid slacks and the blouse she'd wear under the sweater that picked the hot pink color from the slacks. In a few minutes, I knew she'd bound down the stairs again, rattling her keys, and utter a quick but cheery good-bye—if anyone happened to be nearby to hear it. So I lingered near the bottom of the staircase, busying myself winding the iron cord and beginning to fold the ironing board, which Caron had left in the living room, when I remembered the new certificate of deposit that I had opened the day before in preparation for college years. I had brought home the bank's proprietor signature card but had forgotten to have Caron sign it, so I retrieved it now and set it on the ironing board with a pen, in hopes of obtaining the signature before she left.

Despite her enthusiasm, Caron was less rushed than she sometimes is in the morning and had time not only to sign the card but also to chat for a bit as she donned her new coat and scarf, pulled on her gloves, and preened before the mirror in the foyer, pulling long golden curls out from under her collar. She was thrilled to have earned a place again this year in the Livingston County Honors Band, and this morning she would drive to the next town northwest from us for the second of three practices this weekend, culminating in a concert Sunday afternoon. She was chattering excitedly about a new friend she'd made in the Brighton High School band. She always had so many friends that it was hard for me to keep up with all their names, and while Lauren was a name I recall having heard, it had only been recently. I didn't remember having met this girl, and now Caron was relating to me that she'd be picking Lauren up this morning for the band practice. Early in Caron's driving career, we had established that passengers were an unnecessary distraction, and that on rare occasions when she felt a need to offer someone a ride, we wanted to know about it beforehand. So now she was dutifully reporting such details as first and last name and address; but she had been driving for over six months now, always responsibly, and I'd relaxed somewhat on the passenger issue. Consequently, I didn't commit to memory the information she was giving me. And now, noticing the time, she said good-bye, gave me a little peck on the cheek, and left smiling, oboe and music in hand.

After watching her car disappear over the expressway overpass, I too glanced at the clock and made a mental assessment of the time that was still mine this morning. My son's soccer team had an indoor match in Farmington at eleven, and it would take a half hour to get there, so Matt would need to be awakened by nine thirty. Before leaving for the soccer match, I could shower and dress and still have the better part of two hours to read textbooks for a couple of graduate classes I was taking.

I was engrossed in the study of recursion in the computer language, LOGO, when the telephone next to me rang. Pencil poised in hand and the text open at page 71 in my lap, I jumped, startled by this intrusion. Who would call the home of teachers and teenagers so early on a Saturday morning? "My name is Teresa Pugh," came the answer to my unvoiced query. "Your daughter has been hurt in an auto accident."

CHAPTER 2

"DO YOU KNOW THE PASSENGER'S LAST NAME?"

S o poised was the voice I couldn't see, that it didn't occur to me that this was something more serious than a fender-bender, giving Caron a scratch or two or, at most, a broken arm. The textbook's print still swimming before me, I calmly penciled on page 71 the directions to the scene of the accident, then reached for the keys in my purse, in preparation to go help my daughter file the police report and make arrangements for car repair. I was relieved that a close friend of the family had talked us into an older model car for Caron, a car with a sturdy frame under its outdated appearance. At the slightest collision, the newer compact cars compliantly accordioned, as for crating.

"Do you know the passenger's last name?" the voice continued. Why didn't she just ask Lauren? or Caron? *or wasn't this possible?* The impact of this question sent a shot of adrenaline pulsating through me, and I was out the door and on the road immediately. Did I even remember to say good-bye or thank you? Did I hang up the receiver? These questions played interference on more urgent ones plaguing me as I pushed the car to a speed it didn't know it could reach. Where traffic and pedestrians weren't present, I ignored stop signs, red lights, "no turn on red"—whatever was in the way of my destination.

It was an eternity before I spotted the flashing lights, yet it had been not quite three miles, and in fewer than that many minutes. A crowd had gathered, their abandoned cars strung out along the shoulder and blocking my view of whatever lay ahead. I screeched to a stop at the end of the line and had to run a considerable distance, all the while searching, searching, but not finding the object of my search, that pea green antiquity that Caron affectionately called Bart. It wasn't here. This was the wrong accident! Her car wasn't here. Running toward the confusion, I had caught the attention of a state trooper as I started to shout, "My daughter—" But in realizing that this couldn't be the right place, I had stopped midsentence, pivoting for the return dash to my car.

"Are you Mrs. Schreer?" the question followed me. *No, my name is Teahan*, I thought. My daughter's name is Schreer. But how would he know that? This was the place! Where was Bart?

Spinning to face the trooper, I focused more coherently on the crowd beyond him. They were gazing downward. Now I spotted the car—or the remains of what had been one. It was lodged in a marshy area at the bottom of a steep embankment dropping from the road's shoulder. The driver's side door was scrunched around a tree—the only tree for a quarter of a mile in either direction. (Additionally, weeks later, I would discover that this was the only embankment alongside the eleven-mile stretch of road between Brighton and Howell—and there was no guard rail. Following Caron's accident, a guard rail was installed. Now the entire area has been filled in to accommodate a new housing development.)

Caron's car, totaled, viewed at the dump

While one could still see the resemblance of a pea green automobile on the passenger side, the driver's side was so thoroughly smashed that it was inconceivable that anyone seated there could have lived. Coupled with this realization was the *fait accompli* of Caron's seat belt allegiance: I couldn't even delude myself by hoping that perhaps she'd been thrown clear before the crash. No, she was dead. My daughter was dead. I froze, my body paralyzed by the weight of this realization, but my mind still racing. *How does one handle this?*

"Your daughter is on her way to McPherson Hospital in Howell," the trooper's voice broke my paralysis. "You should proceed directly there." Nearly reaching my car, I remembered that I'd forgotten to inquire after Lauren, and out of the corner of my eye, as I'd turned from the trooper, had I seen a completely covered body on a stretcher being brought up the embankment? Suddenly everything became real, and I was ashamed to have been so thoughtless. Again I raced to the scene of the flashing lights, catching the same trooper as I tried to catch my breath. "Lauren,"

I begged, "how is Lauren?"

"Lauren. Lauren?" He seemed confused. "Yes, Lauren! Is she dead?"

"Oh, Lauren! No, she's fine." Simultaneous to his understanding came mine. It was at that moment that the stretcher I'd previously been unprepared to acknowledge neared the top of the embankment and was passing us. A black and hot pink plaid pant leg sticking out from under the blanket caught my eye, and what followed was the bloodied face of a young girl, probably recognizable only to her mother. Whatever shock, denial, or functional paralysis had incapacitated me dissipated instantaneously. There was no room now for myself, no time. This child needed a mother. No one else knew her. Whoever else I was vanished as I stepped out of emotion and into whatever levelheaded action was now needed from Caron's mother.

"May I speak to her?" I inquired respectfully of the trooper.

His responding gesture indicated a "why not?" but he quickly reconsidered and gently motioned me to wait as he stepped ahead to ask the paramedics, who were now lifting the stretcher into the ambulance. "NO!" screamed the female paramedic emphatically, and then repeated, "NO!"

"Meet them at the hospital," came the trooper's interpretation. Helpless, I again retraced the steps to my car, this time in no hurry. I was reluctant to leave, as Caron was still here. I continued to brace myself for her death, as it looked inevitable, and I just wanted to be with her. But already, I could stand in the paramedics' shoes and understand two things: Their duty was, thank God, to Caron, not to me. And they couldn't perform their functions so effectively with a hysterical mother in the way. No doubt, hysteria was more common than not among family members at scenes like this one. They had no way of knowing that I would be different.

My car moved out of the line of curious onlookers' cars and into the westbound traffic lane, creeping past the crowd and the flashing lights of the police cars and ambulance. Now I averted my attention to the rearview mirror. Expecting the ambulance to pull out any second, I wanted to be ready to pull over and let it pass with its precious cargo. Why didn't it pull out? What were they doing back there? Plagued with the fear that Caron would die in the ambulance, I could not proceed directly to the hospital as I'd been instructed. First, I needed to know that the ambulance was, indeed, going there.

Just ahead, there was a boat dealership—and a telephone booth out front. I pulled in next to the booth. I could still see the flashing lights from here. Determined to keep busy while standing sentry, I deposited a quarter into the phone and pressed some numbers.

When I'd received the call at eight forty-five from Teresa Pugh, she'd asked the passenger's last name. But if Lauren truly were fine, as the trooper had said, she could have given her own last name. Her parents needed to be notified. What *was* her last name? Caron had told me less than an hour ago, but I couldn't remember. Who would know? Ah yes, now I recalled Caron telling me that Lauren was a very good friend of Karen Herbst. Karen's father owned the pharmacy we frequented in Brighton, and Caron worked there a few hours a week, so I knew the number by heart. When Bob Herbst's voice came on the line, I spilled out the necessary details and asked the question about Lauren's last name. Right off hand he didn't have it either, but he assured me that he would find it and call the parents. I was confident that this would be his top-priority mission until accomplished. This man had invented the words "community service" in Brighton. To the very best of my knowledge, he's never failed anyone.

The next call was to Matt. I told him what I knew, which wasn't much, and asked that he stand by for further updates. At fifteen, his life was soccer, and he voiced perturbation with me that I wouldn't commit to taking him to his soccer match. I couldn't very well take exception to his not grasping the gravity of this situation, when less than a half hour before I had at first responded to the notifying call with thoughts of "fender-bender." No doubt this was the point at which my son was now, and his point of view was further exacerbated by his being a teenager, up earlier than teenagers usually arise on Saturday mornings, and faced with the aggravation of a thwarted goal. I suggested that it was still early and he could probably find a ride with a teammate if he was determined to go.

The ambulance remained stationary. There was nothing I could do. Resignedly, I got into my car, started it up, and steered it onto the highway. I crept along Grand River toward the hospital, which was less than a mile short of Howell High School, Caron's original destination this morning. When I arrived, I exited my car quickly, and as I approached the desk just inside the emergency entrance, the sight of a familiar face mollified my anxiety considerably: here, at the volunteer desk, was my friend, Mary Schild, a close teaching colleague, her classroom next door to mine. The ambulance had not arrived, so I had no "duties" for the time being. Mary's presence enabled me to relax a bit. I didn't yet know the full weight of unremitting responsibility, but already I could welcome a momentary respite from it. Mary brought me some personal care items, including tissues and a toothbrush, which I'd requested. Not too many years ago, Mary had been through what I was now going through, with her own daughter, who had not lived, just as I feared Caron would not. Mary knew all the right things to say and do. In this short wait, which seemed agonizingly long at the time, I thanked God for this ray of light in what had otherwise turned out to be a very bleak morning. In time to come, God's grace would be shown again and again through countless other people, the next of whom would be Caron's band director.

Freshened up, thanks to Mary, I was able to watch the ambulance's arrival with more appreciation than apprehension. Anxiety would return soon enough as I sat in the waiting room—waiting for what? There was no news, no news, no news. Mary, a visitor information volunteer on Saturday mornings, wasn't allowed in the emergency rooms, so there was no way for me to get information about what was going on in there. An hour is interminable when one is waiting for the unknown. The best I could do was to keep busy so as to make the time appear to pass more quickly. I called Larry at the Charles Cameron Pool in Chelsea, but there was no way he could get away, as he'd arrived there on the school bus with the team.

Soon, Carl Klopshinske arrived. He was Caron's band director, affectionately called Mr. K by all. As it turns out, Teresa Pugh, who had placed the phone call that rerouted my day, was a trumpet player in the Brighton band and had been en route to the same honors band rehearsal as Caron. In fact, she had been behind Caron all the way through Brighton and for the three miles beyond—to the scene of the accident. After making the phone call, Teresa had continued on to Howell High School to alert Mr. K about what had happened. He immediately left the rehearsal to the other county band directors and came right away to the hospital, where he was a great comfort to me. As he waited with me, he encouraged me to make some phone calls inquiring about Lauren, and we were able to determine that she had gotten out of the car independently and, while obviously shaken, appeared to be uninjured. Her parents had somehow been contacted and had taken her to McPherson-McAuley Health Center in Brighton for an examination. Muscular aches, as well as bruises from her seat belt, would be with her for a while, but she was otherwise physically unhurt, praise God!

A new concern arose with the arrival of the trooper who'd been at the accident. According to him, Caron had been speeding.

Normally fairly objective about my children, recognizing always another side to the story, I was at once defensive now. The trooper surely thought me one of those overprotective and annoyingly enabling parents. Superimposing the "not my kid" syndrome, however, was the reality of the highly mature degree of responsibility my daughter had carried from an early age. Most recently, it was she who had convinced me, a claustrophobic, to wear a seat belt, and she who lectured me whenever my speedometer needle advanced too far to the right, or whenever I had but one glass of wine with dinner. This kid, sometimes tiresomely opinionated, was one who, to a fault, abided by rules. She had not been speeding. It was urgent to me that I impress this upon this trooper. There was nothing else I could do for Caron at this time. The least I could do was protect her reputation. Fortunately, Teresa had come with Mr. K to the hospital, and she now spoke up: She'd followed Caron for over three miles, and as her own speed had been fifty-three (in a fifty-five-mile-per-hour zone), she knew Caron's to be that, also.

Furthermore, she said that Caron had slowed almost to a stop at the yellow blinking light at Sylvan Glen Mobile Home Estates—just beyond which was where the accident had occurred. It had to have happened as she was accelerating to resume speed. I've tried it many times since that day, and there is no way that a car that had just come "almost to a stop" could have been speeding where Caron's car left the road.

Later that morning, I talked with Lauren on the phone. She confirmed that they'd slowed almost to a stop at the yellow blinking light and that it was when they were accelerating to resume speed that the car found a melting frost spot on the road and "went onto the dirt on the side of the road. Caron was scared, but she did everything right. She got the car off the dirt there, and then she was afraid she was going into the other lane, so she corrected that, and that's when . . ." Lauren was understandably upset and couldn't continue. We determined that it was at that point that Caron lost control of the car. It skidded off the right side of the road, turning 180 degrees in the process, for when it was stopped by the tree at the bottom of the embankment, it was the driver's side of the car that took the full impact. Caron sustained a severe blow to the left side of her head, which mangled her left ear . . . and what else? When would they tell me how she was?

Both Mary and Carl were with me when someone came in to give me a preliminary report: Caron was conscious at the time of the accident—moaning, not talking, and head injuries were suspected. She was now unconscious, but moving all extremities. Vital signs were good: they were monitoring blood pressure. She had been intubated for breathing. Chest tubes had been inserted, right and left. IV lines had been established. She had been brought here to be stabilized, but they would be airlifting her to St. Joseph Mercy Hospital in Ann Arbor.

I called Larry again, and he had arranged for transportation. I told him to meet me at St. Jo's. And now that I knew "something," I called Caron's father in Arizona. With the time change, this call intruded on his Saturday morning more prematurely than the phone call I'd received earlier. He was calm and said to keep him posted.

Meanwhile, the Howell band director had arrived, talked with us for a while, and taken Teresa back to the practice with him. Now the helicopter was here. I felt I'd put in at least a full day already, but it was only 10:30 a.m. I'd been asking to see Caron, and hospital staff had been consistent in their refusals. Now that preparations were being made to take her away by helicopter, and I'd not be allowed to accompany her on the flight, I implored them once more, voicing assurance (which may not have compared to my demeanor) that "I'm not a hysterical mother. I feel she needs to know that she's not alone in this. I simply want her to know that I'm here."

They were reluctant, but relented when, as they tried to forewarn me of the gruesome scene in the ER, I responded, "I saw her at the accident. I know what she looks like. I need to let her know I'm here with her." But I surprised even myself when, in the ER, I was able to take her hand, hold back the tears, keep my promise of composure—and even interject a little humor into the one-sided conversation: "Hey, sweetie! You get to ride in a helicopter, lucky you! I've never been in a helicopter! You'll be at St. Jo's in twelve minutes! It's going to take me closer to an hour to drive there!"

Mr. K refused to let me drive. He insisted on taking me to St. Jo's. We started right away, as it would take us considerably longer than the helicopter. Before we'd even traveled as far as Brighton, the helicopter passed us overhead.

CHAPTER 3

"YOUR SON IS HURT."

A ll hospitals should have a "Valerie service" with their emergency rooms. It's very reassuring for the helpless waiting family—and must relieve other hospital personnel of incessant interrogations (for which they usually are not privy to the answers anyway), not to mention the load off the doctors, already overburdened. Larry had arrived as I was finishing giving the receptionist the insurance information required, and he and Carl and I were ushered into a private consultation room, where we were assigned our own private liaison to the emergency room. What a wonderful idea! Valerie went in and out between the emergency room and our private consultation room, getting answers to our questions and supplying us with little tidbits of other information—nothing, really, but tremendously reassuring to us: Caron was alive and receiving ongoing care.

The time passed quickly with regular bulletins, and it didn't seem long before Valerie was moving us to a new location: consultation room 1 off the critical care waiting room. Caron was ready to be released from the ER to the SICU (surgical intensive care unit), which meant that she was ready to undergo surgery. Valerie bid us good-bye and good luck. We'd really miss her in the next hours, as there would be no Valerie counterpart between surgery and our new location.

A doctor arrived to inform us of an exploratory laparotomy, surgery needed to arrest abdominal bleeding. I signed the consent form. The surgery was to have taken about two hours, but it was over four hours later before anyone came to tell us anything. We were restless but thankful to have been joined by the pastor of our church and one of the members of the congregation, who had heard about the accident from her daughter in the band, then called our pastor. I had also made a few phone calls—the first of which was to Caron's father, who promised to be on the next plane to Michigan. Other calls made were to close friends who live near us, to arrange for someone taking Matt in for the evening, and for someone to feed and walk the dog, as we might not be able to make it home.

Somewhere in the anguishing wait came the second adrenaline-stirring phone message of the day. This time I could enjoy no momentary calm, as I was now a veteran at responding to emergencies. The message, "Your son is hurt," prompted an instant image of myself spending eternity racing back and forth between two hospitals, for my mind was stuck in the rut of thinking that the only possible cause of bodily injury is an auto accident. Matt must have found a ride to his soccer match and had been in a crash. Hospitalization would have been elsewhere as St. Jo's is not in the direction he'd have been traveling. What more was God going to ask of me? Could I handle this? I thought not.

Fortunately, God never gives us more than we can handle if we just trust in Him. Matt had, in fact, made it quite safely to his indoor soccer game, whereupon he injured his ankle in his first play of the game. So when our friend, Mark Benner, arrived to pick up Matt as per my call for help, he had had to take him first to our family doctor, where Matt was put in a half-leg cast and given directions, "Come back next week when the swelling goes down, and maybe we'll give you a *full* cast!"

Now Dr. Ranval, first assistant to the surgeon, had arrived to report on the surgery, which in fact had been completed two hours earlier, but Caron had subsequently been taken somewhere else for an angiogram. I could tell already that I was going to learn a lot during Caron's stay in this hospital. (*Angiography*, we learned at a much later date, is the broad term denoting visualization of the heart and surrounding arteries via injection of a radio-opaque dye and subsequent x-ray photography. More specifically, the diagnostic procedure used on Caron was an arteriogram, because the dye was injected into an artery.)

Dr. Ranval explained that they had found Caron's spleen to have been ruptured (from the pressure of the seat belt), so they had performed a splenectomy: they had removed it. Without a spleen, he went on, she would be at a slightly higher risk for pneumococcal strep and other bacteria (because the spleen is an instrumental organ in the immune system); so she'd need penicillin whenever her teeth were worked on, and people would need to know that she had no spleen if she ever got an infection of any kind. The greatest risk would be in the next two years. Also, she would need regular vaccinations, but he admitted that medical sources were still not certain as to what "regular" was; and I forgot to ask, vaccinations of *what*? Presumably penicillin; but in any case, she'd just had one, so a regular revaccination would be down the road a piece, time to ask later. For now, I was trying to absorb something Dr. Ranval was saying about their having discovered that Caron had three other teeny-weeny spleens (one-to-two-centimeter "accessory spleens"), a phenomenon found in about 15 percent of all people. They're also sometimes referred to as "satellite spleens." While these probably would not be of much practical protection to her, they wouldn't hurt either.

Next, Dr. Ranval told us of more "disturbing things" that they'd found. There was a bruise on the upper part of Caron's neck (left side), so they had done an arteriogram to determine if there was any internal injury. They had found that the left carotid artery to her brain had a small tear in it (in an inner wall of the artery). Further, there was no way to reach it surgically. The immediate risk was stroke. If she did not suffer a stroke at this time, the next time of risk would probably be in six or seven days. (Whenever there is a loss of integrity—or break—in an arterial wall, the body's response is to close it with a blood clot. If this clot becomes too large, it may break off and float into the brain vessels, become lodged, and cut off the blood supply to the part of the brain normally served by the blocked brain vessel—thereby causing a stroke.

The risk of stroke is both immediate and delayed: if the body doesn't respond immediately with a massive clot, then a smaller clot could be slowly added onto until it reaches a significant size to break off. This could happen in six or seven days, and sometimes a little longer than a week.) Alternatively, the carotid artery could be tied off, but this was a more drastic technique and wouldn't be considered except as a last resort, as a life-saving technique. (Tying off the left carotid would guard against a blood clot entering the brain from there, and because she was a young person, with more resiliency in her vessels than an older person, it could be expected that the right carotid artery would compensate for the loss of the left by carrying more blood to the brain. However, the surgery itself offered risk of stroke.)

Dr. Ranval felt that heparin, an anticoagulant (medication which blocks the formation of blood clots), would be helpful, but they couldn't put her on full-dose heparin because she had "too much else going on": she had DIC (disseminated intravascular coagulation), mildly, which he explained as meaning that "clotting and anticlotting are out of whack: she's not clotting where she should be but *is* clotting where we don't want her to be."

A computerized tomography (CT) scan had been done, and Dr. Ranval's summary of Caron's neurological condition included "some brain swelling"—part of the treatment being "we dehydrate her a little bit." He was careful to be positive and never did say "brain damage." I would learn at a later time, when I'd be better able to accept it, that swelling, or edema, can cause neurological damage (developing at some time after the injury itself), because the skull does not allow for expansion of the brain. This would compound the brain damage Caron had sustained in the accident impact, when her head had hit the window support frame. To further assess damage, she was scheduled for another CT scan between 7:00 and 9:00 p.m.

When she'd been taken into the operating room, she was demonstrating purposeful movement. It had been necessary to medically paralyze her during the laparotomy, splenectomy, and arteriogram to immobilize her muscles, as she was trying to pull out the tubes they had inserted.

At some point in his review, Dr. Ranval used the words "hopefully wakes up." I don't remember in what context, but the words made an impact, and I jotted them down in my notes. Having seen the car, I couldn't comprehend how Caron could live; yet I couldn't really accept that she might die, either. Though stated in the kindest and most encouraging way, the words "hopefully wakes up" were, in effect, the first indication from someone in a position to know that the possibility was there that she might not. While a sadness crept into some of the parts of me, which had up until now held only fear of the unknown, I was thankful for Dr. Ranval's honest evaluation, and for his patient explanations of so many terms that were new and foreign to me. I've heard many times that ignorance is bliss, but the state of not knowing is torturous for me, to the point that even sadness is a relief. To be able to combat the enemy, one must know who or what the enemy is. Caron was in a coma, from which she might or might not wake up. The medical experts were doing their best for her. Much remained in God's hands. There must be something I too could do to help. In the days to come, ways to help would show themselves to me and to many others who loved Caron.

It had been late afternoon before Caron had completed her tours of the emergency, surgical, and radiology units at St. Jo's and was returned to the SICU. It was late afternoon before Dr. Ranval left consultation room 1 of the critical care family room. And just minutes after his departure, here was another doctor bearing yet another consent form for surgery: Dr. Austad was the plastic surgeon assigned to care for Caron's left ear. He too was very kind, but I was beginning to get the picture that hospital news was destined to be bleak: he didn't know how much of the external ear would survive, so my consent to surgery would include the possibility of amputation if he met with too much dead tissue. At a later date, I learned that the original diagnosis had, indeed, not been hopeful—the ear described as *resembling raw hamburger*.

This surgery was done at Caron's bed in SICU, and before an hour had passed, Dr. Austad himself returned to report that no part of the ear had been removed, but that we'd have to wait and see how the body would accept the parts that had had to be reassembled and reattached. A lot of dead tissue had been encountered, and there was no guarantee that the ear would live, because the body treats dead tissue as foreign and tries to break it down and eliminate it from the body.

Word traveled fast in Brighton, and we were not lacking in visitors to help keep our minds occupied as Caron went in and out of surgeries, procedures, and CT scans. More women came from the church and more band parents. Two volunteered to rescue my car from the McPherson Hospital parking lot and to bring it to St. Jo's. Caron's oboe teacher came, anguishing almost as much as I over Caron's tragedy. One of Larry's sisters came to offer her support, and the following day both sisters teamed to retrieve Larry's car from the Novi High School parking lot, where he'd left it to board the school bus to the swim meet. My good friend Merry Jane Benner stopped in, offering the warmest empathy one could possibly receive at a time like this, and I was thankful that Matt would be in such loving care tonight. Everyone was so kind. But eventually they had to go home to their families. Before long, even the doctors went home, and we were finally allowed to sit by Caron's bedside.

Each patient on SICU is assigned a primary nurse, who is the patient's main caregiver and who does all the record keeping, as well as selecting which nurses will take her place when she is off duty. Laurie Kadish, an angel disguised in a nursing uniform, was assigned to be Caron's primary nurse. Laurie was to have gone off duty at 7:30 p.m. and had a husband and small daughter waiting for her at home, but so conscientious was she that at 8:30 p.m. she was still there, completing Caron's chart and giving instructions to Jeri, the nurse who would take over for the night.

I felt the hospital go to sleep around me. Lights dimmed. Footsteps in the corridors ceased. Only the hum, bleeps, and drips of the various apparatuses to which Caron was connected continued. Physically exhausted but mentally alert, I sat in the darkened room holding Caron's hand until at eleven Jeri finally ordered me to go get some sleep. Fortunately, this hospital complex included an attached hotel, the McAuley Inn, for the purpose of accommodating patients' families, and Larry had already checked us into a room. Because of the nature of the hotel and its composite of residents, it was very quiet here, and under other circumstances would have been most conducive to sleep, even for an insomniac like me. Tonight, however, I could little appreciate the conditions, and as I lay in the dark wrestling with sleep in one sense, in another sense I was struggling to wake up from a horrendous nightmare.

CHAPTER 4

"I WANT YOU TO KNOW MY DAUGHTER IS HERE."

Mesmerized by the lighted dial of the bedside clock as the nightmare raged within my tensed body, I could not sleep, and 1:00 a.m. found me retracing my steps back to the SICU unit. During the day, the main floor of the hospital was filled with hustle-bustle as visitors scurried in and out bearing gifts and flowers—or made a hasty stop at the hospital gift shop across from the elevators before pressing the elevator call button. Ambulatory patients often wandered down here by day for exercise, to buy candy bars or personal articles, or to visit with friends and relatives in the large sunny lobby. Patients with a dietician's pass took their meals in the bustling cafeteria, with visitors and hospital personnel, instead of in their rooms. But now the cafeteria wafted forth no smells—either to invite one in or send one hurrying in the opposite direction. Day-use offices along the way were closed, locked, dark. The long, wide hallways were lit but deserted. Even in tennis shoes, my footsteps echoed back at me.

On the second level, in the area of the intensive care units, there were occasional signs of activity, but only those necessary to sustaining life. When I pressed the large metal plate outside the surgical ICU, the doors swung open noisily, signaling an intrusion to the nurses and patient-care aides within. Jeri poked her head out of Caron's room and waved me in. Thankful to have been admitted, I sank quietly into the chair in the corner. *There must be visiting hours here*, I thought, *and surely they don't include 1:00 a.m.! I must make myself invisible.*

I watched as Jeri busied herself checking all the equipment that had become a vital part of Caron, just for the time being, I tried to reassure myself: the respirator whooshing its oxygen-rich air into Caron's lungs, the oscilloscope monitoring Caron's heartbeats, the IV tubes (intravenous lines) that kept the fluids coming in, the catheter tube and Foley bag to dispose of urine drainage, the chest tubes and Pleur-evac for chest drainage. How frightening it all was, even more so in the eerie calm of night—and, still, how very reassuring. If any monitored part of Caron ceased to function or anything went amiss with any of the machines, bells would ring and people would come running to help.

When Jeri had completed her equipment check, she left the room. I moved to Caron's bedside and took her hand in mine. Hers was so cold. I rubbed it, trying to revive her circulation, and then the other hand. She didn't stir. I covered her hands with the sheet and made a mental note to ask Jeri for a blanket. Then I leaned on the bed rail and just watched. It was the middle of the night. Jeri's only direction before leaving was that I let her sleep. *She'd slept all day!* I thought. I was impatient for her to wake up. But I wouldn't interfere. I'd just watch quietly.

I studied my little girl's face. Nothing. I couldn't find peace there. But I didn't see a struggle, either. Emptiness. I wanted to pray but wasn't sure what to pray for. I prayed that God hold Caron in His grace and that His will be accomplished. I hoped His will was the same as mine and that a miracle would happen here. I couldn't imagine—and didn't want to—life without this child.

There was nothing attached to Caron's head at this point, although the possibility of implanting a monitor in her head to measure intracranial pressure had been discussed earlier on Saturday evening. She did have on a neck brace, as it had not yet been determined if there had been any injury to her neck or spinal cord. And her wrists were tied to the bed rails to prevent her from pulling out tubes. I knew from what Dr. Ranval had told me that this was necessary, as Caron was making purposeful movements; but I ached for her, for her loss of independence. I don't really understand people who are *inherently* calm and easily contented. Larry was an enigma to both Caron and me: we admired the tranquility he modeled, but we were unable to pattern after it. Caron, like her mother, had always needed elbowroom—some space for creativity, some room to be different, to try new things, to explore things others might think out of reach or unimportant. Without question, Caron would not approve of these wrist constraints if she were to awaken tonight. Oh, Caron, please wake up!

Jeri was back. It was 2:00 a.m., and she told me I should leave in ten minutes and go get some sleep. Perhaps she knew that would be impossible, for she has two little ones of her own; but as a nurse, she also knew that mothers must be forced to take breaks, for their own physical and mental health, if they are to be of any future use to their children, after all. Later in the day, when Laurie was back, I'd ask when visiting hours were on this floor. Laurie would tell me, "Ten minutes at eleven, ten minutes at one, ten minutes at three, ten minutes at five, and ten minutes at seven . . . but we make exceptions." It seems that I had already passed the tests of invisibility (when the nurses were busy in the room) and perceptivity (about when to get out).

I was surprised to awaken at 5:00 a.m. So I had fallen asleep after all! But the nightmare was still with me. I hadn't been able to shake it. I pulled on my blue jeans and sweatshirt and ratty gray tennis shoes, dashed some water on my face, and quick-stepped back to the SICU. All still quiet. For a short time. By six, the corridors would be filled with doctors making their rounds. Caron would have so many looking in on her that we wouldn't be able to learn all their names. One trio of residents that would be quite regular we would nickname "Smith Et Al; or Smith, Et, and Al." Well, such is the destiny of residents who neglect to wear their name pins and overlook the courtesy of introducing themselves to the patient's parents.

The doctor in whom we were most interested was the consulting neurosurgeon, Dr. Farhat. He was most elusive, and no matter how tight the shifts Larry and Ron and I would set up in the days to follow, Dr. Farhat most usually seemed to slip in and see Caron when we weren't there. It was frustrating to us, as we held great reverence for this man and really wanted to hear his prognosis from his own lips. The unanimous appraisal of the nurses was that he was a man of few words, apparently shy in oral analyses—but that Caron was in the best of hands. Having missed him this morning, we had asked the nurses to tell Dr. Farhat that we'd like to speak with him. He did contact us by phone later in the morning and, true to the nurses' words, he was short on prose, but we were cheered by his message: the heparin and hyperventilation were working well—the swelling in Caron's brain was beginning to lessen—so the monitor implantation didn't seem necessary at this time.

I sat with Caron most of this first of many Sundays that she would spend in this hospital. Larry took up a position in the critical care waiting room, where visitors had to check in. The SICU, for obvious reasons, did not encourage visitors other than family, but family members could bring anyone they wanted to bring into the patient's room. We decided at the outset that we wouldn't allow any visitors except family and a few people very close to the family. We didn't want to take any additional chances that Caron might contract a complicating illness such as flu. Also, we felt it our responsibility to protect her dignity. She wouldn't want people looking at her as she now looked. Many people came, and we visited with them in the waiting room. We were grateful not only for the relaxing diversion from our bedside watch but also for the knowledge that Caron was obviously well loved. I wrote down every name of every visitor and saved every card and letter sent to her so that she could bask in this love later, when she woke up. Additionally, this secretarial work gave me something to do, something to take my mind off the tragedy that had struck not only Caron but our entire family and those close to Caron and to us as well.

Waking up from a coma is not, we would discover, like television portrays it. I wanted Caron to open her eyes, focus on me, and say, "Hi, Mom! Where am I?" That's the way it happens in the movies! In fact, however, that's not often how it happens in real life. (Keep in mind that movies are usually only about two hours long, so actual events must be speeded up, sometimes at the expense of reality.) A coma is a deep state of unconsciousness that may last hours, days, months, or even years. In coming out of a comatose state, a person may respond to touch or sound along a fairly predictable scale from generalized to localized to varying degrees of confusion and agitation and appropriateness. This is referred to as "lightening" and is indicative of the patient's increasing cognitive functioning. It does not happen instantaneously but, rather, over some amount of time, which differs from patient to patient and is not predictable. Loved ones must wait without knowledge of for how long or for what.

The family that prepared to wait for Caron included her stepfather and me; her father, having flown in from Arizona; her brother, Matt; and Mr. K, who would be Caron's most reliable visitor and supporter. He was already here, helping Larry to field telephone calls, take messages, and entertain visitors in the critical care waiting room, when Ron and Matt arrived. Matt wielded his crutches well already, but he was unprepared for the sight of his sister, one year his senior, in a coma. In self-defense against the bossy blond toddler at our house, Matt had learned competitiveness at an early age; and in his fifteen years, he'd always envied his sister's seeming evermore a step ahead of him. In fact, despite her being older, he was forever catching up and occasionally even surpassing her—in height, strategy games, spelling skills, math logic, athletics. But if he realized these things, it was never quite enough. He wasn't secure that he measured up. Yet he did find some comfort in the guidance of an older sibling. It was Caron—not our educational system—who, through "playing school" with him, had taught him to read; Caron who taught him that possession is nine-tenths of the law; and Caron who protected him from his fears (such as snakes, spiders, toads, and mice, which didn't bother her in the least!)—and from hurts: she was quick to protect him from potential offenders and danger and to help him when he suffered real hurts—even the ones for which she was responsible. But who would protect him now? Certainly not this helpless lifeless girl. Life would be harder for Matt now. There was inevitably going to be a role reversal, and he'd had no preparation for it. Head injuries do this to families: they hurt everybody, not just the brain-injured one.

Younger brother smiles after older sister wipes away his tears

The Livingston County Honors Band Concert was to be at three this afternoon. Caron's father and brother felt it important that she be represented there. I walked them to the waiting room area and said good-bye and thanks. They departed for Howell, where Ron would speak to the band and audience alike, saying, "I want you to know that my daughter's here. And she'll always be here with this crew."

If one dreams or thinks while in a coma, surely Caron would have been willing herself there that afternoon. I returned to her room, wondering if persons in comas were able to hear or feel or think or remember. When she came out of the coma—however long from now that would be—would she remember anything said to her or done for her during her time in SICU? I decided not to take any chances. On even the remotest of possibilities that some cognition was taking place—and might even be fostered—I decided to bombard this little gal with stimuli during her convalescence. During every moment that should have been one of her waking moments, I would talk to her and treat her as if she were awake and listening. Perhaps deep inside her, someplace, she would hear or sense that people who loved her were calling her back.

Laurie was a step ahead of me. She had posted a sign above Caron's bed:

My name is Caron.

**Please talk to me when
in my room and caring for me.**

I thrive on positive strokes.

She asked me to write some specifics about Caron so that interested staff could learn some things about her and choose conversational topics of interest to her. I wrote the following:

Hear ye! Hear ye!

When Caron becomes conscious, she will want answers to these questions:

1. **How is Lauren?** (Lauren was the passenger in the car Caron was driving when the car hit a frost spot Saturday morning, 1/28.) Lauren got out of the car on her own two feet and was uninjured . . . and Lauren still praises Caron for her level-headedness and conscientious driving!

2. **Where's my oboe?** It's safe. Lauren's mother took it home with her that day and has since returned it to us.

Extra! Extra!

In addition to being the solo oboist in the wind ensemble at Brighton High School, Caron

1. plays piano beautifully;
2. plays bells in the marching band;
3. is active in the Lord of Life Lutheran Church youth group;
4. manages the church nursery;
5. works part-time in a position of responsibility in a local drugstore (the pharmacy at Uber's);
6. speaks French well. She's visited in France twice, and in her senior year in high school, she'll be taking a French course at University of Michigan;
7. is an excellent student (all A's except a B+ in chemistry and a B in trigonometry);

8. earns 1s in social conduct/citizenship; and
9. is never too busy to help someone else who needs help or to extend a kindness. She's one super kid, and I will say so myself!

Caron's Mom

Laurie was already at work on the common philosophy at which we had each arrived independently. Intent on getting Caron's hair washed, she explained, "It can't be very comfortable having that blood-matted hair pulling on her scalp." Laurie had been impatient to get back the results of this morning's x-rays, hoping that the neck brace could be removed and a special hair-washing board slid under Caron's head; but after a wait of "too long," she decided just to go ahead with her mission, neck brace and all. "I'm compulsive this way," she laughed as she sponged hair in small areas at a time with a hydrogen peroxide-water solution. Afterward, she did the same with baby shampoo and, finally, with a water rinse. A lot of blood washed out—and not just a few shards of window glass. As I helped Laurie comb out Caron's hair (and was glad she'd gotten a haircut the week before), I joked with her that Caron had her own special brand of shampoo and wouldn't approve of the hospital brand Laurie had used. "Well," replied Laurie, "that's all the more reason for Caron to get better—so she can wash it herself with her own choice of shampoos!"

Speaking of choices, Matt had brought Caron's radio/tape recorder and a couple of her tapes, and Laurie put them right into service: teenage music, not my choice, but I resolved to get used to it. Larry teased Caron that if she didn't wake up soon, he was going to bring in some country music tapes. Ordinarily, that kind of threat would have gotten a rise out of my now-unresisting daughter.

Before going off duty, Laurie wrote an order allowing Caron's father and stepfather and me to go in and out of Caron's room at will, but she cautioned that we must extend the courtesy of asking any relief nurses if our presence would be acceptable to them before automatically entering. An important point to remember is this: nurses, like anyone else with expertise in a field, take pride in their domain and, as a rule, don't welcome intrusions but are quite receptive to people who acknowledge the territorial rights.

When Laurie introduced me to Cathy Kolpachi, the nurse who would take over for the night, my first reaction was alarm: "Oh, my! I'm going to have to stay awake all night watching over this sweet young thing!" Truly, she was probably still asked often to show her driver's license. Who would believe that she was out of *high* school, let alone nursing school? She was as cute as cute could be: dimples, sparkly eyes, and a long dark ponytail complete with a big bow. As she went to work, it didn't take long to see that she was as efficient and knowing and caring as she was darling. I put my mind at rest; we had, indeed, been blessed with fine nurses, and when I learned the next day that Cathy would be Caron's primary weeknight nurse (with Jeri working the weekend nights), I was thrilled.

Cathy's voice seemed especially appealing to Caron. She twitched more, and a softness came over her face when Cathy spoke. It was a voice very much like that of my sister, Caron's idol, Aunt Susie. In fact, this sweet young nurse looked a lot like my little sister too, except that Susie's hair is blond.

Cathy let me help give Caron her bath (in bed, of course), and I felt infinitely more useful than I remembered having been in thirty-some daylong hours. Wistfully, I remembered washing these same precious fingers and toes when they were wee ones. They were ever so much less cooperative then.

Ron arrived at ten, armed with enough entertainment materials to last the whole night through. I turned Caron over to him and retreated to the McAuley Inn room for my second night's stay. With her father sitting at her bedside, I felt more at peace and was able to sleep for a few hours.

CHAPTER 5

"THEY'RE NOT REAL DOCTORS YET, ANYWAY."

onday was Caron's third day in the hospital and the first day after her accident that her classmates would return to their classes at Brighton High School and she would not. I had talked with the high school principal on Sunday regarding rumor control. Anyone who was curious and had gone to view Caron's car would know that the accident had been a serious one, but I couldn't see any productivity in her friends' worrying. I asked that, in his morning announcements, he state, simply, that Caron was "stable and making good progress. The family asks for your prayers." I promised to keep him posted with regular updates.

This was also, for me, the first of I-didn't-know-how-many days of not returning to my class of first graders. So convincing are the movies' coma scenarios that I was still in a state of believing that Caron might wake up at any time and that I'd be back in school shortly thereafter. Some people call this denial. In truth, after shock, denial is a frequent reaction families of brain-injured patients go through, but I wasn't experiencing denial in the true sense of the word, for I simply did not know what to expect and didn't even know enough to formulate the right questions to ask. Fortunately, the principal of my school was able to enlist the services of a substitute on a week by week basis until my return. Still unaware of (or really denying?) the severity of Caron's injuries, I brushed off his words, "even through the end of the year, if needed."

Awake at 4:30 a.m., I showered and changed into some of the clean clothes one of the ladies from church had brought me, and I was back in room 2436, SICU, at 5:15 a.m. All was still and dark. Ron, a blanket wrapped around him, was asleep at the bed rail by Caron's right hand. I sat down quietly on the closer side of the bed, on a little footstool by the door. Soon, he awakened, for the unit was beginning to prepare for the doctors' impending arrivals: the intensity of the lights was increased and nurses' skirts and rubber-soled shoes whisked and squooshed in quick time up and down the corridors. "Brr! It's *cold* in here!" Ron began, then described the night he'd spent as (other than the cold) "delightful": Caron had been more active. Cathy would describe it as "lightening up." Cathy's voice continued to be a stimulant to Caron, and Ron had seen our little girl's eyes shoot open momentarily when Cathy was talking. At six o'clock, Cathy breezed in and went straight to the head of the bed with a sweet little cajole, "Caron, will you open your eyes for me?" as she routinely began to replace the near-empty IV bottle. Now I too witnessed Caron's eyes shooting open on command. And then, just as quickly as they'd opened, they closed, and Caron was out again.

Smith Et Al took this opportunity to arrive, gave our daughter cursory glances, and the spokesperson in the trio murmured that she was about the same. I must have looked terribly downcast, for as they were leaving, Ron remarked cheerily, "*You and I* know she's much better than yesterday. Who cares what *they* think? They're not *real* doctors yet, anyway!"

Real or not, it disturbed me that these men didn't talk to Caron while they were in the room. As a teacher, I'm well aware of the self-fulfilling prophecy, and I worried that because she appeared unreceptive, doctors might think her not worth their efforts. Certainly, if she were at all cognizant of her environment, their not talking to her would buttress her own feelings of nonexistence, if not also *their* feelings along this line. Laurie had forewarned us to never say things in the room that we wouldn't want Caron to hear. This being the case, shouldn't we then be *sure* to say things that we *would* want her to hear? I stepped over to the bed, took her hand, and greeted her with a cheery, "Good morning, Caron! It's Mom here. You look rested. It's a beautiful day outside. Just take a look out the window!" She didn't respond, but I didn't give up. Laurie and Cathy and Ron and Larry and I had decided upon aggressive support, and we intended to continue regardless of Caron's lack of physical response.

Next, the EKG machine was rolled in on a cart. Patients in ICU units are often monitored with electrocardiograms to determine if their hearts are functioning normally, so I wasn't concerned about this.

Ron waited two additional hours in hopes of meeting Dr. Farhat, but by 8:30 a.m., we were both betting that since this important doctor wasn't here yet, he would probably wait until after the scheduled 2:00 p.m. CT scan to make his assessment. So Ron left to take his turn at sleep and then to pick up our hobbling son from high school and go shopping for high-top tennis shoes for our girl: Laurie had suggested these to prevent drop foot over the end of the bed, and Ron had quickly volunteered to buy them. It would give Matt an opportunity to be helpful too.

Dr. Farhat walked in at about the time Ron would have been pulling out of the hospital parking lot, and Larry had just joined me. (He hadn't gone to school that day, wouldn't go for the next couple of days, and would even feel bad about going back on Thursday.) Dr. Farhat commanded Caron to open her eyes, and she did! Similarly, he induced movement of limbs. He told Larry and me that she was coming along well, but almost in the same breath he was talking about the crash impact and the resultant insult to the left hemisphere of Caron's brain. He was referring to the fact that she didn't move her right leg independently and that her right hand was not moving or grasping so readily as the left. Damage to the left hemisphere of the brain affects movement on the right side of the body and vice versa. On the other hand, damage to the brainstem often affects function on the same side as the insult. One example of this is eye movement. Whenever Caron opened her eyes, albeit briefly, they always rolled to the right. This indicated injury to the left side of the brainstem: the muscles that would control movement to the left were not receiving the correct signals, so the eyes always rolled to the right.

I worried all day: what other activities controlled by areas of the left hemisphere and left side of the brainstem might have been affected by the blow? I prayed that mental capabilities would not be among them. Later that afternoon, it was a nurse I'll call Fay who cleared up some things for me and eased some of my fears. Later, we would all come to pray that this nurse would be on duty somewhere *else*, or off duty altogether; but on this day, I was thankful for her presence. She was speaking to me of Dr. Farhat. I hadn't solicited this conversation. She had begun of her own volition and continued that we were so fortunate to have him and so lucky that he was making positive predictions about Caron, for all the nurses took note of his apparent gift of sixth sense: whatever he says seemed always to come true—and he'd only written positive remarks on Caron's chart, so "she'll be fine," Fay summed it up.

I etched those words on my heart, and they sustained me for days, even weeks, but now I questioned Fay about the meaning of this morning's report from the doctor. Yes, Fay explained, Caron had damage to her brain, just as she'd had damage to her shoulder: there was a bruise in each place. As a bruise gets better, she went on, there is increasing movement in that area. As the bruise on Caron's left shoulder healed, mobility in her left shoulder and arm would be enhanced. And as the bruise on her brain healed, mobility would return to her eyes, right hand, and right leg. This may have been a simplistic explanation and perhaps not totally factual. Brain "bruises" *don't* heal just like bruises on other parts of the body do. Brain cells, once damaged, never regenerate. Some brain functions can be re-tracked. Others cannot. This, we were yet to learn, is the reason that no one ever totally recovers from a head injury.

Also, we wouldn't understand until much later that the reason some improvements *are* seen over time, following a head injury, is that, while the direct specific area of the brain that is damaged is, indeed, dead, the *surrounding* area (which swells up, pinching neurons and causing them temporarily to stop functioning) is not dead. Because the neurons in this surrounding area weren't directly damaged or broken, these functions often do return when the edema (swelling) subsides. This type of recovery is sometimes very slow, making it appear that the patient is relearning things that were lost when, in fact, they were not lost at all.

Regardless of the simplicity of Fay's explanation and its straying somewhat from accuracy, I couldn't have understood anything more complicated at this time, and God knew I needed some encouraging words.

In our era of lawsuits, most hospital personnel are overly cautious not to say anything that might later be misconstrued as an unfulfilled guarantee—so our ears had been crying out for some positive words to fall upon them. Prior to this, about the most encouraging words I'd heard were from a Baptist minister, a personal friend, who'd visited the day before. I was telling him how Caron had always been a religious inspiration to our family—the person who got us up on Sunday mornings and dragged us off to church even when the sun was shining and we weren't so willing as usual. After the early service and the hospitality hour, Larry and

I would come home, but Caron stayed through the late service, because she managed the nursery during that hour. She was active in the church youth group, and within her circle of friends in the high school, she often found opportunities to witness for God. And so I'd bounced my theory off Reverend Swink: Wouldn't God want to keep such a fine ambassador as Caron here on earth? She had so much more work to do for Him! And the good reverend responded by saying, "Hang on to your hopes! Keep your faith! We're all praying!"

In fact, if prayers in and of themselves could heal, Caron was destined to walk out of this place in short order. We're Lutherans, and our entire congregation was praying for this special young lady that everyone knew and loved. Larry was Presbyterian before marrying me, and his Presbyterian friends were offering their prayers. The Benners were Methodists and had initiated a prayer chain in their church, as had Mr. K and our friends the Dentons and Crossmans at the Wesleyan church in Brighton. Reverend Swink had his Baptist church praying. We had good friends in the Episcopal and Nazarene churches too. Sister Mary-Therese on the hospital staff stopped by every day with her rosary, and St. Patrick's Church in Brighton was praying as well. Caron's stepmother is a Christian Scientist, her paternal grandmother is a Jehovah's Witness, my school principal is Jewish, and a family for whom Caron babysat is Mormon. All of them were pulling for Caron. It gave us a warm feeling of reassurance to know that in Heaven an ear was being bent so persistently.

Nevertheless, it's sometimes hard to hang on to your hopes and keep the faith when faced daily with increasing new concerns. On this particular morning, following the EKG, a cardiopulmonary person came in to do an echocardiogram—a technique utilizing ultrasound for the purpose of diagnosing lesions or physiological abnormalities of the heart. He instilled still further concern by voicing frustration that he might not be able to get good pictures, as he thought Caron had developed emphysema (a lung disease that decreases the elasticity of the lung tissue and thereby affects breathing). Soon after he left, a lung specialist came in; and later, he returned with an associate. These two said nothing to me, but left me with new dread.

Nothing ever came of the cardiopulmonary person's foreboding, and I never again saw the lung specialist or his associate, so after a while I relaxed regarding heart and lung injury. The presence alone of so many white coats is frightening. It would be helpful if they would simply identify themselves and succinctly state the purpose of their visit as "routine" or "precautionary" . . . or, for some, "unnecessary": the honesty might draw a much-needed smile.

Dr. Austad was encouraged by the healing he was already seeing in Caron's left ear. He wasn't yet making predictions, but his warm smile was encouraging, as were his words, "The longer the body continues not to reject the reconstructed tissue, the better the likelihood that the ear will survive."

The neck brace came off on this third day, and we were relieved that there were no spinal injuries. Now that the special hair-washing board could be used, Laurie washed Caron's hair again. Then she conveniently got tied up in paperwork, leaving me to comb out the snarls—an unpleasant job when the subject is a squirming child in a hurry; but now I had time on my hands and enjoyed the assignment, talking to Caron as I combed and combed, until her hair was nearly dry. Laurie had a knack for servicing both patient and parent in one simple gesture.

Not so Fay. When she took over for Laurie, who actually *did* have lots of paperwork to do, she lectured me on Caron's need for REM sleep, and from her tone and emphasis, I decided that REM sleep must be a euphemism for "don't touch or talk to the patient; patients are not to be stimulated for their own benefit, but only for the convenience of doctors' examinations and nurses' care." I sat dutifully on the stool all afternoon, not touching, not talking. It wasn't a very fulfilling afternoon for me, to be sure; but more importantly, I felt a loss for Caron: something inside me felt she really *needed* and *wanted* the stimulation. I just knew she could hear us and that she must be frightened and hurt and needing to know that we were there.

Larry and I left for a half hour and discovered a private restaurant in an adjoining office building. We would later find this place a welcome respite from hospital atmosphere, but in studying the menu our first day there, I lost my appetite: One of the entrées was called Bart's Best. My thoughts turned to Caron's now-trashed Dodge Dart, Bart.

Fay extended her coverage of Caron's room into Cathy's early-evening hours and made it clear that she didn't want anyone around when she was bathing Caron and tending to her ear. We retreated to our room for a while. When we returned, we found Ron in the critical care waiting room, writing furiously in his cramped left-handed backhand: Fay had kicked him out too.

At least we weren't at a loss for people to talk to. There were always visitors here, and Caron alone kept the waiting room receptionist in a job at the telephone. At first, the calls had come to the SICU desk, and there were so many that sometimes I'd be on one line and the nurses would signal calls for me on the other lines too. They said they didn't mind summoning me to the phone, but I was worried that this would become tiresome and they'd generalize to the conclusion that Caron Schreer's family ought not be on the floor except for the regular ten visiting minutes every two hours, daylight hours only. Fay would enthusiastically spearhead that one! So I asked that all calls be directed to the waiting room instead of to the unit—and now the family in the waiting room was kept hopping picking up the phone.

Mr. K—Carl—had arrived just as soon as he could after school and before Fay began tending to Caron's bath. He was tickled to be bearing a poster board-sized card that must have had messages inside from a hundred band members. The large computer-generated message was this:

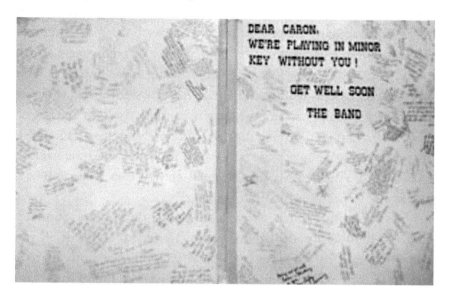

I noticed the play on words right away, but Fay wasn't so appreciative, so Carl pointed it out to her, reading out loud, "Look, it says right here: 'Dear Caron, We're playing in *minor key* without you! Get well soon. The band.'" He chuckled, delighted with his cleverness, and even Fay couldn't suppress a small smile. She was less than thrilled, however, when we set about hanging this masterpiece on the wall—just about where Caron's eyes seemed to rest when they shot open from time to time, pulling to the right. So there: forty-four inches by twenty-six inches of wall space covered . . . only a couple hundred square feet left to go.

The messages on this oversized card were very touching, and the humor in some of them indicated that the morning announcements at BHS had assuaged some fears. Perhaps the message that touched me the most was this one from the bassoonist: "I'm really glad to hear you're doing great. You had everyone on the edge of their seats for a minute. I can't wait to see you again. You add some spice in all of our lives. I thought you'd like to know we'll still try the quintet and get a *"1"* for you. Love, Mike Walsh." The quintet of which he spoke was a group of band members who had been practicing together for the District Solo and Ensemble Festival coming up in less than two weeks. In past years, Caron had always entered as a soloist. This would have been her first time in a quintet, as well, and she had been very enthusiastic about it. Other members of the quintet wrote similarly light messages. From the clarinetist, "You're the only oboe we've got—and most of my percentage of conversation in government class! Come back—this instant!" And from a French horn player, "Get well soon so I can give you more tips on oboe playing!"

As we read through all the comments, the tape of Sunday's Honors Band concert filled the room. I cried to think of all the upcoming musical experiences Caron would miss: both district and state solo and ensemble festivals, as well as the district and state band festivals. Caron has always enjoyed life to the fullest, and music has held the largest and most special place in her heart. She would be very sad when she realized what she had missed; but I knew that I would be ecstatic when she was well enough to make such a realization.

Larry arrived with chicken he'd gone home to cook, and we decided we may as well eat and turn in for the night, as we couldn't get back into the room with Caron anyway, and Ron was here for the night shift. We all took a walk to Caron's room where we found the door shut and a sign posted on the door: "It's time for me to sleep now. Please let me have my rest." Fay begrudgingly let us in to say good-night to Caron before we retired, and of course she warned us not to disturb her; but outside, in the corridor, Cathy whispered to Ron that she'd call him from the waiting room as soon as Fay left.

When Fay left, Cathy would restart the tape that Fay had turned off, and Ron's words, spoken shakily but bravely, would fill the room, in hopes of enticing Caron to return to us:

"Good afternoon, everyone. In spending the last day and a half with my lovely daughter in Ann Arbor—it's, of course, every parent's nightmare, and it comes *true* occasionally. But luckily, we wake up from nightmares, and this is one that—uh, that young lady, she's a fighter, and she's going to battle through this one. The critical is critical, but it's improving hourly. I was thrilled when I looked at the program just a moment ago and saw that the first piece to be done and directed by Mr. K from Brighton is 'Irish Posy.' My daughter, on her mother's side, is a Hathaway, and she's got the stuff that all Irishmen are made of. And I'm bringing . . . my daughter's love to all of you. She squeezed my hand twice today[1]: once when I told her that her friend Lauren was just fine, and the second time when I said, 'Honey, I'm going to your concert.'[1] And so I thank you for coming to honor these students, who are the best representatives of music in Livingston County. And I want you to know that my daughter's *here*. And she'll *always* be here with this crew. Thank you."

---

1 Caron may have squeezed reflexively, possibly even in response to the familiar voice, but probably not in response to the meaning of the messages. Nevertheless, saying this offered hope and made a positive impact on these young people who had a concert to perform this afternoon. It effectively fulfilled the intent of Ron's presence at the concert: It helped her friends feel that she was, indeed, there with them in spirit. We knew she *would* have been—if she *could* have been.

CHAPTER 6

RUMOR CONTROL

Ahhh! Cathy was still here! The Honors Band music was resounding from wall to wall, and there was the sweetest little smile on Caron's face. What a relief it was to see the strain gone, replaced by such a serene comfort. The band concert concluded, and I slipped in the tape of oboe selections that her oboe teacher had brought in the day before. The doctor parade began, and as always, the first to arrive were Smith, Et, and Al with their daily report of "the same." They'd have to learn better bedside manners, I remember thinking, if they expected anyone ever to want to learn their names.

Laurie ordered us off the hospital grounds for a couple of hours. Not just out of the room, but off the grounds! Not the same implications at all: Laurie knew I needed a change of scenery for my own sanity. But she didn't know Judd, our yellow lab puppy suddenly living alone in a house that used to be filled with people. Labs are people dogs: very affectionate and demanding lots of attention. I cursed Laurie when we walked in the front door of the house: Judd had left messages all over the house that he was not happy with our prolonged absence. Larry began picking up the pieces.

Poor Judd. He knew something was wrong. He sat in front of me and laid his head in my lap, gazing up at me with confused and doleful eyes, his tail doing a slow rain windshield wiper on the floor behind him. Even a puppy can sense when excitement is out of place and therefore must be contained. He must have been so glad to see us, but he kept his excitement in check.

Later, when Merry Jane stopped by, he jumped on *her*. That, he must have felt, was appropriate enough. He hadn't yet been to obedience school.

We took Judd for a walk uptown. Only a week before, on a freezing-rain evening, Caron and I had taken Judd on this same walk, slipping and sliding all the way. Passing His House storefront, she had stopped to admire the Precious Moments dolls, wildly inflecting, "I *love* these!" (Ooh! Ah!) I had told her they were too expensive but, as usual, I had tucked the idea away in memory for some special moment—maybe her birthday in May. But now, on an unseasonably warm last day of January, Larry and I were walking Judd to His House, specifically to buy a Precious Moments doll—for it would, indeed, be a precious moment when Caron came out of the coma.

Along the way, Larry bought Judd a rawhide bone (to replace the coasters and other household items that no longer existed for us to leave lying around for Judd's chewing pleasure). After we'd made all our purchases, we went on to Caron's bank to run an errand for her. She's always been so organized: Mark Benner had retrieved her purse from Bart, and in it we found her bankbook with an envelope of money tucked into it. On the envelope were written instructions (originally intended for herself alone) to deposit the contents, plus ten of the eighteen dollars payment she was expecting to receive in the mail for doing the church nursery, plus ten dollars she'd written "that Mom owes me." I deposited the envelope contents plus twenty dollars. Also in her purse was her church collection envelope, filled and filled out, all set to have been put into the collection plate on Sunday. The kid was in a coma and *still* finding ways to get us to church on Sunday mornings! All right, so we'd go next Sunday and deposit her offering.

Lauren's mother had called on Monday, concerned for Caron and asking when Lauren would be able to see her. At first I suggested that it might be too much of a shock for Lauren to see Caron as she now was. Then I realized that Lauren's mind held a picture that must have been far more terrifying. At least we would be able to explain all the tubes and devices. Hopefully, Lauren would be able to understand that everything here was to help Caron recover.

So now it was Tuesday, day number 4, and Lauren was here to visit. She was marvelous! What a trooper! She took Caron's hand without qualm when I offered it to her, and she spoke to Caron as if expecting her to answer right back. She kept this up for a remarkably long time, considering that she was receiving no responses. Then she put on a microcassette tape that she had gotten several band members to help her put together in school that day. Delightful! It included cheers (of the "Chigaroo! Chigarah! Rah! Rah! Rah!" variety); encouraging words ("we know you're a really strong person, so we know you're going to pull through this really mean stuff."); threats ("beware . . . we're going to come and drag you out of your bed!"); lots of well-wishing, some in French; and music, lots of music! One barbershop quintet hammed up "Goodnight, Sweetheart," complete with "Do-do-do-do-do . . . ," but with made-to-order new words: "Wake up, sweetheart. Well, it's time to come home . . ."The bassoonist played the ever-familiar childhood torment, "Na-na-na-na-na-na" (C-C-A-D-C-A) on just his double reed; then nagged, "The double reed department is kind of lonesome so you'd better get back—real quick!" Another band member played a creative version of Chopsticks, inserting comments at the ends of all the phrases: "Hi, Caron! . . . This is

Tim . . . you know, from 'First Hour' . . . you know, Analysis . . . heard you were feelin' kinda bad . . . Get well soon! . . . You've got a lot of homework to make up, you know . . ." Her friends seemed to know just what it would take to get Caron back on her feet!

Cards and letters were already pouring in via the postal system too. That evening Laurie gave me the go-ahead to read Caron some of the many cards that had arrived. I began with excited anticipation, as something very encouraging had happened before Larry and I had left the hospital for the afternoon: I'd been sitting alone with Caron, and she was "out." Unless a doctor or nurse or other attendant came into the room to do something to her, she usually remained this way, but when someone disrupted her in any way (such as moving a tube, changing an IV, removing adhesive tape, or changing a dressing), she would react irritably. It was only during those times that occasionally she might be responsive to a "Caron, open your eyes," or "Caron, squeeze my hand." All her responses had been during periods of disturbance. While I was sitting with her this morning, however, she had abruptly opened her eyes and gazed at the window she faced. I took her hand, and she accepted mine! When I said, "Caron, it's Mom. Can you squeeze my hand?" she gave me a very emphatic cruncher! And then she was out again. But what *joy*! That one crunch sustained me all day, and I was now eager to be privy to more good news from Caron.

I described each card, told her who'd sent it, read the verse and any additional personal messages of encouragement; but she offered no acknowledgment. I was disheartened but not willing to give up. When the last of the cards had been read, I opened our favorite book of poetry: Shel Silverstein's *Where the Sidewalk Ends*. Her expression lightened with each poem that I read, and during "The Bagpipe Who Didn't Say No," the facial equivalent of a chuckle spread over her face. She was becoming lighter and lighter. Several poems later, her father and brother walked in, and each said hi. She opened her eyes wide, staring up at the ceiling. This in itself showed a physical improvement, since the blow to the left side of her head had previously caused her eyes to roll always to the right. Matt took her left hand, which was closest to the door. I continued reading the poem in progress as I walked around the foot of the bed to the other side of the bed, and her eyes followed me! What a moment! We were all ecstatic! And that was the end of Caron's grace. All totaled, she'd had her eyes open for maybe two minutes that day—but that was two minutes more than on the previous day. When a loved one has suffered a head injury, one must be encouraged by small portions of progress.

I spent that evening with Matt in our McAuley Inn room. We ordered in pizza and watched *Matlock* on TV. Matt had many fears and worries concerning his sister, but the only ones he was able to voice were "Will she die?" and "Why does she stare up at the ceiling when she opens her eyes?" He wanted answers, but what *were* the answers? He wasn't comfortable with "I don't know" or with any replies that weren't definitive or that required speculation and/or patient waiting on his part. He was much more comfortable relaying facts—tales of how he'd been dispelling rumors about Caron around the high school: one rumor was that she had developed gangrene and had had both of her legs amputated. We laughed to think of the possibilities for responses, among them, "Then I would say a miracle has happened, for I saw her toes wiggling at the end of the bed today!" Someone else was spreading rumors that she had a broken neck. And Matt had also heard that one ear had been amputated. Since there were bandages over her left ear, Matt wasn't sure about this one, and he had to ask if it was true. I was glad that Matt was spending the night with us. It was hard to imagine what he must have been going through, and I was glad to be able to share just a small part of his frustrations, and to try to help.

CHAPTER 7

"BREATHE!"

The alarm malfunctioned, and Ron had arrived to pick up Matt before any of us were awake. While Matt showered and dressed, Ron briefed me on his night with Caron. So both of us missed the doctors' rounds. We joked that we weren't sure how we'd survive the day without our morning dose of the Three Stooges' pronouncement of "same." Somehow, we managed. And by the following morning, Smith Et Al seemed to have dissolved as an entity. The monotonous "same" voice was the only constant in the group, and now there was an attractive young black woman whom we would come to know as Dr. Judith.

Rather than simply glance at Caron, Dr. Judith stepped up to the bed and asked Caron to hold up just the right finger on her right hand. Quite a complicated direction. None of us held our breath. And when, in fact, Caron did it, Smith's monotone murmured, "She's the lightest I've seen her."

Dr. Judith also made verbal mention of Caron tracking: a term we learned meant "following objects with one's eyes." Well, Caron had followed my voice around the foot of her bed as I read from *Where the Sidewalk Ends*; did that count as "tracking"? I decided to believe it did and that, as usual, we were ahead of these young "whitecoats" in our observations. But I was very impressed with this new doctor, who had actually spoken to my daughter.

On the next day, Caron did her usual trick of zonking out just before the young residents came in the door. Dr. Monotone Smith was leading a new group of whitecoats, and I was disheartened to observe that Dr. Judith wasn't among them. They noted the lack of activity, shook their heads, and left. I surmised that one day they'd stumble in on Caron walking and talking, and they'd mutter, "She's quite a bit lighter today."

In these three days, which finished off Caron's first week in the hospital, Caron seemed to plateau, cognitively speaking. I didn't detect much lightening up. Of course, my senses had dulled. I was exhausted. While I'd had a couple nights of sleep when Ron was able to spend the night with our daughter, some of the nurses, following Fay's example, were now beginning to resist visitation during the night; and whenever I knew Ron had been denied entry, I couldn't sleep. What if Caron woke up in the middle of the night in this unfamiliar place? Wasn't it possible that the resultant anxiety might traumatize a head-injured patient? My heart bled for my little girl, who had not yet even noticed her surroundings, let alone registered any reaction to them.

Weary, unable to appreciate or even notice small positive signs, I concentrated on factual information. Much was beginning to happen with regard to the important bodily functions of breathing and eating. In this first week, Caron had remained on respiratory assist. And no nutrition had been given; there were other "more important" concerns. (If she could only know, I chuckled, that these people thought that there were more important things in the world than eating! Wait until she finds out that they deprived her of food for over a week, I mused. She'd never believe she could live so long without pizza. We who could think and feel and talk had to joke about these things, as our only hope of getting through this ordeal sane was to put our senses of humor on overtime.)

Caron had been on a respiratory assist of fourteen. This had been raised to sixteen on the second or third day, but the respiratory technician had protested that this wasn't necessary, that she was doing fine on fourteen, and so it was immediately reinstated to fourteen. On the fourth day it was reduced to twelve. The number refers to how many breaths per minute are provided by the respirator. While on respiratory assist, patients can take breaths of their own, but the respirator still provides the number of breaths to which it is set. In this way, the patient is guaranteed at *least* the set number of breaths each minute, even if (s)he takes no breaths independently.

The night before her fifth day in the hospital, a decision was made to begin to wean Caron from the respirator. She was transferred to IMV = IMV differs from respiratory assist in that whenever the patient takes a breath without the assistance of the respirator, this breath *substitutes* for one of the machine-programmed breaths. Therefore, the patient is guaranteed only the set number of breaths. In order to get eleven breaths per minute on IMV = 10, the patient would have to breathe eleven *independent* breaths.

On Caron's fifth morning, the respiratory technician on duty came in to measure respiratory parameters. It must have been a panicky feeling to a body accustomed to having breathing assisted by a machine, but he and I both talked her through it, and she did fine, taking breaths on her own, on command. It couldn't be guaranteed that she would continue to breathe automatically, without cuing prompts, so of course she was put back on the IMV = 10 after the testing session. Before leaving, Cathy explained to me that the IMV would be systematically reduced to eight, then six, then four—and then to BRIGS, where Caron would be breathing entirely on her own but with supplemental oxygen added to her breaths.

When I arrived at 6:00 a.m. on the eighth day, Ron announced, "She's on her own!" (He had been allowed to stay the night because it was Kurt, another of our favorites, who was the night nurse.) The respiratory technician and night nurse had conspired in the night to take Caron off the respirator. With her father spending the night, she would have a full-time coach, even when Kurt might have to leave the room to tend to another patient. So Lynn, the RT, had disconnected the respirator, and Ron had spent the night timing breaths and coaching Caron to "breathe!" So now she was on BRIGS, 30 percent oxygen. Precisely the reason we had originally decided to have one of us with Caron at all times: Certainly the hospital could not afford to staff so that each patient received undivided one-to-one attention. And if parents were willing to follow nurses' and doctors' directions, then wouldn't that patient have a better chance of a more complete recovery and sooner? Any nurse or doctor willing to register an answer to that question responded affirmatively, and many told us how lucky Caron was to have parents so devoted to pushing her to reach her best potential—but while some would agree in theory, in practice they really did not want their domain intruded upon by parents. I often wondered if these same nurses actually stayed out of their own children's teachers' territory. If so, I felt sorry for the children, for all of Caron's parents are educators, and we all know how much more beneficial it is for a child if the parents support the teacher and their child's education—and pitch in helping! This is all that we wanted to do for our daughter, here in the hospital. We had no intention of getting in the way of the experts in her medical care.

Laurie, Caron's primary nurse, was gone for five days, to a family wedding. Before she left, Ron and I joked with her about who she was lining up as Caron's nurses until she returned on Monday (which would be Caron's tenth day). She hadn't decided, so Ron interjected, "Just so her name isn't Fay!" This led us into a discussion of nurses and how Laurie, Cathy, Jeri, and Kurt had spoiled us. Laurie always remained very professional, never making derogatory remarks about co-workers. So while she admitted that she was one to become emotionally involved with her patients, she also wanted us to understand that there were some fine nurses who didn't . . . and, once again, Ron had a dry comment: "Fay is a *fine* nurse." The period that terminated his sentence was about as pregnant as any period I've ever heard.

Before Laurie left, we set the Precious Moments doll on the bed stand with a five-inch-by-seven-inch picture of Caron at two and a half: long blond pony tails, winning smile . . . and these words:

Here's just one of many:

PRECIOUS MOMENTS

with Caron . . . what a little sprite she was at this age! Help us to celebrate the *next* precious moment in "The Life and Times of Caron Colette Schreer."

If *you* are with her when she comes into consciousness, please give her this *Precious Moments* doll that she was admiring in the window of His House bookstore just a week ago. (At the time, I told her that she couldn't have it ... but, well, it'll be a pretty *precious moment* when she's *back*!)

Laurie's eyes watered as she cried, "What are you trying to do to me?" But now Laurie was gone for a few days, and we would experience a host of substitutes—most of whom were one named Fay.

We couldn't help but compare the sensitivity of Laurie with the insensitivity of Fay, who, on her next tour of duty, entered Caron's room, commented on an odor, lifted the covers, and proclaimed for all the world to hear, "She pooped!" Caron may have been comatose, but we know she had some level of awareness, as she had demonstrated an ability to breathe on command, lift a particular finger, raise a designated arm—not always, but sometimes during her lighter periods. Didn't this woman realize, or care, that this young girl might understand what was said, or at least the tone of voice, and that she did deserve to retain some semblance of dignity while confined to this bed and at the mercy of others? The rule of thumb that we had chosen to follow was that we must assume that Caron could understand everything. Obviously, this nurse didn't subscribe to such a philosophy, and as we were at her mercy regarding visitation privileges, we didn't admonish her or even voice disenchantment. We did cringe inside.

Larry had been the parent on duty just before Fay arrived, and he'd reported having had to *fight* with Caron: she had thrashed about, tossing her legs back and forth, trying to push herself onto one side or the other by pressing on the mattress with the hand behind her. Larry said she was so strong that he had difficulty restraining her. Later, when we realized what had happened, we also realized that there was some level of consciousness operating within Caron, enough for her to feel uncomfortable about having a bowel movement in bed. *And what other awarenesses and feelings were trapped inside her silent body?*

From the very beginning, Caron's wrists had been tied to the rails of the bed, due to her purposeful movements. Despite this, she had discovered how to scoot down in the bed, bringing distasteful objects to the wrists that couldn't move to the objects. In this way, she had managed to pull out her left chest tube one night. She was put under close surveillance, and it was determined that the chest tube did not need to be replaced: her left lung was fine. A few days later, some doctors came in to remove the right chest tube.

A dietician came to talk to me on the sixth day about nutrition for Caron. Doctors had tried to insert a tube for feeding purposes, but it had become coiled around in her stomach and was, therefore, ineffective for feeding at this time. The doctors hoped that stomach contractions would push the tube down into the small intestine, which was where they wanted the food deposited, as this would reduce risk of upset and vomiting. (When the brain is injured, autonomic functions [involuntary movements, such as gastrointestinal movement] may behave unpredictably, even crazily. The doctors wanted to get past the stomach, beyond the pyloric sphincter, into the small intestine, because once past the pyloric sphincter, food does not reflux; it stays in the gastrointestinal tract and becomes digested.) The hoped-for movement did not come about, so the tube was removed. On Friday, they tried to reinsert it via fluoroscopy, an x-ray technique of sorts. Apparently, this didn't work either, because Caron continued without nutrition until the following Tuesday, when her doctors approved hyperalimentation as a means of providing nutrition. This would supply vitamins, minerals, amino acids (protein-building blocks), lipids (other essential fatty acids), and electrolytes, in addition to glucose. She had been on only an IV of glucose and electrolytes, not sufficient to maintain weight.

Meanwhile, we had other concerns and lots of time on our hands to do something about them. As mundane as they might have seemed to doctors whose concerns were the more important ones of saving her life (and doing so without interfering any more than necessary with what the quality of that life would then be), our small concerns were all that there was within our realm of know-how, and we felt more useful when trying to tend to these matters, no matter how trivial the medical experts may have thought they were. After all, we couldn't know what to do to save our little girl's life. We had to leave that most important job to the doctors and nurses, trusting implicitly in their doing their jobs well. Not liking to feel useless, we looked into the less important things, such as teeth. Caron had just completed some years of orthodontic work and had been wearing a retainer to train her teeth to stay in their new positions. Obviously, she couldn't wear the retainer while in a coma due to the danger of it becoming dislodged and her choking on it. I called her orthodontist. What could we do? Not to worry, he reassured us: what had been done before could be done again; bring her back after she was out of the hospital.

Vision was another concern. Caron had been wearing contacts—that she had proudly purchased herself, rather than to wear glasses, which annoyed her. We had mentioned the contacts in the beginning after all her procedures and surgeries had been completed. A doctor had looked for them, and he had reported that they must have popped out upon the impact in the collision. But now, as Caron was beginning to open her eyes from time to time, we realized that this wasn't going to be a very rewarding experience for her if she couldn't see anything, anyway. Ah, the educator in us was creeping in again! Optimal conditions enhance learning—and when conditions are less than what they can be, learning is impaired. We didn't want our daughter to decide that opening her eyes was an exercise in futility, so it was obvious (to us) that she ought to have a pair of glasses.

It was Ron who called the ophthalmologist to request that a pair of glasses be made up with Caron's most recent prescription. In the ensuing conversation, although agreeing to make the glasses, Dr. Heinze stressed that it was *highly* unlikely that those contacts had dislodged themselves, and he suggested that we enlist the services of someone sensitive to contacts to "look again. They're there." That night, Kurt was Caron's nurse. He found and removed the contacts. What a guy! *And* he believed in the family support concept, so Ron had been welcomed in to spend the night. That was the night that Caron came off the respirator—and we proved, on *two* accounts, how valuable parent support can be.

I drove Matt back to Brighton that night. He was staying with friends of the family. Driving him back gave Ron some evening time with Caron, and it gave me a chance to chat with Matt. It's easy to feel disconsolate when one's child is in a coma. But it's ever so much more constructive to look for positive outcomes. I was pleased to see that Matt was growing in compassion and in consideration as a result of what we were all going through. He indicated an awareness of the financial situation by volunteering to forego new clothes for the Winterfest dance coming up. He'd be getting a full cast on his leg on Monday and would neither be able to get into dress pants nor be able to dance, anyway, so he figured he could just suggest a movie to the young lady, instead. The only glitch was that the young lady, who had invited him, already had purchased a new gown. Well, perhaps, under the circumstances, she could save it for the next formal dance. Everybody had to make sacrifices. Some were easier than others.

Matt seemed to understand that this whole ordeal would certainly cost a lot—in dollars, as well as in the toll it would take on Caron, on our entire family, and on others. In just the first five days, the hospital stay alone (*not* including ambulance, helicopter, surgeries, anesthesiology, x-rays, CT scans, arteriograms, doctors' fees, our room at the McAuley Inn, and so on—in other words, the

SICU room alone) had cost much more than we'd have been able to put our hands on. Larry did the initial legwork on insurance processing. As frightening as the five-day-stay amount was to us, it looked like most everything would be covered by insurance. Ron's insurance would be primary, as his was the first birthday in the calendar year. Caron's car insurance, with a reputable company, would be secondary, as her birthday was in May. If anything remained after the coordination of benefits between the first two companies, then Larry's and my excellent teachers' medical plan would process the claim. In fact, in the next two years, close to a million dollars worth of bills would accrue—and would all be covered by insurance. Still maintaining our humor, we'd call it our *million-dollar baby* experience—may we never have to have another one!

When I returned to the hospital complex that night, I stopped to say good night to Caron before going on to our hotel room. Kurt put his arm around me and inquired, "Are you going to get some sleep? I've heard that you're not sleeping."

"Only when Fay won't let Ron spend the night here with Caron. When I know he's here with her, I sleep well. Thanks!" I slept well that night.

CHAPTER 8

THE MAN NEXT DOOR...
AND NO MORE NIGHT VISITS

Eighth day. (This was the morning Ron announced, "She's on her own!" after coaching Caron's breathing all night.) Larry had come with me early this Saturday morning. He felt guilty about not having seen Caron in the past two days and nights. He had returned to teaching Thursday, was involved in swim meets both evenings since, and had another one to attend later in the afternoon. He asked to sit with Caron for the morning hours, so I left to take care of some paperwork and to return phone calls. There were so many kindnesses for which I wanted to extend personal thanks.

People had been so good to us. "Friends who care," one card read, donated three nights' stay at the McAuley Inn, "to ease the burden of staying away from home." Caron's employer, Bob Herbst, always so very thoughtful, contributed an answering machine on which we could record daily updates on Caron's condition, so as to not have to spend all our time on the phone after we moved back home. The Benners arranged to have a second phone line installed so that we could reserve that one unlisted number for doctors' use, thereby being assured of receiving any urgent messages from the hospital, even if we were on our regular line or if the answering machine was running. The Dentons cleaned the house and did our laundry in preparation for our return. A teaching colleague contacted the president of our local teachers' union to request that a sick days' bank be established on my behalf so that I wouldn't have the added hardship of loss of pay. (The last of my leave days would be used on February 21.)

Josh, Mark, and Eric Benner were indispensable to us, as was Merry Jane Benner, who sent along such scrumptious meals when 'the boys' came to work at our house.

Many friends took turns spiriting me off to lunch each day, to be sure I'd eat something nutritious. (Other friends, who knew me well, sent me life's staple: dark chocolates!) A couple of friends were invaluable in educating us about what to do on Caron's behalf. They had lost a son three weeks after an automobile accident just two years before, and while it must have been painful for them to visit us in the hospital, their doing so meant a lot to us, and we heeded well their advice about turning and repositioning Caron. This discouraged pressure sores from forming and warded off pneumonia—to which coma patients, especially those on respirators, are vulnerable, because they are prone to aspirate (breathe in) saliva, mucus, or other fluids, which then find their way to the lowest area of the lungs, thereby creating an opportune environment for pneumonia.

The cards kept pouring in, a couple dozen every day, including wonderful poster-sized cards done by some of Caron's high school classes (the teachers either instrumental in organizing this, or at least supportive when students asked to do it). Religiously, every other day for a couple of months, the Uber Drug Store gang sent a card—signed by everyone working there in the previous forty-eight-hour period. Each day, Caron kept her eyes open for increasingly longer periods of time, albeit mostly gazing blankly up at the ceiling. It was when her eyes were open that I'd read her the day's mail. Often, there was no reaction, although she seemed to become more alert at the mention of certain names. One day, when I was counting out all her mail and commented, "and none of them have little plastic windows," she smiled. After reading the cards, I hung every one of them on the walls. Dispassionate toward the drab walls underneath, the nurses cheered me on.

As I left Caron in Larry's care this particular morning, I was nabbed by the SICU unit's environmental control specialist, who began, "Your daughter has lots o' cards, doesn't she? C'mere, I wanna show ya somethin'." She led me to the opposite diagonal of this unit so she could show me how one woman was displaying her husband's cards: it appeared to be a yardstick covered with felt, with holes punched below, and yarn threaded through the holes; the cards were attached to the hanging yarn strands. This piqued my interest and sparked my love of invention. I was almost suckered into devising something similar for Caron (but it would have to be much bigger to hold all of her cards) when this ECS inadvertently blew her own devious scheme with the additional comment, "It's so hard to get the tape off the walls." How could she have known that for twenty years I'd been battling custodial staff interests vs. kids' better interests—and I wasn't about to lay down the sword when it was my own daughter's battle! While Larry stayed with Caron, I visited the hospital gift shop and invested in a new supply of tape!

Wherever there weren't cards, there were stuffed animals, surrounding the lone Precious Moments doll. We joked that we could open a stuffed animal pet store, but we knew that Caron would never part with a single one. Her favorite at this time, or perhaps it was the nurses' favorite, because it was big enough to prop Caron up against, was a pink bunny from her friend Amy. And always, music or teenage chatter filled the room. Her friends, whom we were still not admitting to the room in person, did the next best thing: they continued to send tapes of themselves in conversation or playing their musical instruments for her, some excerpts from class lectures, lots of joking and cajoling her to hurry back. These many gifts of the voices and music of teenagers were enjoyed by all who entered the room. We'll probably never know how much of it Caron actually took in at the time, but a comforted look on her face compelled us to continue to play these tapes over and over and over. I believe I memorized some of them. Certainly I'll never forget her friend Leeann, who was taking mostly advanced-placement classes and would be the class valedictorian, bemoaning her perception of herself as a procrastinator.

Sometimes parents brought their offspring to the hospital, imploring us, "He's crushed that you won't let him see her. They're such good friends," or "She *needs* to see Caron." The teenage daughter made this latter one easier by saying, "Mom, *all* the kids do, but there are too many of us to make that practical." Usually, it was, indeed, difficult to turn people away, but it was a necessary thing. Had we not done this, the hospital staff would have limited visitation, from the beginning, to those five ten-minute visits in each twenty-four hour period—and Caron would have been deprived of all that one-on-one help we were able to give her. Incidentally, during one of our "no, we can't let you see her" explanations, we learned where the amputated ear rumor may have been born. In chatting with one of the women who'd been with us in conference room 1 the very first day (when I signed Dr. Austad's consent-for-surgery form), I was now telling her about getting Caron glasses, when the woman interjected, "How will they stay on with one ear gone?"

Finished returning some phone calls and having written all the thank-you notes my writing hand would allow me to write, I returned to Caron's room to release Larry to his afternoon swim meet. He was disconsolate. The respiratory tube had been removed, but the early-morning hours had begun with so much wrestling and coughing on Caron's part that the tube had been replaced. Larry felt, however, that all her writhing and gasping were due to her having to have another bowel movement, not wanting to do it in bed and not being able to tell anyone. Perhaps the gasping was an attempt to talk. (We had been forewarned that she wouldn't be *able* to talk for a while due to the inflammation of tissues in her throat from the irritation of the tubes.) He felt that it was unfair and premature of them to have reinserted the tube, and he was also feeling inept as her guardian during that time. Realistically, however, we both understood that medical expertise was not one of our gifts, and we had to continue to trust doctors' decisions. This was out of our territory.

Meanwhile, because of the inflammation of Caron's vocal cords (due to the intubation—the breathing tubes), the doctors were now discussing doing a tracheostomy: a surgical incision of the trachea, through the throat. I grabbed the first respiratory technician I could find, who allayed my fears by explaining that this surgical procedure is done below the vocal cords and does not affect them; but fear revisited me when he went on to say that it's "usually not permanent." On Monday I would call Brighton High School's nurse (who would assure me that I need not worry about an "ostomy" or an "otomy"; it's an "ectomy" about which I should be concerned, as "ectomy" indicates the removal of something.) Also on Monday, a team of otolaryngologists would be in with a consent form for me to sign, for the surgery to be performed Wednesday. Meanwhile, they would prescribe dexamethazone for the purpose of reducing the swelling of the vocal cords. On Tuesday morning I would arrive at 11:00 a.m. to find that the drug had done its job, the respiratory tube had again been removed, Caron was tolerating it well, and the tracheostomy wouldn't be needed after all. God was indubitably keeping the upper hand here!

A hospital ophthalmologist came to take a look at Caron's eyes, as per our request, since her contacts had not been discovered and removed until a week after her accident. He reported that her eyes had not been damaged and that the ointment that the nurses had been putting in them could be discontinued.

Meanwhile, Dr. Farhat had been in to speak with me about a sixth-nerve palsy. I had no idea what this was. As nearly as I could ascertain, it's the sixth nerve that controls lateral (sideways) eye movement, and because of the blow to the left side of Caron's brainstem, her eyes were not yet traveling their full ranges. This must have been the palsy, a paralysis, to which he was referring. Fortunately, he spoke of it as a temporary thing. He also mentioned that because her eyes had different ranges of motion, she was probably seeing double at this time, and this could continue for a couple of months.

The unit was understaffed on this, Caron's first full Saturday here, and perhaps because I had established a reputation for being dependable and not leaving the unit without notifying someone where I could be reached, Caron's assigned nurse for the day kept busy in other rooms, and I was alone with Caron. No one came in to cleanse Caron's ear, apply ointment, and change the dressing. Her left inflatable sock (to enhance circulation) deflated, and no one had the time to replace it.

She kept scooting down in the bed, and no one was available to help move her back up or reposition her. Normally, all these things would have been done like clockwork, or even more often, for on SICU nurses often have only one patient, and usually not more than two. They must really have been understaffed, for I'd never seen anyone here who was remiss about anything. I did all that I could to help, but I felt insecure without direction. I rubbed Caron's back, exercised her limbs, and put on the ludicrous turquoise and yellow high-topped tennis shoes to prevent drop foot; I think her brother and father may have purchased these as a means of keeping Caron awake once she began to survey her own body parts, and perhaps to entice her to talk too, if only to say, "Egads! Get those atrocities off my feet!"

I didn't leave for lunch, knowing that the nurses who were on duty had more than enough to do with newer, more critical patients. For Caron, delayed risk of stroke was no longer a major concern. The day crawled along—interminably long! People who'd said they would stop by at lunchtime or early in the afternoon didn't come until evening, or not at all. This too was unusual. My nerves were on edge from the stress of being uneducated in IC work but in charge for the day of my only daughter. Probably not having had breakfast or lunch also contributed to my being out of sorts. At 6:00 p.m., the IV machine began to ding. No cause for alarm. This was a signal that more liquid should be added. If a nurse was not in regular attendance in the room, adding liquid when it became low, then the machine was programmed to ding at the end of an hour, when it would be close to having emptied. Usually someone arrived within a minute or so to tend to this task. But today five minutes dragged by, and that relentless bonging was beginning to be annoying. I stepped to the doorway, hoping to get the attention of one of the many nurses, aides, orderlies, doctors, EKG technicians, respiratory technicians, pharmacists, nutritionists, and so on, who could usually be found in numbers in the corridors. Nobody! No one at all was visible! Highly unusual! There wasn't anyone at the desk, either. No problem. This wasn't an emergency; someone would come when they could.

As I retreated to Caron's room, I noticed the man in the room next door to hers beckoning wildly to me. There was unquestionably a problem *there*, so I hurried down the hall, looking in patient rooms for a nurse. Several doors down, I found one, tending to a patient, and I ventured, "Excuse me, but—"

"You can't come into other patients' rooms," she snapped at me. I looked instantly down at my feet to ascertain that they were still planted firmly on the tile of the corridor, and not within the hallowed area of this nurse's private jurisdiction. Yes, my feet were being well behaved. Confident that the injustice had been inflicted upon me, rather than executed by me, but brushing this aside in my concern for the gesticulating gentleman down the hall, I told her that the man in room 2437 needed help, and then I returned quietly to room 2436.

Caron's own nurse for a day arrived soon after this, and while refilling the IV, she gave me a gentle (but, under the circumstances, aggravating) lesson about not going into other patients' rooms. Though I was not guilty, I didn't offer rebuttal. Rather, when Ron arrived shortly thereafter, I left to refrain from exploding, regain composure, retain sanity . . . and grab a bite to eat.

When I returned to bid Caron good night, the night substitute was ushering Ron out and wouldn't let Larry and me in, either, not even to say good night. We surely missed Laurie and Cathy! It was becoming obvious that "floats," while medically efficient enough, often didn't hold the same philosophy as those who made SICU their vocation—the philosophy that credited these patients with understanding, even though they appeared to be out of it. I had told Caron I'd be back to say good night. Now, for her sake, assuming that she had comprehended what I'd said, the promised should take place. How long would it take, and in what way would it hurt? It could only help. But the nurse was unyielding, explaining only that "we need our rest." We tried to explain that "this is how we *get* our rest," whereupon she switched to some other excuse. I was becoming upset, and she became upset. Finally she told us to wait in the critical care family room, and she'd send the head nurse or a doctor out to talk with us.

The head nurse *and* a doctor arrived in just a few minutes. Same arguments—and the same switch in the story each time we effectively countered the argument at hand. These people couldn't even claim that we were a nuisance to the staff or a disturbance to Caron; everyone, even the nurses who didn't like having parents around, had to admit—at the very least—that we'd always been very perceptive about when to remove ourselves from the room and that we had not disobeyed any of their directions with regard to Caron's care. But the bottom line was this: no more night visits, *regardless.*

I didn't sleep that night.

Since Ron had been robbed of his night shift, he spent Sunday morning with Caron, and Larry and I went to church—to deposit the offering Caron had had ready for the previous week and to enjoy the comfort of friends. However, exhausted from not having slept much or well, tears that I'd been saving up for a week flowed freely and constantly throughout the service and afterward. I came home feeling like a failure: I hadn't painted a very convincing picture of faith and hope that morning.

At home, I put the first message on the answering machine, which had been installed since I was home last: "This is the Schreer-Teahan residence, C. J. speaking. Today is Sunday, February 5. Caron is still in intensive care and is still serious, but no longer critical. She is still progressing steadily. Cards and prayers are welcomed. Caron will not be receiving visitors for quite a while yet. Please be patient. Leave a message after the long tone if you'd like."

When Larry and I arrived at Caron's room, the same nurse was here who had been here the day before, and she told us that after she returned from lunch, we'd have a little talk about visiting hours. Meanwhile, Ron told us that our daytime visiting hours had been reduced to two two-hour blocks: eleven to one and five to seven. Great. Just great. Having been with Caron all day every day for a week, I could attest to eleven to one being her most regular and very soundest sleeping time—after the exhaustion of doctors' and technicians' rounds and nurses' routines.

Maddie returned, as she'd said, after her lunch, and Ron left. Maddie repeated the same logic we'd heard the night before: "*You need your rest,*" "If we let you, then we have to let everybody," and so on. But she was very kind in her presentation, and when I offered a counterproposal of 11:00 a.m. to 7:00 p.m., she didn't hesitate before agreeing to it. Ah, even hospitals are not immune to politics!

When we returned to Caron's room, some nurses had her sitting up in a cardiac chair, wearing her eye-popper high-tops. But her eyes were closed. Her left arm propped by Amy's bunny, and the rest of her padded with and wedged between pillows, she kept slipping down farther and farther, with each slip her eyes shooting open momentarily. After a half hour, enough for the first time sitting up, two nurses came to put her back in bed, whereupon, it being after 1:00 p.m., she began to lighten up a bit. Having finally taken up the realization that comatose patients in real life *lighten* up rather than suddenly *wake* up, I put Caron's glasses on her and placed the Precious Moments doll in her hands. (We were now permitted to untie the wrist restraints when we were in the room with her, as long as we hovered over her, ready to prevent her from pulling out tubes if she suddenly attempted to seize one.) As she was examining the doll's face, I said, "She has big feet, doesn't she?" and Caron's eyes dropped immediately to the doll's feet! My heart leaped: my daughter *does* understand!

Since we would only be permitted in SICU for eight hours a day, and no nights, there was no longer any point in our staying in the McAuley Inn; and as I couldn't appear until 11:00 a.m. anyway, I spent Monday morning packing up everything that we'd accumulated, carrying it down to the car, and checking out.

Caron was still awake when I arrived a little before eleven. She looked miserably uncomfortable in the cardiac chair, as the chair's back had only been cranked up to about forty-five degrees. When the nurse commented on how comfortable she looked, Caron knit her brow! Ah, my spunky little gal was beginning to express herself! But Millie didn't catch the expression, so I helped Caron out by saying, "I don't know . . . she usually prefers to sit up straight . . ." at which Caron immediately demonstrated by grabbing what she could grab with her hands and pulling her torso away from the chair's back. No doubt, she would have been successful in pulling herself upright except for her wrists being tied to the chair arms, the chair back being so far down and the padding of so many pillows being in her way. But this was enough to convince Millie. She moved some of the pillows, cranked the chair back to a perfect ninety degrees, and re-situated Caron so she was, indeed, comfortable—whereupon Caron fell asleep, upright, for her most predictable nap of the day, "the eleven to one."

While Caron rested, I talked in the hallway with Millie, sharing with her some of the responses I'd seen from Caron, and my concern that she was more capable than the hospital staff was giving her credit for. "Hold up one finger" was getting old. Caron seemed to me to be frustrated, but she wasn't able to vocalize yet, so she had no way of expressing herself except in response to these simple commands. Wasn't there something that we could do?

When Caron was no longer sleeping and had been returned to her bed, Millie initiated a communication system for her to use: one finger for "no," two fingers for "yes." It was a start. While there weren't many issues about which Caron cared enough to cast a vote at this time, at least she now knew how to do it. She learned this code without too much rehearsal, and when her father and brother arrived later in the afternoon, they tested her with some simple yes-no questions, and she responded by holding up one or two fingers! We were so proud! Our daughter was on her way back!

When they had arrived, Matt in his new full-leg cast (so he'd borrowed a wheelchair at the front door), Caron had been awake and sitting straight up in her cardiac chair. They hadn't yet seen her sitting up. Ron winked at her, and slowly, with much concentration, but surely, she winked back! When he asked if she could wink the *other* eye, that took more concentration and required a more intense effort—but she accomplished it! We smiled as she slowly crossed her left leg over her right and then, even slower, her right leg over her left. In our ordinary day-to-day lives, we never think about these simple movements, but for Caron they were milestones.

Matt was beginning to relax somewhat while visiting. The hyperalimentation had been started today (after ten days of Caron having received no nutrition. She was quite alive and improving daily, so perhaps we've given regular eating more credit than it deserves!) Matt noticed the introduction of this bottle of yellow liquid and the additional tube now leading into his sister. He questioned what it was, to which his father teased, "Mountain Dew, pure Mountain Dew."

Matt wheeled over for a closer view and exclaimed, "Twenty percent *dextrose!*" Then, turning on me (the nutrition-preaching mother who'd never allowed pop and seldom allowed junk food into our house), in half-mocking derision but total indignation, he accused, "And *you're* allowing her to *have* it? NO FAIR!" But he recovered quickly, retreated to the foot of the bed, and busied himself writing "Get well soon, Caron" on a huge Etch A Sketch he'd brought for his sister's future use in communicating with us.

Caron really was becoming more alert every day. The next morning, before leaving home, I left this message on the tape: "Caron is becoming more and more conscious every day, and for longer periods of time. The rehabilitation people are anxious to start working with her soon after she's released from intensive care, which doctors and nurses estimate to be within the next few days. Thank you for your prayers and cards. They're working! Leave a message after the long tone if you'd like."

When I arrived at the hospital, Laurie reported that Caron—steadied by two nurses—had supported her own weight for the two steps from bed to chair. They were now using a straight-backed chair with a student desktop that snapped across the arms. I placed all the mail that I'd brought with me, as well as all the mail that had been sent directly to the hospital, on this desktop. Caron beamed and reached immediately for a bright red envelope. She couldn't open it, but once I'd slit it open, she was able to maneuver the card out of the envelope, whereupon she handed it to me to read to her. She smiled in recognition of the sender's name, one of her favorite guitarists at our church. She stayed alert for quite a few card-openings, assisting in them, and particularly delighting in a comment one friend had written on the card from her entire French class: "I'm actually learning something from doing my French on my own. Scary thought. I hope you'll come back soon. Becki."

When Ron arrived, Larry and I left to allow him some time alone with his daughter, as this was his last visit. Caron was convalescing well: she was no longer on the critical list and seemed to have gotten safely past the time period in which she might have suffered a delayed stroke. Ron had been away from the Arizona elementary school in which he was principal for a week and a half now; he'd be returning on a morning flight the next day. We would come to learn that Caron's post-traumatic (after the accident) memory was short; in less than a week she would ask why her father had never come to see her in the hospital. For a long time, Larry and I would need to be Caron's memory for her, and the patience that, as teachers, we had learned to show with slow learners would be put to the ultimate test. While Ron said good-bye to Caron, we spoke with a health care service's nurse consultant, who had been appointed to be our liaison to Caron's car insurance company for the purpose of facilitating payment of benefits, including loss of pay from her part-time job.

The night nurse was an unfamiliar face to us. When she entered the room, she whistled, "I've never seen a room in this unit so covered with cards!" Ah yes, that reminded me: If Caron was being moved off the SICU soon, I'd better make haste in getting all those cards off the walls. I stayed until I was kicked out that evening—taking down and stacking cards and posters and calculating how much it was going to cost in tape to put them all back up again. One of life's more delightful problems!

CHAPTER 9

STEPPING DOWN

Big day for Caron! She was being moved off the SICU to a step-down ward, the neurosurgical unit. Before leaving home to go help move the menagerie of animals, the stacks and stacks of cards, and a dozen helium balloons with various messages on them, I left this message on the home tape: "Today is Wednesday, February 8. Caron is being transferred out of intensive care today! She'll be on the 6000 unit for a while. You'll be glad to know that she has regained that beautiful smile of hers and she's using it liberally. If you're sending a card, add a humorous note; it's good to see her laugh! Thanks and God bless you all, you've been such a source of strength to us through this."

I also made a quick stop at Meijer's to pick up four large scrapbooks for the many cards Caron had already received. She now had so many big posters, computer-generated banners, and other well-wishing signs to decorate the walls that I had decided to store the cards in scrapbooks: one book for cards from her friends and teachers at school; a second one for cards from our church friends; another for cards from relatives and close family friends, including her Uber's family; and the last for cards from

89

people she may not know but who wished her well all the same, such as students in my classes, past and present.

Caron had already been moved to the sixth floor before I arrived, so I had only to go fetch all of her paraphernalia. She was resting peacefully and continued to do so all day. When I had called SICU earlier in the morning, the night nurse reported that Caron had been perky at 1:00 a.m.—smiling, responding, laughing—and that at 3:00 a.m. she had become agitated, so she had been given medication at that time to help her sleep. Little wonder she slept all day! Additionally, this morning a medical student had removed the CVP (central venous pressure) port, as per a hospital regulation that to guard against infection, ports must be changed every-so-many days. Another was to be put in on the left side at any time, so the nurses had to keep Caron in ready position—prone and in bed—for the doctor who would put in the port. Whoever this was never arrived. Rather, the leader of Smith Et Al came by at about 6:00 p.m. to let us know that it would be done; he didn't know when or by whom. (Thanks for the information.) Meanwhile, in not being moved to a chair, Caron had had no stimulus for awakening or being alert part of this day. I suppose she may have needed the rest, but the mother and educator in me couldn't help but think, *Wake up, Caron! Time's a-wastin'! There's so much to be learned, let's get on with it!*

At lunchtime I was able to pump a half a cup of tomato soup and a third of a cup of runny eggnog into her—her first hospital feeding by mouth. For dinner she accepted four ounces of chocolate ice cream. In between, she just slept. I busied myself taping cards into scrapbooks and hoping she'd wake up.

Caron's blood gases were good this morning without additional oxygen, so she was taken off BRIGS, and now there were no tubes at all running to her face. Also, by definition of having been removed from the SICU, she was no longer wired to a monitor. She was still catheterized and still on IV. Cotton-stuffed mitts had been substituted for the wrist ties so that she had more freedom of movement but wasn't able to grasp anything with her fingers. Caron could wear these mitts when someone was in the room with her; but when she was left unattended, the bed rail wrist ties would still need to be utilized. I vowed to be there as much of every day as I would be allowed. So far, no one had said anything about visiting hours on this floor, and I didn't intend to ask about them so long as no one was objecting to my presence.

Just before 7:00 p.m., Caron's new primary nurse, Lisa, came to invite me to the second meeting of an eight-week Wednesday-night series on traumatic brain injuries or, more simply, TBI. Larry had just arrived, so I was free to leave, and I joined Lisa for my first Family Education Night. The speaker was Dr. Owen Z. Perlman, a physiatrist, the physician in charge of physical medicine and rehabilitation. I had not yet met him and wasn't aware of how important he was going to become to us. Fortunately, I was instantly impressed by this relatively young doctor who seemed both brilliant and compassionate, two qualities not often found together. However, his topic was heavy, and while I had regretted missing the first meeting in this series, it didn't take long for me to realize that I might not even now be ready for the information being disseminated. They were wise not to have invited me on February 1!

Dr. Perlman was speaking on technical topics of which I had no prior knowledge: among them, coma scales and scales of cognitive functioning. It was very disturbing to me, and the more I tried to understand, the more disturbing it became for me to understand. The Glasgow coma scale,[2] a gauge of levels of consciousness, assigns numerical scores from the poorest, 1, to a best score of 4, 5, or 6, respectively, in these three areas: eye opening, verbal response,

2 Dr. Bryan Jennett and Dr. Graham Teasdale, "Assessment of Coma and Impaired Consciousness," Lancet, 2:81-84, 1974.

and motor response. Thus, a perfect sum would be 15. Dr. Perlman stated that a sum of 8 or below was generally indicative of a coma, and that a sum of 9 or above would indicate that the patient was probably not in a coma. So far, the information wasn't portentous. Caron obviously was in a coma at the time of her arrival at this hospital. This was fact. But the *implications* of that coma, from which I had been protected previously by my ignorance, were threatening to me: there were statistics, derived from actual patients' scores, which reported the outcomes associated with these patients' best levels of responsiveness in the first twenty-four hours after the onset of a coma.

I had no idea what sum Caron had actually attained, only that it had to have been 8 or less. I looked at the scale, and studied the patient responses for each score in each of the three areas. Based on what I'd seen in Caron's first twenty-four hours after the accident, I would not have been able to give her more than the base 1 in eye opening and verbal response, and I hadn't a clue as to the best motor response: 1? 2? 3? 4? So this admittedly untrained eye would have seen a total of 6, at best, and a mere 3 as the worst scenario. On a table that associated sums of 3 or 4 on the coma scale with the eventual outcomes of actual patients, nearly nine out of ten had died or lived on in a vegetative state; fewer than one in ten recovered to the status of moderately disabled. Even among the patients studied who began with sums of 5, 6, or 7, over half fell into the dead or vegetative category and barely a third into the moderate disability/good-recovery category. Having taken data analysis courses, I knew, rationally, that these statistics could *not* be used for *predicting* future patients' outcomes. Nevertheless, the large part of me which was enveloped in being Caron's mother forgot to be rational, and I found myself fearing that the odds weren't so good as I'd talked myself into believing that they were for my daughter. I left the meeting early because I couldn't face any more of what I was perceiving, without foundation, to be reality.

Sometimes a little knowledge is not better than none at all, and this is particularly true when one is emotionally involved. I realized my mistakes in logic but could not separate myself emotionally so as to reject them as providing misinformation.

Having slept all day, Caron was awake when I returned to the room, and Larry reported that she had been quite uninhibited while I was gone: pulling up her hospital gown and scratching at her crotch. The catheter tube seemed to be annoying her, and she was determined to get at it. Larry said he spent the entire time pulling her hand away from her target area and pulling her gown back down. Eventually, a young male patient-care assistant noticed what was happening and brought waist-tie baggy britches to match the hospital gown. Caron scowled at him, but Todd would become a favorite sight to her in the coming week. I couldn't help but reflect back to another portion of Dr. Perlman's presentation, that of the Rancho Los Amigos Hospital Levels of Cognitive Functioning. On this eight-level scale (from "no response" to "purposeful and appropriate" responses), the third level, localized response, described the patient, in part, as showing "a vague awareness of self and body by responding to discomfort by pulling at nasogastric tube or catheter or resisting restraints."

This had been a disappointing day for me. I prayed that tomorrow would be better. In fact, tomorrow Dr. Farhat would tell me that head injuries improve like the sun passing behind the clouds and then back out again: there would be bad days as well as good ones, but in the total picture, the good days would become more plentiful and the bad ones less frequent.

Larry and I returned home late to find homemade vegetable soup waiting for us in a pot on the stove; fish crackers, rolls, and cookies on the table; and a beautiful fruit salad in the refrigerator. The ladies of the church and other friends had begun a catering service as soon as we'd moved back home, and we were so thankful not to have the added chore of preparing meals when we came home exhausted. No matter how discouraged we became, there were always rays of sunshine—in every single day.

The next morning, I left a message on the tape about Caron having had her first hospital meal, and I hurried along to share my daughter's thirteenth day in the hospital. It was another discouraging one. She was very confused and agitated much of the day. When she was in her chair, she writhed and squirmed and struggled to get out of it. In bed too, she contorted herself this way and that, not being able to get comfortable. Mealtimes were a source of distress to her also. She was on an all-liquid diet, and I couldn't get anything into her. She refused to try to drink through a straw. Any liquids transported by spoon were either boxed away by a padded mitt or upset upon arrival when she clenched her teeth and lips tightly together and shook her head vehemently back and forth. This routine seemed vaguely familiar to me, from a time some sixteen years earlier.

The only enlightenment during the day was that one of the nurses reported Caron's face having lit up that morning when asked if she'd like a shower. Strapped in a chair placed under the shower stream, Caron assisted in scrubbing her own hair and then in toweling herself dry. She must have been ecstatic about being allowed to shower. At home she would shower at least once a day. Throughout all her morning and evening sponge baths here in the hospital, it hadn't occurred to me that if she could think about it she probably missed her shower ritual.

On the drive home I appealed to God that if this whole thing had been staged in order that I should learn to be more patient, then it was working; I *was* learning to be more patient, but I really needed some encouragement—*tomorrow!*

That evening—over Merry Jane Benner's fabulous shrimp and crab quiche, spinach salad with mandarin oranges and sugared almonds, and bran muffins—I reviewed the Rancho Los Amigos

Hospital Levels of Cognitive Functioning and was surprised to find that level 4 is labeled "confused, agitated." If Caron's confusion and agitation was normal progress along a continuum of levels of cognitive functioning, then perhaps this hadn't been such a bad day after all. Ah, God in His wisdom knew that I didn't have enough patience to wait until tomorrow!

The following morning I could turn the previous day's disappointments into a positive answering machine message: "Caron's letting those nurses know that she wants to do more than lie around in bed! She's now assisting with her showers!"

Most of the morning was spent doing business on the phone: calls to the state police, WHMI 93.5 FM (our local radio station), school nurse, and so on; everybody wanted updates on Caron. At ten, as I put the receiver down, the phone rang before I could locate the information needed for my next call. I was upset to find that it was one of the doctors at the hospital calling on our regular line, and he'd apparently been trying since before eight. I had given the hospital the new number reserved for the hospital's exclusive use and had that number been used, he'd have reached me on the first try. Luckily, this was no emergency, and the only cost was the doctor's time. Caron had been scheduled at ten for a two-week follow-up angiogram (regarding the tear in her left carotid artery), but no one had thought to get written consent beforehand, so they now needed me to come there and sign a consent form.

The angiogram was done at noon, and then Caron had to lie flat and still for four to five hours—no sitting in a chair, no shower, no nothing, just lying still and flat. This would have been next to impossible if she had acted as confused and agitated as she had the day before. But all went well. She was alert to and from the radiology unit. I pointed out windows and sights to her, and she strained left and right to see. She was the most conscious I'd seen her, and she scrutinized my face thoughtfully, for a long time.

I gave her a choice of reading material, and she deliberated long in making her choice: eyeing carefully each of the four books I'd propped up in front of her. Finally, she batted the Steinbeck book *Of Mice and Men* with her mitt, then lay back to recuperate from that difficult decision and physical effort. She remained alert through most of the reading of the first two chapters—forty pages!

During this reading, many people came and went. Perhaps it was the many disruptions that kept Caron alert, rather than the book itself. I'll never know. She doesn't remember—and cannot, in her wildest imagination, conjure up an image of her "prim old mother" reading her that book!

Many of the visitors were here on the business of nutrition. I had been protesting Caron's liquid diet, as the staff was suddenly interested in Caron's intake, and I—the feeder—didn't really think that the calories Caron knocked all over the sheets and walls were going to fatten her up any! Betsy, from the dietician's office, brought menus for me to fill out, then returned later to pick them up. Meanwhile, a nutritionist came by to discuss how we might increase Caron's kilocalorie intake; and later she too returned, to question some of the choices I'd made on the menus Betsy had brought.

After our reading and the nutrition visits, Caron was becoming restless and inattentive, so I put in the tape of the County Honors Band Concert she had missed the day after her accident. She perked up immediately, and though there was some confusion in her expression, there seemed to be recognition there too—and between the two was woven pain, deep, emotional pain. As Mr. K's voice sat upon her ears, saying what a fine oboe player Caron was, tears welled up in her eyes—her first tears in two weeks. Throughout her father's speech and on into the music, "Irish Posy," the tears ran down her cheeks and dripped upon her gown. I didn't disturb her by wiping them away. This was the finest moment of cognition I'd seen since two weeks before when this little miss bounded from our front door to go make music, love of her life. We had all suspected that music might be the key to calling her back.

She kept searching my face with the pained expression of memory resurfacing, yet through this pain there was that very peaceful look, that look of understanding. Whenever the oboes played, she leaned closer to the tape player, so I started turning up the volume at these points. Once, when the oboe faltered, she raised her eyebrows, and when I said, "They needed you there, honey," she smiled her acknowledgment.

Later, I had the volume turned way up again so we could hear the small voices of the oboes, and I'd forgotten that this was the *Phantom of the Opera* piece in which the young French horn player, who had offered to give Caron some tips on playing the oboe, showed even further versatility in the solo "screamer" part. Suddenly, that scream pierced the calm in room 6029 and raced up and down the 6000 unit corridor! Caron wasn't at all startled—as I was and as one *would* be if not anticipating this portion of the piece; but rather, she was genuinely amused as I fumbled to turn down the volume, and two nurses came running in to see what had happened! Larry took over at four, after a full day of teaching school, so that I could get Matt in to see our family doctor, as he was complaining that his four-day-old full-leg cast was falling apart; well, what did he expect when he refused to wear the protective shoe that was part of the deal? (But it wasn't *cool*.) He was in a bad mood, quarrelsome, and not at all pleasant to be around. The good doctor described him as "stuck at the preschool emotional state where he was when his father left the house." She also posed some interesting possible explanations for his increased aggravating behaviors: his father traveled all the way back from Arizona—but not for *him*, "and when was the last time he ever saw you two *together*, for any purpose?" (Again, it wasn't for *him*.) She may well have been right; and then there were the compounding problems of his sister's condition, his own insecurity about what lay ahead, and a mother who seemed never to be home for him. I ached for him but couldn't pull myself much farther in two directions.

We laughed out loud when we arrived home to see what a pill Judd had been in everybody's absence. (All else we could have done was to cry, and laughing is oh, so much healthier!) He had cleared the kitchen table for us: five apples, three or four bananas, an orange, and a whole package of wheat crackers had disappeared, as well as the remainder of the cookies that had come with dinner the night before. A can of cinnamon was sprinkled all over the kitchen floor—I could just *see* that can clenched between his teeth and him furiously shaking it! He had punctured several grapefruit but decided not to proceed any farther with those. We found the banana peelings in the basement, as well as the shreds of the cracker box and wrappings, but no further remnants of the crimes. Well, if this appeased the lonely puppy, I supposed it was at least better than chair legs and bedspreads! Ah, both the young males at our house had seen better times!

One of the better times, however, had not been mealtimes. As we sat down to a scrumptious lasagna, spinach salad, garlic toast, and mint chocolate-frosted brownies, all of which had arrived shortly after we'd gotten home and cleaned up the kitchen, Matt commented, "This sure is better than what I usually get to eat around here!"

Larry arrived later, after saying good night to Caron at the hospital. He reported that she had eaten well—all liquids, again, but a nurse had cut a straw in half so the intake would be quicker, and she'd welcomed the chance to do for herself. Later, she cracked Larry up when he handed her a napkin, telling her to wipe some dripping gravy off the side of her mouth—and she, instead, took a big swipe around her mouth with her tongue, an act that our sixteen-year-old daughter would never before have performed! Disinhibition, a common trait of head-injured patients, was creeping in.

RANCHO LOS AMIGOS HOSPITAL

SCALE OF COGNITIVE FUNCTIONING[3]

I. **NO RESPONSE**
Patient unresponsive to stimuli.

II. **GENERALIZED RESPONSE**
Patient reacts inconsistently and nonpurposefully to stimuli. Responses are limited and often delayed.

III. **LOCALIZED RESPONSE**
Patient reacts specifically but inconsistently to stimuli. Responses are related to type of stimulus presented, such as focusing on an object visually or responding to sounds.

IV. **CONFUSED, AGITATED**
Patient is extremely agitated and in a high state of confusion. Shows nonpurposeful and aggressive behavior. Unable to fully cooperate with his treatments due to short attention span. Maximal assistance with self-care skills is needed.

V. **CONFUSED, INAPPROPRIATE, NONAGITATED**
Patient is alert and can respond to simple commands on a more consistent basis. Highly distractible and needs constant cueing to attend to an activity. Memory is impaired with confusion regarding past and present. The patient can perform self-care activities with assistance. May wander and need to be watched carefully.

VI. **CONFUSED, APPROPRIATE**
Patient shows goal-directed behavior, but still needs direction from staff. Follows simple tasks consistently and shows carryover for relearned tasks. The patient is more

---

3 Adult Brain Injury Service, Rancho Los Amigos Medical Center, Downey, California. A revised version of this scale is now available at http://www.neuroskills.com/rancho.shtml.

aware of his/her deficits and has increased awareness of self, family, and basic needs.

VII. **AUTOMATIC APPROPRIATE**

Patient appears oriented in home and hospital and goes through daily routine automatically. Shows carryover for new learning but still requires structure and supervision to ensure safety and good judgment. Able to initiate tasks in which he has an interest.

VIII. **PURPOSEFUL APPROPRIATE**

Patient is totally alert, oriented, and shows good recall of past and recent events. Independent in the home and in the community. Shows a decreased ability in certain areas but has learned to compensate.

CHAPTER 10

FIRST WORDS

I got started early on Caron's third Saturday in the hospital so as to be able to feed breakfast to her. Weekends always brought a changeover in staff, and sometimes a shortage of staff. Additionally, I expected that this would be the day Caron's *real* meals would begin. How disheartened I was when, instead of pancakes and bacon, which she would have devoured, the breakfast tray held Cream of Wheat, milk, and mashed bananas! The label at the top of the menu read "Puréed Diet." Was this a baby step forward or a giant step backward? She could bat this stuff to as-yet unchristened areas of the walls—but she couldn't drink it through a straw. In all honesty, however, breakfast didn't go too badly. Caron had always been fond of Cream of Wheat and had never outgrown an occasional craving for a jar of baby food bananas or peaches. (She would sometimes even purchase these herself if she thought she wouldn't run into anyone she knew in the grocery store!) But lunch consisted of puréed green beans and puréed casserole, which was also green; and there was no way she was going to eat either!

While I was, in fact, learning much about patience that no one who knew me would ever have believed possible, I was also beginning to dabble in another quality I'd always admired in others but had been insecure about trying myself: assertiveness. I knew that there was a fine line between being assertive and being obnoxious, and I can't honestly say which side of the line I was falling onto more often than the other, but I was also coming to an understanding that my feelings about what other people thought of me had to be secondary to what I knew to be right for my daughter. These people were well skilled in their jobs, but they didn't know my daughter. They were good at saying, "Go home. Rest. You must take care of yourself." But a mother's sense of well-being is bonded with her children's well-being, and how could I take care of myself at this little gal's expense? No one here could know who she was. Even had there been one nurse constantly with her, that nurse could only know her as she was now, and this was not the real Caron. There was a more frequent changeover of nurses on this floor than in intensive care, and on this first Saturday morning here, I didn't recognize any faces from the previous few days.

After breakfast, Caron fell back asleep. Patients are no problem when they're sleeping, and had I not been here, I have little doubt that she would have been allowed to sleep all morning. But I was here, and when a new nurse popped in on some small business, I cornered her with my concerns about the puréed diet, and she passed the buck to the dietician, who wouldn't be back again until Monday. All right then, I'd drop that line of questioning and go on to my next topic. "Is Caron going to have a shower this morning?"

"Oh, she can't have showers yet because—"

"She had one the day before yesterday," I countered. Caron got her shower.

The doctors made their rounds a little later on Saturdays. Caron had returned from her shower, squeaky clean, and I'd combed out her hair. Dr. Judith was among the three doctors today, and when their examination was complete, I asked when the catheter might be removed, as it was quite an annoyance to Caron. Dr. Judith replied that this couldn't be a decision of the doctors alone, as it was the nurses who would have the increased responsibility if it were removed. She flagged down a passing nurse to ask what she thought and received the answer, "She's not ready." Now, how would this nurse know anyway? To my knowledge, she'd never met Caron! I knew Caron was ready. It was the nurse who wasn't ready. I asked how a patient's readiness was determined. Her reply was "when the patient can tell us that she needs to use the bathroom and when she can walk to the bathroom." No telling how long it would be before the swelling in Caron's vocal cords would go down enough to allow her to talk. And had anyone tried to help her walk? No one since Laurie on SICU. Larry and Ron and I had exercised Caron from the very first day, moving limbs and extremities as we talked to her in the SICU, but nonetheless, we would expect her to have lost quite a bit of muscle tone.

I also asked Dr. Judith about Caron's diet plan. Why couldn't she have real food? The answer was twofold: No one was convinced that Caron could chew and swallow without choking. And Caron's food intake wasn't yet of sufficient caloric amounts to justify moving her to foods that were harder to consume. *Harder* to consume?!!! *They* should be here at feeding time, trying to force-feed liquids and mush to a strong young adult! And as to the issue of choking, what safer environment could there be than a hospital? For those trained to do it, choking is not difficult to remedy.

I began reading aloud chapter 3 in the book *Of Mice and Men*. When the lunch tray arrived, I placed a bookmark at our stopping place and reached for the tray. Caron mouthed an unvoiced "No ... noooo!" Thinking that she was getting ready to put up a fuss about eating, I proceeded with some positive comments about lunch (which is pretty hard to do when everything looks like week-old leftovers from St. Patrick's Day) while I opened the milk carton and pulled a large food syringe out of the drawer in the bedside stand. One nurse had given this to me a couple of days before, demonstrating that when one pried open Caron's mouth and delivered the liquid into her cheek with this thing, she then had only two choices: either swallow it or drool it out all over herself. I knew Caron wouldn't make the second choice if she remembered anything at all about the person she once was, for she had always been fastidious. Even as a baby, she would shake her fingers disgustedly if any of the food got on them, and she'd refuse to take another bite until I wiped her hands. Grandma Schreer, who always did the cakes in our family, was disappointed on Caron's first birthday, as her previous three grandchildren had delighted in messing in their first birthday cakes, but Caron refused to touch hers again after her first tentative touch told her it was messy. (Grandma was delighted with Caron's little brother when *his* first birthday came along: he was ecstatic about this mushy brown art goop, and while nobody else got to eat cake on Matt's birthday, he had enough chocolate to last him the rest of his life, and we washed frosting out of every crease in his roly-poly body that night.)

The syringe had been dormant in the drawer of the bedside stand since that nurse's demonstration. If our positions had been reversed, I would have felt terribly degraded to have someone squirting food into my mouth with a syringe. I didn't want to do this to my daughter. On the other hand, this might be my only hope of getting Caron onto a standard diet. There would be no changes in her diet until she had taken in 2,500 calories a day for three days, Dr. Judith said. 2500 calories! That was considerably more than what Caron usually ate! How would I ever succeed at pumping 2,500 calories into her? Unless I *literally* pumped them into her! Well, just three days, I rationalized, and then *real* food— if we could somehow also convince some doctor that she could swallow and wouldn't choke.

Having filled the syringe with green gunk, I turned toward Caron and was simultaneously met with sight and scent of the real reason she had mouthed those long "noooos." Nothing had escaped untouched: chair, gown, pillows, legs, floor; everything had to be scrubbed, and it wasn't the delectable brown goop Matt had gleefully messed in fifteen years before. Caron looked mortified when her favorite male patient-care assistant appeared with a mop. He had just arrived for work. Welcome to patient room 6029, Todd!

Caron was disconsolate when the cleanup brigade had finished, changed her gown and pj's, sprayed the room, and left. I couldn't get her to take in more than four ounces of applesauce and the carton of chocolate milk. Caron, like her mother, could never turn down chocolate.

Sensing what she must be thinking and feeling, I reminded her of what the nurse had said this morning: that things would change when she began to voice her needs. "Try it," I coaxed. "Say after me, 'I have to go to the bathroom.' I . . ." But she didn't mimic. I picked up the book and began where we'd left off.

Larry arrived soon afterward, and we were discussing some things when suddenly Caron grabbed my arm, and a hoarse, raspy voice coughed out, "I . . . have . . . to . . ." She took a big breath. It had taken a lot of energy for her to say just three words. It was obviously painful, but she had to do this in order to meet another goal.

"You have to *what*, Caron?" (As if I didn't know.)

She spit the words out in a rapid flow, each word weaker than the one before it, but all seven words were there: "I have to go to the bathroom."

I raced out into the corridor and hailed the first nurse I saw. It just happened to be the nurse who had said no this morning to the catheter question. "My daughter just spoke!" I exclaimed. "She said she has to go to the bathroom!" Every muscle in this woman's body cried out that she didn't believe me, but I wasn't about to give up. "You don't understand," I started. "Where I'm coming from, when the child performs an act you've been trying to elicit, you *reward* this so as to encourage the child to learn it. We've been waiting for two weeks for my daughter to speak, and now she has. Her first words were, 'I have to go to the bathroom.' Now, are you going to help me help her to the bathroom, or am I going to do it by myself?"

Reluctantly, she followed me. At first she tried to get Caron to repeat the sentence; she wanted to hear it herself. *Come on!* I silently urged. It was painful enough for her to say it the first time. The nurse seemed to be weakening until Caron nodded affirmatively to the question "Do you have to urinate, Caron?" at which point the nurse turned to me with an explanation that the catheter would handle this. *Please*, I implored with my eyes, and she asked one more question, "Do you want to sit on the toilet for a while, Caron?"

Todd had overheard the corridor conversation and had followed us to the room. When Caron rasped a frustrated but determined "*yes!*" he moved forward to assist. Caron was wobbly, but she bore her own weight all the way into the adjoining bathroom, with Todd steadying her, and the nurse pushing the pole with the catheter apparatus on it. No one's efforts went unrewarded, despite Caron's performance before lunch.

Speaking of performances, I had to dash off, as I'd promised Caron I'd go listen to her quintet play in the solo and ensemble festival in Fowlerville—an hour's drive from the hospital, and they were scheduled to play at two forty-four. In parting, I made one more promise: I'd be back, and we'd pursue this bathroom thing some more.

Gina was nervous, as she had gotten a 2 on her solo and was worrying that she would blow the quintet's chances. The four older members had earned 1 ratings on their flute, clarinet, French horn, and bassoon solos. Gina, a freshman, had agreed to play the oboe part that Caron was not going to be there to play, but Gina was afraid of letting the group down. Carl had shared this with me, so

I popped into the warm-up room to offer some encouragement. I introduced myself to Gina and told her that Caron was so pleased that she had agreed to give this a try so that the quintet could play after all. She seemed relieved, and she did just fine. The group earned the 1—just like Mike Walsh had promised in his message nearly two weeks before. All the quintet members agreed that Caron deserved a medal too, and Carl was able to give the go-ahead. On the way back to the hospital, I stopped at a local jeweler's and had it engraved, using Mike's sentiments from January 30:

**We Did It
For You!**

"Caron's quintet", which did earn a "1", the highest rating! Front: Sonya, clarinet; Gina, oboe; Tricia, flute. Back: Mike, bassoon; Susie, French horn.

The medal needed no explanation: when I held it up for Caron to view, she beamed from ear to ear!

In the three hours that I was gone, Dr. Judith had come and gone again, and Larry was distressed that she spoke of trying to insert another food tube into Caron's stomach for the purpose of delivering nutrition. This served as incentive for Caron, and when the dinner tray arrived, she made awful faces, but she downed all of the puréed beef (which was gray—uagh!), all the lumpy whipped potatoes, all the puréed peaches, all her chocolate milk and chocolate ice cream (no problem here!), and a piece of soft white bread with butter. She chewed just fine and had no difficulty swallowing.

I was feeling gutsy after Caron's meal, and when a nurse popped in to say a cheery hello and to ask if there was anything we needed, I decided to go for it. Summoning all my courage (for lying isn't one of my fortes), I said, "The doctors okayed removal of the catheter today, but no one has been in to do it yet. Could you do it now?" Well, it wasn't *too* far from the truth. After all, Caron *had* said, "I have to go to the bathroom," and she *did* support her own weight into the bathroom, and Dr. Judith *had* said that catheter removal had to be a joint doctor-nurse decision, so if this nurse agreed . . . And she *did*! What a relief for Caron! Less than a half hour later, she told me again that she had to go to the bathroom, and when the nurse took her, she made good—and then, wobbly as she was on her feet, she tied up her own drawstring pants in a bow.

Tired from all the events of the day, Caron then zonked out for the night, wearing her new medal with the blue ribbon.

Before we left, we surveyed the room. Posters and banners covered the walls, and there were floral arrangements on every available inch of dresser, bed stand, and windowsill area. Flowers had not been allowed on SICU, and as soon as Caron had been transferred to room 6029, the flowers had begun pouring in, many with colorful balloons in them, bearing cheery messages. A new teddy bear had arrived on this day, also, to keep the rest of the menagerie company.

Caron had had a very long-distance call earlier this morning—before she was talking. Five years before, she had gone to France for three weeks as part of a fifth-and sixth-grade exchange program. She stayed with a family named Dalsace, and the oldest Dalsace girl, Camille, had spent three weeks with us too, so the girls had had six weeks to become good friends. Caron had then saved her babysitting money for airfare so she could spend the summer after her freshman year in France—*avec la famille Dalsace*; and the following year Camille came back to us in the summer. Now, upon receiving word from me about Caron's accident, Camille was devastated. Her mother, Jeanne (Caron's "French mother"), told me that she had never seen her daughter in such a state, and the whole family promised to put together a tape of their voices to help jog Caron's memory. When I put the phone up to Caron's ear and she heard Jeanne's cheery "Allo, Caron!" she had grinned a huge grin and listened attentively to everything Jeanne had to say.

But on Sunday, Caron had no recollection of a call from France the day before, and when I asked her who the members of the Dalsace family were, she responded, "Todd and I think Dave." (Dave was another of the 6000 unit's patient-care assistants.)

However, at 6:30 a.m. the phone had rung at our house, and Lisa—Caron's primary nurse, back from a day off—was on the line to say that Caron was talking up a storm but she couldn't understand her. "I think she's speaking French. Do you understand French?" When Caron came on the line, she said, hoarsely but clearly, "Hi, Mom!" After that, her speech became unintelligible— possibly in French—until she rasped, "I gotta go now."

Larry was already on his way to the hospital to feed Caron her breakfast. We were discouraged from having to force puréed foods on her, so we took turns, always prefacing our attempts with "Dr. Judith says . . . ," "Dr. Judith would like . . . ," or even "Dr. Judith will order removal of the IV if . . . ," upon which Caron would sometimes begrudgingly, distastefully, but nevertheless open her mouth. Now that she had begun to talk, she had a few choice comments to make, too, about the food and about Dr. Judith!

Matt and I spent the morning at church, where we were pumped with questions about Caron, and we made a promise that her dialogue class could come to see her after church the following Sunday.

Marci Neuman had brought our supper to church with her for Matt and me to take home. She's such a wonderful cook, and I couldn't help thinking about Caron. Why *couldn't she* have food like this? On impulse, I prepared a plate for Caron: roast beef, a twice-baked potato, broccoli, a roll and butter, and a brownie; and Matt suggested I take along a bottle of apple-cranberry juice, as he remembered it having been her favorite drink.

I arrived at noon, just as the lunch trays were arriving. When I lifted the lid of Caron's tray, and strained gray meat stared blandly up at us, Caron spit out, "SICK!"

"It's okay, honey. I brought you something better. You eat it all up, and we'll prove to those doctors that you can eat normal food."

I needn't have said that. It took no coaxing whatsoever to get her to eat *this* food!

Later in the day, no doctors having appeared, I asked a nurse if Dr. Judith would be around.

"Dr. Richmond?" the nurse asked.

"Yes . . . Dr. Judith. Caron wants to see Dr. Judith."

"I do?" Caron queried.

"Yes." I smiled. "Remember what you wanted to say to Dr. Judith? About how wonderful the meals are around here and how you gobble them right up?"

"Oh yes!" Caron now shared my smile.

"What do you want to say to Dr. Judith?" The nurse could hardly wait to find out.

"I want to tell her where to go!"

CHAPTER 11

"HOW DID THIS HAPPEN?"

John Maurer, back from several weeks' business abroad, came to see Caron on the afternoon of this third Sunday that she was in the hospital. He was a close friend of our family, and Caron looked upon him as another father. He had taught her to ski and water-ski and sail. He had taken her for seaplane rides and cooked hamburgers on a grill on his pontoon boat for her and her many giggly girlfriends on her birthdays. When he learned that they couldn't go otherwise, he chaperoned Caron and Matt on an airplane to Arizona to see their paternal grandfather before he died. It was John who had bought Bart for Caron. She was closer to John than to almost anybody. But when he left after visiting, I asked her if she knew who that was. She answered affirmatively, yet not convincingly, and I pursued it further:

"What's his name, honey?" "I forget."

"It's John."

"Oh yes. I remember."

"Do you remember where John lives?" "No."

"He lives at Whitmore Lake." "Oh."

"He has something that you love to ride in. Do you remember what that is?"

"No . . . a car?"

"No, it's not a car, but it is something you ride in. John takes you up in it—just you and him, because it only has two seats. It's red-and-white . . ."

"I don't remember." "It's a seaplane."

"No, I don't remember."

"That's okay. Something else about John: he's the person who gave you Bart. Do you remember what Bart is?"

"A red-and-white seaplane?"

We had been aware, of course, of Caron's anterograde amnesia—her inability to remember things since the accident. Now that she could speak, it came as quite a shock to us to witness such a blatant example of the extent of her retrograde amnesia— loss of memory from before the accident. For half of Caron's years on this earth, John had been an important person in her life. That she could not recall his name, or bring to mind all the joys he had shared with her and Matt, or even remember her beloved Bart and that John had given it to her . . . These revelations were devastating!

On the other hand, it was encouraging that she could remember small details from a simple dialogue, and she had obviously retained some skills in logic, which helped her make guesses based on the way the conversation was going.

It was later on that same day, when Mr. K was with us for his daily visit, that Caron impressed us with her brightest revelations yet—two hours' worth. Carl hadn't heard her talk yet, so he was enthralled. He had arrived at dinner time, and I'd said, "Oh, good, Carl! Eating hospital meals isn't one of Caron's favorite parts of the day, but she'll be on her best behavior while *you're* here." (She was still on the hospital's puréed diet; they didn't know yet about the lunch she'd had that day.)

As I spooned and squirted puréed beef and beans into her, as well as other equally appealing accompaniments, Caron became more and more lucid. Carl occupied himself looking at all the posters, banners, and oversized cards on the walls. We had hung those by strings attached to the metal trim at the wall-to-ceiling junctions, because the textured wallpaper here resisted tape. All the regulation-sized cards were now stored in four large scrapbooks sitting on Caron's bed stand. When Carl had finished studying all the wall hangings and made comment about the number of them, I handed him one of the scrapbooks. Caron had watched me assemble these, and I'd told her about each card as I taped it in the book, but now she seemed to have no recollection of having seen these before. She was intrigued, so Carl shared the book with her, and she read the large print of the title page aloud: "Educational Stuff: cards, letters, and messages from friends at school, school staff, and past teachers."

We went through the book quickly, as I knew that Caron's attention span wasn't yet very long. She'd normally drift off after five or ten minutes, maybe a half hour at best. So we just looked at the cards, I told her whom each was from, and we didn't read them unless she specifically asked. She made comments on some, surprising us with her selective memory: "He was a good teacher." "I love her. She's so sweet!" "I liked her. She made us work hard." "I'm not surprised." When we came to the French class's card, she asked to hear some of the comments when I mentioned particular names. When I read Becki's comment about actually learning on her own, "scary thought," and hoping Caron would come back soon, Caron interjected, "She *never* studies—*never!*" At the mention of another name, Caron's disinhibition began to show as she exclaimed and gestured with wide-spread arms: "She's *big* . . . *really big!*" This isn't a comment the Caron I knew would have considered important enough even to make, let alone emphasize as she did, but now she needed to express herself and to prove—to herself? to us?—that she could remember. She was grasping at anything remotely familiar and voicing it.

When we came to the hand-drawn Woody Woodpecker card from her whole AP Biology class, Caron pulled that one close and read several of the messages herself. Her eyes were still not working together, so she was seeing as one sees with crossed eyes, but it seemed important that she try to read some of this herself. Many of her closest friends were in this class, and she adored the instructor; it was one of her most enjoyable classes. So I was surprised when, after giving us some briefs on some of the classmates who'd sent their wishes, she moved on to the topic of the instructor's lectures and said, "They're boring."

"Kind of like Mr. K's messages?" asked Carl.

"No," she returned, without looking at him, "Mr. K's lectures are rather interesting."

"They are?"

"Yes. He's different. He's fun. I like Mr. K. Did you know that he's been up to visit me often?"

She was conversing with *me*, and I was worried. Didn't she know that he was here? And that he had been here every single day, all sixteen days so far, cheering her on? Was it possible that she didn't know who he was? At this point, I wondered if she really knew who I was, or if she had simply accepted me as a friendly visitor who came regularly. Tentatively, I gestured toward Carl and ventured, "Who is this?"

"Mr. K." She grinned. She had been toying with us all along.

We looked at our watches. She had been quite alert for over an hour, breaking all previous records for lucidity. Mr. K stayed awhile longer, long enough to witness Caron slipping down in her bed and accidentally hitting the button that raises the head of the bed with her toes. He laughed, "Hey! I'll bet you could play the oboe with your toes! Those are pretty talented toes!"

"I'm looking forward to playing my oboe, period. But it'll be scary." Carl had been concerned about what to do in his bands. Caron had been the only oboist in the wind ensemble, the band composed of the most experienced players, usually only juniors and seniors. He didn't want to betray her by replacing her, but district and state band festivals were imminent, and the band needed an oboist. He had asked me several times what he should do. I longed to be able to tell him that Caron would be back, but I was finally beginning to come to grips with the fact that head injuries aren't quick to heal, and we were looking at a long recovery period here. In addition to this, the angiograms were showing no improvement in the tear in the inner wall of her left carotid artery, and I was beginning to sense some uneasiness on the part of the doctors whenever I mentioned Caron's oboe playing. So I urged Carl to move Gina up to the wind ensemble.

Rarely does a freshman ever have the opportunity to enter this elite band, and it must have been frightening for Gina, but when Mr. K asked her, she agreed to give it a try. Mr. K knew she was shy; after all, she was but a ninth grader. But Gina would show spunk and determination, and she would be a fine asset to the band. The band would, as usual, take *1* ratings in the spring competitions. We did decide, however, not to mention this change in the bands to Caron at this time. She adored Gina, but we couldn't know what Caron's emotional state was, how effective her logic and planning abilities were, and, in short, how she would handle this situation. Certainly, if she could return to band, the wind ensemble would simply carry two oboists, but we weren't sure if Caron would fully be able to understand all this, so we chose not to complicate things, not to mention it.

Shortly after Carl left, the phone rang, and a voice from Arizona said, "Put me on to Cari." Caron's face lit up when she heard her father's voice on the phone, and she responded to questions he asked, but after he hung up, she asked, "Why doesn't he ever come to visit me here?"

Caron had been intelligible now for an hour and a half, and she showed no signs of drifting off, so I pulled out two more carrots we'd been using—in addition to the Dr. Judith one—to keep her eating: we'd been promising her that once she was on real foods, she could invite some friends to come visit, and we'd have a pizza party. Now, thinking Caron would certainly be on real foods by the day after the next, I asked her if she was ready to begin thinking about which friends she'd like to invite to her pizza party. She clapped her hands in the same glee often displayed by preschool children on Christmas morning.

We had been through all the pictures in her wallet; and with not too much confusion, she was able to identify all her closest friends. Now the job was to narrow them down to four or five, as patient rooms in a hospital aren't very big. Leeann's picture was on top, so she named Leeann first. After that, she became a bit more judicious, and eventually added Kellie, Kathy, Amy, and Cindy to her list. She had already been alert for over two hours now, and it was plain that she was fatiguing. She began losing her train of thought and asked me, again and again, to go over her "guest list." At one point, when I named Kellie, she interrupted, "Oh, wait! If you invite Kellie, then there's somebody else you have to invite. They kind of go together. Let me think, who is it? . . . Oh yes! Kathy, um . . . Kathy Lane!"

"Kathy's already on the guest list," I reminded her. "She is?" she asked in disbelief.

"Yes, she is."

"Well, good, because they can entertain each other. And Cindy and Amy . . . they'll get along. But Leeann might drive everybody crazy."

When I suggested that we could erase Leeann's name from the guest list if she'd like, she was relieved. This alternative had not occurred to her. I was beginning to see some of the rigidity often associated with head injuries, even before I was informed of it: To Caron, the fact that Leeann's name had been written on the list made the invitation irreversible. Reluctantly, I erased Leeann's name. She had always been one of my most favorite of Caron's friends. But in making the list herself, Caron had taken one giant step in planning skills and a small step toward understanding that things are not usually etched in stone. I also remembered that Leeann was a friend whom Caron had always enjoyed on a one-to-one basis rather than in a group, and being myself a person most comfortable with one-to-one relationships, I respected her concerns regarding throwing this special friend into a group of other friends from other contexts. Leeann was special to all of us, and we'd invite her to come alone to visit Caron.

Caron dropped off to sleep after her pizza party guest list was complete. Virginia, one of the weekend-only nurses, and one who had helped Caron into the bathroom once this particular day, stopped by on her way to check out. She wanted me to tell Caron that she wouldn't be back until the following weekend and that she wished Caron good luck. Of me, she inquired, "Is your daughter's personality *normally* like this?"

"Normally like what?" I asked.

"Well, when I helped her in the bathroom, she had such sweet manners. She kept saying, 'Please' and 'Thank you,' 'I'm sorry,' 'Sure,' and 'Excuse me.' Is she normally like that?"

"Absolutely," I was proud to say.

"I just wondered," she went on, "because so many TBI patients go through personality changes, and I wondered if the TBI had changed her in this way." No, although more naive, Caron's emerging personality was as kind and sweet and positive as it had always been (except, of course, for the disinhibition episodes). But so far, she really was not aware of the ramifications of her being here, or of the time frame. In retrospect, judging by things she had yet to say and questions she still had not asked, I would have to say that up until this point, and for some time beyond, she was still functioning as if in a dream—removed from reality, yet aware of some parts of what was real, piecing the real and the unreal together, as dreams do.

Several days before, I had bought some large two-sided Valentine's Day shapes: hearts, cupids, flowers, boxes of candies, and so on. I suspended them from the ceiling with invisible thread and paper clips attached to the metal bands supporting the suspended ceiling tiles. Some hung quite low so that Caron could see them, and the doctors had to dodge them to get to her bedside when they made their morning rounds; but the nurses all agreed that this was an excellent way to help Caron regain her memory. Other patients walking by enjoyed looking into this room, and perhaps the décor reminded their visitors that flowers or a box of candy on February 14 would lift the spirits of their loved ones too. All in all, it cheered the place up. But as I turned out the lights to leave tonight, the Valentine hangings were but shadows crouching over and around Caron's bed, and I was sad for how much of her exciting teenage life she had already missed and would continue to miss . . . for how long?

As I drove home, I prayed—for Caron, for Matt. Caron was going to be playing catch-up for a while, and there were no guarantees as to how much she would regain. So I prayed especially for Matt. Something good had to come out of all this. I prayed that it could be that Matt might continue to learn compassion—he was beginning to show some of this already—some aspect of service toward, and/or concern for others. He needed to move away from the self-centeredness that was somewhat typical of his age but even more indicative of his developing character. I wanted him to know that I loved him, yet right now I didn't have enough time to show him. I hoped that he could somehow know it anyway and learn to return love and kindness. I really hoped that in seeing his sister's recovery he would find some peace in understanding and that he might come to see God working here, as we did.

The next day, Caron remembered neither the pizza party nor whom she had invited. And despite all the conversation about her room décor in the past week, when I asked her what holiday it would be the next day, she could venture only a guess: "Thanksgiving?" I refreshed her memory on everything, being careful to remind gently so as to not make her feel a failure. In this type situation, it's sometimes best just to speak of everything as though it were the first time it's being mentioned.

Perhaps when one has been in a coma, one comes out of it sensing a loss of time. During this same week that Caron had thought Thanksgiving must be coming up, she was also persistent about her senior pictures, insisting that she must get them signed and passed out. But she wasn't a senior. She was missing the second semester of her junior year. Senior pictures weren't due to be taken for another half year, with picture exchanges happening in the months after that—the months surrounding Thanksgiving. But no amount of reason could convince Caron that she was not a senior, she had not had senior pictures taken, and there was no set of pictures waiting to be signed and passed out. At this same time, she was also confused about home. When someone asked her where she lived, she had responded, "In a subdivision . . . on Wide Valley Drive . . . in a pink house." We had never moved, in all the years since Caron's birth. When we brought our baby girl home from St. Joseph Mercy Hospital in Ann Arbor almost seventeen years ago, she had come home to a white house on the main street of the city of Brighton, and none of this had ever changed. We tried to re-educate her about this too and even brought lots of pictures from home to help, but over a week later, when asked her address, she would reply, "I don't know. They haven't told me my new address yet." And when prodded about why she thought we must have a new address, she'd answer, "Well, they *must* have moved by *now!*"

I had brought with me a collection of valentines so that Caron could make selections for her friends who had been invited to come for a visit the next night and some additional ones for other people to whom she might like to send Valentine greetings. She first selected cards for Kellie, Kathy, Amy, and Cindy, but as she was signing her name to each, she kept forgetting whose it was and which ones were already done and which ones were yet to be done. It looked like this was going to be one of those days Dr. Farhat forewarned us about, when the sun would pass behind the clouds. This was especially discouraging after such a bright day as the one before. Caron was fading fast and began babbling about someone named Martha. Martha *who?* I'd never heard of a Martha. She pouted and said she was very sad that I hadn't invited Martha to the party. I'm sorry, Martha, whoever you are.

The fifth and last card she signed before falling asleep was one for everyone at the high school. While she slept, I added a note about her progress, and a "Thank you for your continued patience regarding our 'no visitors' policy. As Caron becomes more conscious and begins talking more about people, we'll begin to allow a few people at a time to come chat with her for a few minutes." I attached a copy of the Rancho Los Amigos Hospital Scale of Cognitive Functioning, with notes regarding the stages through which Caron seemed already to have progressed. She seemed to me to have reached level 5: confused, inappropriate, nonagitated. In this level, the patient is distractible and needs constant cueing to attend to an activity, but can perform simple self-care activities with assistance. Caron was, in fact, assisting in her morning showers now and going to the bathroom. On the school's copy I didn't write details, just dates that she seemed to have moved from one level to the next, and I concluded by drawing an arrow pointing to level 6 (confused, appropriate) and saying, "Caron is trying to move into this stage. She is successful a couple of hours a day." The next morning I would post these messages outside the band room door, as so many of her friends were in the bands; and the office would make an announcement about it being there.

Caron slept most of the afternoon. Meanwhile, doctors and nutrition personnel came in and out. The doctors were still concerned about Caron's calorie count not coming up—and yesterday one of her trays had been returned to the kitchen untouched, they reported. "Oh, I can explain," I said, as I pulled out the list of foods—real foods—that Caron had consumed the day before, from Marci Neumann's kitchen. "And later she ate a candy bar," I added. I braced myself for a well-deserved scolding. It didn't come. Instead of chastising me, they did some quick calculations on calories, adding mine to the kitchen count for the day, and they seemed satisfied. Then they asked questions about her ability to chew and swallow, and when I told them there'd been no problems whatsoever, they wrote the order for "real food" and said they'd ask the dietician to come see me with regard to food preferences and menus. *Whoopee!*

Larry had called me at three: Matt *wanted* to come to the hospital with him. This was new. Since his father had returned to Arizona, Matt had been resistant about coming. The problem on this particular day was that after stopping at the hospital to chat with Caron for a little bit, Larry had to continue on to Eastern Michigan University for a 7:00 p.m. graduate class he was taking, so Matt might be stuck here for the entire evening. Even when he had come with his dad, he was reluctant to stay for more than a few minutes; after fifteen minutes, he would become irascible.

"Does he know he might be stuck here for a while?" I asked. "I don't know."

"Well, make it clear to him, and if he still wants to come, bring him." Maybe God was opening a window, in answer to my prayers the night before.

So Larry and Matt came, bearing Chicken Divan from the kitchen of Karen Dei, another of our many friends from church— *all* of whom were proving to be much better cooks than I. After we'd all eaten together, Larry left. I had dropped out of my graduate classes the first week after Caron's accident, but I encouraged Larry to stay in his, as he had more hours yet to earn than I did toward his Master's Plus 30. As it was, he had stepped down from his swim coaching position because of Caron's accident: he had exchanged titles with the assistant coach, so as to hold less responsibility in the team's management in case he was needed more to help out with Caron.

Matt annoyed both Caron and me with some of his familiar habits: cracking his knuckles, flicking through the television channels repeatedly with the remote control device. *Click, click, click, click, click, click.* But he was uncharacteristically amenable when asked to stop. He also showed empathy toward his sister during dinner: "Don't make her eat those carrots. She hates carrots!" and "Don't make her eat any more! That's more than she usually eats! Can't you see that she's miserable?" Later, whenever he noticed that she had scooted down in bed, he would help me pull her back up again; and when she dozed and became uncovered, he covered her back up again. I reflected on my prayers from the night before and was thankful to see that God had listened and was working within my son.

In the moments that Caron was awake that evening, various aspects of her memory and lack of memory amazed me. She could remember details of her friends' personalities, but not the color of the house she had lived in all her life. She remembered that she was expecting a $25 check from Uber's and an $18 check from church, and she could name friends whose pictures were in her wallet, but she couldn't remember her address, and she had no recollection of Disney World, where she had been at least a half-dozen times. She didn't remember ever going to France, either. She couldn't hang on to the concept of Valentine's Day and seemed to have no recollection of Valentine's Days past. My sociable girl: she couldn't remember places or things or concepts, but she could remember her monetary business, and she could remember people's personalities. My responsible little people gal!

Once Matt was engrossed in a television program, Caron zeroed in on some questions that I had known I could expect from her when she really began moving back into consciousness: "How many days of school have I missed?" Her eyes widened when she heard the response. "How will I ever make up my work? Can I go back tomorrow? . . . No?"

She looked hurt. Tears welled up in her eyes. She quavered, "Why not?" She wasn't really receptive to the answers, but she didn't know how to tender opposition. Although she had adult concerns and worries, she had returned to an infantile emotional stage, where Mommy took care of everything. "When can I go back?" she continued. "Next week? . . . No?!" Disbelief. Alarm. Panic. "Well, when?" I couldn't give her dates and times, only "when you're ready," and right now she definitely wasn't ready to handle such indefinite answers! *Oh, help, God!* Like any small child, Caron wanted *the* answer, and she wanted it *now.* "Will I be a senior next year?" she demanded, but I couldn't guarantee that, either. (Indirectly, at least, she was acknowledging that she was not now a senior.)

Getting no place on the school issue, she switched to the topic of finances. "What about my college savings? How can I keep up if I'm here? I'm supposed to get about a $25 check from Uber's and an $18 check from church nursery. When you deposit those, will I be up to date on my college savings?"

Ah, finally, a question I could answer: I had the two checks in my purse. All I needed was her signature so that I could deposit them. (I had previously deposited $10 of the $18 check, as per the written instructions enclosed in her bankbook, which was found in her purse, retrieved from the car by a friend. But I'd now deposit the actual check too.) As she signed the checks, I reassured her that her college savings were in tip-top shape and not to worry, whereupon she jumped to "What about the money I owe the church?" She had pledged a designated amount of money to the church each week, and she was not about to be consoled by comments that the church would understand. To Caron, a commitment was a commitment!

Finally, with moist searching eyes, she asked me, in little more than a whisper, "How did this happen? Is there anything I could have done to avoid this?" Caron was finally beginning to understand the nightmare her family had already endured for sixteen days and nights.

The next day was Valentine's Day. The night nurse reported to the morning nurse, who reported it to me, that Caron continued worrying out loud, off and on throughout the night, about bills and deadlines and commitments. While, yes, this level of responsibility and organization had been modeled for her, Caron had not had to acquire these characteristics. They were part of her character from the beginning. She always had her own way to go about doing things, and she persevered until things met with her satisfaction. As a toddler, she had a wagon of twenty-eight blocks, each with letters ink-stamped on four sides but brightly painted with enamel on the other two sides. Half of the blocks had green on one side and yellow on the opposite side. The other fourteen blocks had blue and red on the two opposing enamel sides. When Caron had helped to put toys away at the end of her busy toddler days, she always took care to arrange the blocks with the green and blue sides up, never the red and yellow, nor the ink-stamped sides.

Sometimes, when it had really been a tiring day, it was easier for her father and me to trundle the kids off to baths and bed, then put the toys away ourselves. We didn't really care which colors were facing up; our mission was just to get things off the floor. But the next morning, Caron would notice immediately that her blocks had not been put away correctly, and she'd angrily whip the wagon off the shelf and rearrange the blocks, all blue and green sides up! At eighteen months, she wasn't stringing words together yet, but she sure could deliver the message clearly that, as keepers of her toys, we parents were failures.

Now, only sixteen years old, she had been equally responsible for her schoolwork, her money, and her promises. Before this time, however, she had never experienced someone or something standing in the way of her achieving her goals and fulfilling her promises. Even at eighteen months, she had had recourse if she was displeased about something. How very heartbreaking it was for her to be in a situation so totally out of her control.

She'd had a busy morning: doctors' visits, breakfast, and shower and hair washing. Lunch arrived, including a real stacked ham sandwich. Caron dug right in without invitation. Her spirits high from this "promotion," she ate her ice cream herself and had no difficulty wielding the spoon. There were a few heart-shaped hard candies on her tray too, in a little paper cup. She gobbled those up and said, just like a little kid, "I *like* those!"

The afternoon was busy also. Caron managed a trip to the bathroom, solo. Later, Larry and I took her for a walk down the corridor, to the nurses' station, and back. There was a steady entourage of hospital workers to clean the bathroom or perform various other regular functions and delivery people bearing flowers and more flowers and a bouquet of Valentine balloons. Larry had brought roses and cards too. Such excitement! Our pastor paid a visit as he had been doing two or three times a week. Jo McDonald, nursing supervisor on the rehabilitation unit, came by to introduce herself and to meet Caron. John Maurer arrived and hooked up a VCR so Caron could watch all the *Cheers* programs he'd been taping for her. Meanwhile, workers in the hallway were furiously pounding their hammers, installing swing-out chairs at the nursing station. Caron complained, "Why are they doing that *now?*"

"It's better than when you're sleeping, isn't it?" "That's true."

Of course, the fact is that Caron was used to dozing off for parts of every day, and today she never had that opportunity. The steady stimulation continued: Grandma Schreer called from Arizona. Mr. K arrived and stayed through dinner. He had no sooner left when Caron's stepsisters, Rachel and Jenny, arrived, bearing Valentine's Day gifts from Arizona. They'd saved theirs to open with her, and they all groaned together over what they'd gotten, but in the end they agreed that being remembered was nice.

By the time her pizza party arrived—Kellie, Kathy, Amy, Cindy, and the pizzas and pop—Caron was exhausted. Her friends seemed a bit disconcerted that she couldn't keep their names straight. This was especially true when they would get up to get another piece of pizza or pour another glass of pop and then exchange places in the room. There weren't enough chairs and with no room to put additional ones, everybody took turns standing up. People changing positions really confused Caron. Her vision was still cross-eyed, and she was really drained from the overstimulation of the day. I should have foreseen the holiday excitement and planned the party for another day. Nevertheless, seeing her friends was a real morale booster for Caron, and while she said and did some pretty bizarre things, she did sit up in bed for a one and a half hour visit with her friends, thoroughly enjoying herself.

I knew she'd sleep well that night, so I followed the party out, reflecting as I drove home on some other events of the past two days. The day before this Valentine's Day party, Dr. Perlman had come in to introduce himself. I recognized him from the previous Wednesday night's lecture series; and because he had impressed me then, it was very satisfying to learn that Caron was now on his service. Further, he stated that Caron would be admitted to the rehabilitation wing "when there's a bed available—probably the middle of next week." This was a disappointment to me, as Dr. Judith had said, "as soon as the IV tubes were out." But I prepared myself to wait out another week, exercising my daughter myself and doing what I could to help her with written and spoken language.

The really good news had come when I arrived Valentine's Day morning: the floor nurses told me Caron would be going to rehab within a few days: *their* doing! They explained that there were currently six candidates for rehab on the 6000 unit, with Caron being last on that waiting list—but they felt that Caron was the most *ready*, and they had recommended that she be moved to the top of the list.

After this, the physician's assistant from rehab came up to ask me some questions. His mission was to get Caron's medical history, and he was surprised that I used all the right vocabulary and had answers to questions that rehab needed to know about Caron. The explanation was simple: we were finally moving into an area I knew something about—education.

Also that morning, before coming to the hospital, I spent an hour at the high school with Kay Kroth, the school nurse. She briefed me on some procedures that had been used a couple of years before when another of our high school students had suffered a head injury: this girl had been IEPC'd into special education and certified POHI (physically or otherwise health impaired) so that a tutor could be assigned. Kay had requested and gotten a special education teacher, Sheila Bradley, whom she described as excellent for this type of service. She said she would do the same for Caron when the time came. As an educator, knowing all the channels one had to go through to be eligible for this type of service, I urged her to begin the paperwork right away so that all would be "*go*" when/if Caron needed this. The referral for special services would be in my mailbox the next day, I would sign it, and it would be back on Kay's desk the following morning.

Things were moving right along for Caron. Now much would be up to her. I had no doubts that she wouldn't let anybody down. She was desperate to regain her independence!

When I got home, I gave Matt his present from the Arizona Valentine's Day package. His reaction was as ungrateful as the girls' initial reactions, but he came around to saying, "Oh, well, it's the thought that counts," a belief he'd never before evidenced. And as *his* Valentine's Day gift to us, he had done the dishes and cleaned the upstairs bathroom, all on his own. I began counting my blessings!

CHAPTER 12

"YOU'RE GOING TO BE IN TROUBLE!"

When I arrived at room 6029 the day after Valentine's Day, great news awaited me there: a room was available for Caron in rehab! I began taking things off the walls right away, and by the time the room had reclaimed its normal drab look, John Maurer had arrived and disconnected the VCR he had just installed the previous day, and Dr. Perlman had come and removed the port on the left side of Caron's chest. She was finally *free! Tubeless!*

John helped Nurse Cheryl and me move Caron and all her stuff to rehab, room 1179. This would be Caron's permanent residence at the hospital for the remainder of her stay. After the excitement of her big move and all the good-byes and good lucks back on the 6000 unit, Caron christened her new bed by snoozing in it for a couple of hours. During this time, I taped up posters, banners, pictures, notes, and balloons that had deflated; and I suspended the Valentine shapes from the ceiling too. I also discovered that there was no dresser or heater register here as there had been upstairs. Closet, shelves, and the heater vents were built into the walls, so there was nothing on which to sit plants, vases of flowers, helium balloon bouquets, or stuffed animals. I called

Larry, and when he and Matt arrived later, they brought two of my bookshelves from my classroom at school, and everything that hadn't previously been hung or put away now had a home.

Larry and I left Matt in charge of his sister while we went to the TBI Family Education Night meeting in the Great Room, just through the double doors beyond Caron's room and to the left. The evening's speaker was a nurse, who spoke on the nurse's role in rehabilitation. I wasn't sure how much of what she had to say was truly factual, for one of her main points of emphasis seemed to be that each nurse was primary to only two or three patients; yet Caron's primary had stuck her head into room 1179 just once today to announce, "Ah'm yer prahmary narse. Ah ahlready hev a heaveh load, but su-u-u-umbody's gotta be'yer prahmary narse, so Ah gieeass Ah'm ee-it."

When we returned to Caron's room, Matt had all kinds of interesting things to tell us. We had been assigned a social worker, and she had stopped in to introduce herself, leaving a lengthy biography to be filled out, and asking that I call her the next day to confirm a 4:00 p.m. Friday meeting with her. Nurses had visited Caron with a scale. Matt had chuckled when they left and Caron breathed an excited, "128! Wow! Only ten pounds to go!" But he was most tickled, in a protective big-brother manner (which was nice to see), at his sister's rather infantile reaction when he told her that he was going to go grab a bite to eat at the cafeteria. Wide-eyed and in a tremulous voice, she had asked, "Are you supposed to leave me all alone?"

"I'll be right back," he had assured her. "It's just down the hall."

With increasing alarm, she had demanded, "Does *Mom* know you're leaving me? Did she say it would be okay?"

"Caron, I'll be right back. I'll grab a sandwich and bring it back here to eat it."

Failing in arousing sympathy, she yelled after him, " *You're going to be in trouble!*"—a scare tactic from preschool years' methods for dealing with little brothers!

She continued this insecurity when Larry and Matt and I readied to leave for the night. We hadn't had this problem when she was on the 6000 unit, partly because she wasn't yet very aware of her surroundings, and perhaps partly because there were no demands made upon her there. Now she was filled with apprehensions: What if they didn't wake her up on time? What if she couldn't do what they wanted her to do in therapy? What if . . . ? What if . . . ? What if . . . ? I was only partly able to assuage her worries by promising her I'd be back at 7:00 a.m. to go through the whole day with her.

On the way home Matt reminded me that I had an appointment to have my hair cut, in Brighton, at 8:30 a.m. It had always been Caron who never was remiss in following her own schedule and meeting her own deadlines—and also reminded her mother and brother of *our* appointments. Now here was her younger brother, stepping up to the plate!

Larry's school system was on its winter break week, so Larry was there for Caron the next morning at seven, and when I arrived at eleven thirty, he said it had been a rather uneventful morning. The therapists had been around to introduce themselves, but Caron had had no therapies. In fact, she had slept most of the morning. Larry described the speech therapist as vivacious and very articulate, the physical therapist as kind and soft-spoken, and the occupational therapist as friendly and patient. Yvonne came in almost immediately after Larry had left, and she was, indeed, vivacious and very articulate! She would be perfect for Caron. She brought with her a black three-ring notebook. This would travel everywhere Caron traveled in the hospital, and everyone who spent time with her would be asked to write in the journal portion of her book to help with her memory. Yvonne made the first entry: "Yvonne came to see me this afternoon and talked to my mom about my journal and my schedule. My double vision bothered me a lot, but I stayed awake the whole visit."

Caron's schedule of therapies began that afternoon: PT (physical therapy) at one fifteen, OT (occupational therapy) at two, and speech at three. In PT, Sue conducted range-of-motion tests and reported that everything looked good and that Caron would just have to work to build up her stamina and muscle strength.

In OT, Laura did some visual tests. Again, there was trouble with the double vision, but with one eye covered Caron did better. Laura asked Dr. Perlman to order an eye patch.

In speech, Caron began a memory test. Later, when Bob Herbst brought Matt, Lauren, and his own daughter Karen for a visit, I told them that Caron had taken a memory test that afternoon, and Caron's incredulous response was, "I did?"

After all the visitors had gone home, Caron buttered her own toothbrush, brushed her teeth, washed her face, and dressed for bed herself. On the 6000 unit, these were not self-care activities that she was encouraged to try. Here, in rehab, patients were expected to do as much as they could for themselves.

While we waited for Larry to come to say good night after his swim meet, I played one of the oboe tapes that Caron's oboe teacher had left for her. I had played it many times in the past couple of weeks, but this was the first time Caron recognized a particular piece and its significance: She was to have played Marcello's Concerto in C Minor for Oboe and Piano at the solo festival February 4. For the first time, she realized she had missed it. Her first reaction, contrary to what I would have thought, was neither sorrow nor disappointment. Rather, she asked, "Was Mrs. VanDommelen ticked?"

What a frightening experience it must be to lighten from a coma, knowing who you had been and believing that this is who you are, but discovering that very little, if anything, around you and about you supports that knowledge and that belief: Words you know won't come to your lips when you want to say them. Facts you once knew don't come to your assistance in conversations. Even your own voice is frightening: hoarse, raspy, flat. Your environment isn't familiar, and everyone seems to be making demands of you. Sometimes they're beneath your dignity: "Caron, can you open your eyes for me? Can you hold up one finger?" But you have no means of saying so. More often, the demands are vaguely familiar: "Spell 'soap.'" And you know that you know how to do it, but when the letters come out of your mouth and your ears pick them out of the air, you realize that you failed. Trifling tasks, demeaning demands—but you fail. You can't even remember the color of the house you've lived in for your entire life—but in trying to remember, you stir up warm, nostalgic feelings of "home," and you want to be there, but "they" won't let you go, and your parents leave you every night to go there, but they don't take you with them. You *know* you're okay; why can't anybody else see it? Perhaps the most frightening thing of all is that you can't substantiate that you're okay. In every experience, in every waking moment, you find yourself failing your memory of who you are, your expectations of yourself. How frustrating, and how very frightening! You begin to react in fear to most everything.

Pat VanDommelen is a taskmaster. She knows her students and their capabilities well, and she never accepts less than their best. This is why her oboists do so well. And it's what defines her as a master teacher in her field of expertise. But she's not an ogre. She never frightened Caron. Yet now, in realizing that she'd missed the solo festival, her first thought was that Mrs. VanDommelen must have been upset with her. This was a fearful response, based on her experiences since having sustained a closed head injury. Sometimes we could talk her into going along with something by cajoling or making promises or using any of the other tactics that parents of preschoolers know well. But we could not effect a significant change in her *feelings*, which were based on her own now-confusing perceptions of what was real. She was, in effect, starting all over again emotionally—from infancy. Only experience itself could eradicate her apprehensions. She had to grow up all over again.

Fortunately, many people loved Caron and were eager to supply the experiences she needed. Pat VanDommelen was no exception. The very next afternoon, she whisked into Caron's room with two gifts which she ceremoniously placed, one at a time, on the table in front of Caron: "*This* one which you would have gotten anyway, had you been at the solo and ensemble festival . . . and *this* one because you weren't at the solo and ensemble festival." Pat always accompanied her oboists at the piano when they played their solos, and she always gave them a little musical gift and a personal note just before their performance. This relaxed them, let them know that she was with them all the way, and gave them courage and self-confidence. But now Caron was getting something extra because she had not been able to participate. As she fondled the charming little pewter box containing a necklace with a G-clef pendant and discovered that the lid of the box converted into a musical staff pin and two tiny eighth note earrings, I know that Caron found the answer to her question, "Was Mrs. VanDommelen ticked?"—and she advanced one giant step in the "Mother, may I?" of growing up.

In the week that followed, Caron was taken to each of her three therapies for an hour in the morning and an hour in the afternoon. Physically, she was weak from three weeks of doing very little, but it was clear that she would regain physical strength, so this wasn't an area of concern for us. Physical therapy was, however, exhausting for her. She did leg exercises on a mat, and walked around the perimeter of the gym first with help, then solo, and finally even pushing a wheelchair. Later, she would advance to a treadmill. She used an arm bike, an air dyne bike, parallel bars, and stairs. For coordination, she had to practice heel-toe walking. Despite Caron's continued progress in physical endurance, a patient-care assistant (PCA) always transported her to her therapies in a wheelchair. She was still confused about where she was and what was happening. Sometimes, she asked questions like "Will we be taking that bus again to get home?" And "home," such as it was, was in the same building and on the same floor as the therapies—just a short corridor's distance away by wheelchair, not by bus. "Home," for now, was room 1179.

The occupational therapist's job was to help the patient readjust to everyday living and tasks of self-help, so Laura's morning time with Caron was, initially, the hour of her arising. The goal was that Caron would eventually become responsible for getting herself up and taking care of her breakfast, shower, dressing, etc., by herself. But the first of Laura's mornings, a Friday, Laura had to wake her up. And at this point, even the inadvertent absence of a spoon on Caron's breakfast tray was a problem with which Caron couldn't yet cope. Laura helped with these things in the morning and made suggestions to us as to how to follow through at lunch, dinner, and bedtime. It was much like starting all over again with a toddler.

In the afternoons of the first week of therapy, Laura administered written memory, math, and perception tests. As Caron struggled to write and noticeably fatigued quickly, I observed quietly, but could really know nothing until these tests were scored and the results shared. However, at the beginning of each session, Laura always asked Caron to remember three things, and in the first week Caron never remembered any of them. Two of the tasks were always personal: "Remind me to give you back your glasses" (or some other personal item Laura would "borrow" from Caron at the beginning of the hour); and "At the end of our session, please remember to ask me when your next appointment is." The third item entailed learning as well as remembering: "Caron, this is a picture of Katherine Taylor. Whose picture is this? . . . Yes, that's right. This is Katherine Taylor. At the end of our time together, I'm going to ask you to tell me the name of this person. Will you remember that it is Katherine Taylor?"

It was the speech and language sessions that were of most interest to me and where I experienced sometimes the heights of hope and at other times the depths of despair. Here, because the tests and exercises were oral, it was easier to observe Caron's strengths and weaknesses. And my being there was sometimes especially helpful because, while there are national norms for students Caron's age, few students perform precisely at those norms. My function was to provide input regarding how Caron might have performed on certain items before her accident. What stood out most dramatically to me was Caron's response demeanor: While she had never been cocky before, she had always been self-assured, even as a toddler. If she hadn't positively known an answer, she hadn't been afraid to admit it, but the asking was always matter-of-fact on her part and never particularly humbling. She had had a healthy sense of recognizing the need for resources, human as well as in print, in order to continue learning. Now, however, while her memory was not good in some areas, this was confounded by excellent memory of her *pre-accident ability* in those areas. This was very humbling and reduced her to childlike behavior and lowered self-esteem. She knew, for instance, that she had been a good speller. But after spelling "conscience" and "particular" correctly, she became hung up on "soap." She struggled with it and finally concluded with "s-o-p-e," but her body language gave away her disappointment at realizing that she had failed to spell this word accurately. Again, on the word "belong," she drew a mental blank, anguished aloud with "I *know* I know how to spell this," and finally finished with this result: "B-o-l-o-n-g. I know that's not right." Sometimes she was way off, as with "physician," spelling it "p-l-a-c-i-s-t."

In one of the earlier sessions, Yvonne discovered a strength in phonetics, which she would draw upon in future sessions to facilitate Caron's memory.

"What is this?" she asked, pointing to a star. "A chair?"

"Look at it again," she encouraged. Incredulously, Caron gasped, "It's *not* a chair?"

"No," responded Yvonne simply, but then went on to point to the star again. "Is this a chair?"

"No."

"So you know when you hear it that it's not a chair. Is it a shape of some kind?"

"Yes."

"Square?"

"No."

"Triangle?" "No."

"Circle?"

"No."

"Does it start with an *s*?"

"S-s-s . . . st-ar!"

Yvonne then showed Caron that there was also a chair pictured on the page (albeit miniscule and tucked unobtrusively into a corner); very matter-of-factly, as if it's a mistake we all make much of the time, she went on to say, "This is probably what confused you." And Caron was able to sit up a little straighter in her chair. My, but I admired how this speech therapist worked.

Yvonne was superb with Caron, sometimes laughing at her responses but always, always applauding her, even while enjoying a good chuckle. One day, Caron was stumped by a picture of an acorn. Yvonne supplied a clue: "It comes from an oak tree."

"An oak nut?" guessed Caron.

"Good try!" chuckled Yvonne. "It's called an acorn."

"That's an *acorn?*"

"Yes, but I like 'oak nut' better."

Yvonne used the black three-ringed notebook often to personalize lessons for Caron. For instance, the night Caron's employer, Bob Herbst, came to visit, bringing with him his daughter, my son, and the friend who'd been in the car with Caron the morning of the accident, each of them had written in the black book. The next day, after reading their remarks in the book, Yvonne asked, "Did you have any visitors last night?"

"Uncle Bob," Caron began, but then turned around to look for reassurance from me. (So as to be most unobtrusive, I always sat behind her.) I shook my head, and in the disbelieving manner that we came to know so well, Caron exclaimed, "It *wasn't* Uncle Bob?" (She does have an uncle named Bob, her father's brother.)

"Bob, yes, but he's not your uncle."

"Bob . . . Maurer . . . Bob . . . Bob . . . Herbst!"

"Right!" continued Yvonne. "And who came with him?"

"Karen Herbst, and one of her friends."

"Yes, and what was the friend's *name*?"

"I don't know . . . unless it was Lauren DiGrande."

"Exactly!"

Each of Caron's therapies exhausted her. Sometimes Laura let her lie down and take a rest break in the middle of her session, or at the end, just before Caron would leave for her speech therapy. Occasionally, Caron whined or cried, wanting nothing more than to go back to her room and go to sleep. Always, when fatigued, she was irritable, and less able to concentrate, remember things, and learn. For these reasons, we still tried (not always successfully) to limit daytime visitors to family (including John Maurer and Mr. K), because we understood her irascibility and could allow her just to "be" and not to have to be "up" for a social performance.

Recognizing that Caron needed to see her friends, we began to invite people for evening visits—although trying, still, to control numbers, because too many at once proved confusing for her, and this confusion was further exacerbated by the double vision still plaguing her. We were learning, nevertheless, some management techniques so as to accommodate larger numbers of people to

Caron's best advantage. For instance, we had promised the teenage dialogue group from church that they could come to visit on February 19—three weeks after the accident. Having learned some things from the Valentine's Day pizza party, we decided to have the dialogue group visit in the large main floor lobby, where chairs could be arranged in a large circle, and everyone could remain seated in one place. This group was especially helpful too, by speaking in turn, one at a time, around the circle. This made it easier for Caron to focus on each speaker and his or her message, to converse with him or her, and to later remember who came.

Our church teenage Dialogue Group, with teachers and chaperones/drivers. Caron, in the front with her black notebook and a gift of flowers, is wearing her turquoise and bright yellow high-tops. Her brother Matt is standing second from the left, back row.

As an added assist, when they wrote in her black book, they did this in the order in which they had sat and spoken. They wrote in the first person, as though she were doing the writing herself, and they wrote reminders to later spark her memory of this visit: where they sat, next to whom, what they were wearing, what they said to her, and so on. The visit was beneficial to everyone. Some of these friends, while worried about Caron, had been afraid to come, afraid they wouldn't know what to say or how to act. All commented, upon leaving, that they were glad they had come. Especially, they said, they were relieved to see that she was well enough to argue with her mother and to tease her brother. I believe they all felt good about themselves when they left; for Caron, who was elated to have a dozen people come to visit her all at once, had bubbled all over the whole time they were there. Afterward, she took a two-hour nap.

When Caron didn't have guests or therapies, we did things to try to help her remember whom she was and what she liked to do before her accident. She had been an avid letter writer from the time she began full-day schooling, so I started transferring the thank-you note responsibility over to her when she arrived at rehab. When she asked for help, I gave it. She couldn't locate the word for "balloon" in her memory bank, and she was at a loss for how to spell "beautiful," for instance. But if she didn't ask, I didn't correct, as it was important for her to feel self-reliance, and pride in having accomplished functional tasks. I trusted that her friends would be understanding. At a later time, she was able to laugh at copies I had made of some of the notes she wrote at this time. Here's one of our favorites, written the eighteenth of February to Karen Herbst, who had visited on February 16:

> Karen, bud!
> Hi bud! Miss you a turn.[4] I hope to see you soon! I don't know how long it'll be, though! I

---

4 She meant "a ton."

miss you a turn!⁵ Thanks again for the beautiful blue flower cape!⁶ I love it! It looks awesome in my shower!⁷ Thanks again! Hope to see you soon!

Love, Caron

In the evenings, we watched Caron's favorite television programs with her or videotapes John supplied: videos of Caron and Matt learning to water-ski, videos of Camille Dalsace and Caron skiing, videos of seaplane rides and our previous dog (Kenya, a black lab) cavorting in the water—all this at Whitmore Lake.

After dinner and before TV or videos, we often went for walks, usually ending at the cafeteria, because Caron wouldn't have walked very far before she would complain, "I'm dying to have a drink," really dragging out the *dying* part. These days she was eager to talk but limited in vocabulary, so whenever she wanted something, it was expressed as "I'm dying to . . ." Sometimes in the evenings, we made hot fudge sundaes, because Caron was *dying* for a hot fudge sundae. She really missed Brighton's ice cream parlor, the Yum Yum Tree!

And always, since having made the move to rehab, when we prepared to leave in the evening, she cried, "I want to go home. *Please* take me home." Failing in obtaining consent, she'd change her plea to "Don't leave me. Please don't leave me here alone."

She had begun to conjure up visions in the evenings about "mice—*big* ones," which "shuffled around" at night. She reported that they began in the hallways, but would work their way into her room and under her bed. We determined that the sound of the nurses' rubber-soled shoes must have been the impetus for the illusions—and the nurses chuckled about the possible Freudian

---

5 Again: "ton."
6 It was actually a helium balloon with a get well message!
7 The correct meaning here was "on my bookshelf."

meaning: that Caron thought of nurses as rats. Nevertheless, her perceptions were reality for her at that time, and she was not ready to believe that they weren't real. One night, Larry and Caron and I went for a walk, leaving Matt behind to trap all the mice. He was happy to have the room and the television all to himself during our absence, and when we returned, he reported having captured every single one of the varmints. Caron checked under the bed and up and down the corridor, determined that the mice were gone, and slept well that night. Quite clearly, she had forgotten that, at our house, she was always the one to empty the mouse traps in the fall, because Matt was afraid to, and I was more than happy to let her do it!

At other times, while she was pleading with us not to leave her, she'd worry out loud, "What if they forget to wake me up in the morning?"

Caron had always been a sound sleeper. And all the family knew better than to try to arouse her from sleep, as one could end up with a shiner or a bellyache if one got too close. But after the accident, her sleeping soundness was magnified to an extreme none of us would have thought possible, and she really was afraid of not waking back up again. On her first Friday on rehab, she was exhausted early in the evening, and she kept dozing off during *Wheel of Fortune* and *Jeopardy*—aired at 7:00 and 7:30 p.m., respectively. Finally, at 8:00 p.m., we kissed her good night and turned off the light. With big tears in her eyes, she whispered, "I want to go home . . ." and began the ritual we'd heard the night before and the night before that. When she got to the "what if they forget to wake me up" part, I tried a new answer, "Do you really think they'd let you get any rest around here?"

"That's true." She smiled, and then she slept.

On the way home, I recounted to Larry my frustrations about therapy scheduling. We both realized that these therapies were vital to Caron. Yet that morning her PT had been cancelled, for a reason we never determined. And when lunch didn't arrive on time, Caron's nurse had taken it upon herself to cancel her 1:00 p.m. PT. She didn't realize how sacred we viewed these therapies as being: when lunch was delayed, I had skipped down to the cafeteria to purchase some lunch so Caron wouldn't have to miss another PT that day. When no transport had arrived by 1:05 p.m., I'd questioned the nurse, found out why, related to her that we had "done" lunch, and she was on the phone fast. By 1:07 p.m., Michael, our favorite transport person, arrived, pushing a wheelchair.

I was positively livid when Larry and I walked into Caron's room the next morning, a Saturday, at 11:00 a.m.: The room was dark. The curtains had not even been opened, let alone lights turned on. Caron was still in bed, in her pajamas, awake, and bewildered, at best. I couldn't read her expression in the dark: frightened? lonely? confused? On a table on the opposite side of the room from the bed was her breakfast tray, untouched. Hospital personnel had told me I needn't come so early every day, but look what happened when I didn't come so early. Friday had been the first day one of us had not been there before eleven, and because her morning PT had been cancelled, Caron had been sleeping Friday morning when I arrived too, but at least she had been aroused, helped to shower and dress, and she had eaten.

Before leaving on Friday evening, I had told the night nurse that Caron had always been hard to arouse, but that that didn't mean she wanted to sleep her life away; it only meant that she slept hard. Please be sure that someone awakens her, I asked, for she wants to get well and get out of here!

Never mind . . . We pulled back the curtains and greeted Caron cheerily. Larry took her breakfast to the microwave in the Great Room, and when he brought it back, warmed, Caron gobbled down everything. I had her in the shower when the morning nurse popped in to announce that Caron had been a sleepyhead that morning. She reported having tried to awaken her when breakfast arrived, but said Caron hadn't responded. I was still pretty angry and feeling spread pretty thin: if I wasn't here from 7:00 a.m. to 9:00 p.m., my daughter's well-being was jeopardized. I tried to calm myself, but my mind was busy wondering why no one had tried again, if not before breakfast became cold, then why not at 8:00 a.m.? or 9:00 a.m.? or 10:00 a.m.? Finally, I ventured a few words: "And what about breakfast?"

"She seemed to need her sleep more," was the reply.

"She'd been sleeping since 8:00 p.m. Do you really think she needed a fifteen-hour sleep stint more than breakfast? Excuse me if I'm confused, but yesterday afternoon a nurse tried to cancel a therapy because lunch had not yet arrived. And now, this morning, you effectively cancelled breakfast so my daughter might sleep round the clock. I don't understand the priorities around here."

I had managed to keep from yelling, if not to truly stay calm, and the nurse did get the message that I was displeased. She promised to do better the next morning, and she was true to her promise. Good thing, for I'd thought there would be an hour after church to get to the hospital and ready Caron, just in case; but the dialogue group decided to dialogue along the way to the hospital, instead of at the church, so they were hot on my heels. And Caron was ready—fed, showered, and dressed, including her shocking yellow and turquoise high-topped tennis shoes. We could have brought some of her own shoes for her to wear; but these were, for us, an important gauge of her real awareness level: when she really became alert, she'd object to those monstrosities!

On the first Tuesday that Caron was on rehab, her seventh night there, Larry stayed with her while I attended Curriculum Night at Brighton High School, to establish class schedules for both Caron and Matt for the following school year. For Matt, this wasn't so difficult. But who knew yet what to plan for Caron? Fortunately, I found that the school was ready to help, in whatever ways were necessary. Teachers were hopeful that she would still return that semester, and many had given thought to how to help her either to catch up or to substitute classes that would be easier to complete in less than a semester, then reintroduce the second semester junior classes into her senior year. Mrs. Rose, who had instructed Caron in English classes before but didn't have her on a class list for the current semester, suggested that an English Independent Study could be substituted now for AP Biology, which could be completed in the senior year, instead. She volunteered to supervise the independent study during her prep hour!

My accumulated leave days were coming to an end, but while I was at Curriculum Night, Mrs. Rose told me she'd donated ten days to the pool, and Mr. K had donated five and said, "If she needs more, *take* 'em!" The teachers' union president, who was Caron's French teacher, reported that all was progressing smoothly toward approval of this pool of days for my use. When I left the high school that night, I was not only overwhelmed with the dedication of these teachers on my daughter's behalf, but I was also immensely relieved and indebted to them for providing the means for me to continue helping Caron for the duration of her hospital stay.

The next day marked the end of a full week of therapy for Caron. Yvonne had begun to assign homework each afternoon to be done before the next morning's therapy. But Wednesday nights were the TBI Family Education Night meetings in the Great Room. Larry and I wanted to go, but Caron was struggling over the evening's three-page assignment, which consisted of many items in which the task was to write a third related sentence to accompany two sentences already written. She was having difficulty applying herself to the task, but every time I suggested we set it aside for a while, she'd protest, "No! I *want* to get it *done*!" So we all ignored her verbal abuse and tried to help. Given the sentences "Marie wanted to make an apple pie" and "The apples on the tree were ripe," she had written, "Marie will make an apple pie just like the one she already has."

Matt looked puzzled. "Caron, read what you just wrote." "It's *right*, Matt," she persevered, "so just leave me *alone!*" "But you've written that she already *has* an apple pie."

"She *does!* It says so right *there* . . ." She pointed to the second printed sentence, which she thought proved her point, and she began reading. When she got to the word "tree," she too looked puzzled. This was obviously not the word she had understood to be here when she had originally read this sentence. But undefeated, she simply tacked an "in the tree" to the end of the sentence she had composed, hoping to have corrected the problem and appeased her brother, and then she tried to move quickly on to the next item.

But of course Matt was not appeased. "Caron, *listen* to what you've written: 'Marie will make an apple pie just like the one she already has in the tree.'"

Caron burst into laughter, and we all joined in . . . but it was still a while before she was able to find a resolution and change her sentence to "Marie will use the ripe apples to make a pie."

The meeting time neared, and because Matt had shown an interest in the work, we asked him if he'd help her. He agreed willingly, but as we actually started out the door, Caron began another outburst of anxiety over the assignment, and Matt looked helplessly at me and whispered, "Do I make her do it or not? What do I do?"

It's interesting how God prepares us for such dilemmas when we listen. The first Tuesday after Caron's accident—when Laurie had ordered us out of the hospital for the afternoon and we'd gone to the shop called His House to buy a Precious Moments doll for Caron—the person working at His House already knew about the accident, and knew me, and she gave me a book entitled *Gold in the Making: Where Is God When Bad Things Happen to You?* I had read the first two chapters while Caron was in SICU, but since that time I had become busy and hadn't taken the time to read. This afternoon, however, while Caron was in PT, I had opened the book to the third chapter; and a passage had jumped out at me as being somehow important. I had highlighted the passage and dog-eared the page. Now, already, there was a use for it. I retrieved the book, flipped easily to the page, and read to Matt:

> "Tom Landry, head coach of the Dallas Cowboys football team, explains his philosophy of coaching this way: 'My task as a coach is to renew the minds of my players . . . and to get them to do things they do not want to do in order to achieve what they want to achieve.'"[8]

I didn't need to say anything else. Matt knew what to do. When we returned from the fourth meeting of the series, Caron's homework was finished, and she and her brother were contentedly watching TV together—no arguments about the program, either.

---

8 Ron Lee Davis with James D. Denney, *Gold in the Making: Where Is God When Bad Things Happen to You?* (Nashville, Tennessee: Thomas Nelson Publishers, 1983), 39.

CHAPTER 13

"JE NE PEUX TE PARLER QU'EN FRANÇAIS."

This was Caron's twenty-seventh day in the hospital. She was well out of a coma, and experts in various fields were doing all they could to determine which skills remained, which had been lost, and how much might be retrieved.

I was doing my own informal assessment too. An untrained observer, I despaired during this dialogue in speech therapy:

"Will a cork sink in water?"

"Yes."

"Is two pounds of flour more than one?"

"No."

"Is a hammer good for cutting wood?"

"Yes."

"Will water go through a good pair of rubber boots?"

"Probably."

"Is one pound of flour more than two?"

"Probably."

"Will a good pair of rubber boots keep the water out?"

"Not always."

"Is a hammer good for pounding nails?"

"No."

"Will a stone sink in water?"

"No."

On the other hand, Caron had now moved into independent reading assignments to prepare for her daily speech and language therapy; and she had decided to continue *Of Mice and Men*, which I'd begun reading to her on the 6000 unit. It was encouraging to know that she could, in fact, read. I didn't know enough about comprehension at this level to realize that she was not really being effective at comprehending what she was reading and that this area was going to require a lot of work.

Caron had recently seen Dr. Austad, and he had removed the stitches from her ear and removed a scab. It certainly looked like the reconstruction had been successful: though red and marked by scar tissue, the left ear was positively on the mend.

And Caron's most joyous moment had just come the day before, when Dr. Perlman okayed her wearing her contacts again. He said he'd order a contact patch too so she wouldn't continue seeing double.

All of the above were indicators of difficulties or progress; but today, the twenty-seventh day, we were finally going to get the straight scoop: we were to attend our first interdisciplinary team conference concerning Caron. I was nervous. I wanted so badly to hear encouraging news, and I was afraid for what discouraging news might be a part of this meeting.

Now here we were. Larry had taken a day off to attend the meeting with me. The hospital social worker to whom we had been assigned was here. She had met with me the previous Friday to describe her functions and to ask if she could be of any immediate help. We also recognized Barbara Zukowski, the health care consultant who was the liaison between the hospital and Caron's auto insurance company. Caron had been assigned a neuropsychologist, who had talked with her only once for 1/4 hour, but she was here too. All of Caron's therapists were in attendance: Sue and Laura and Yvonne. Her primary nurse was not on duty this day, so another nurse was present to take her place. And presiding over the conference was Dr. Perlman.

Dr. Perlman began the conference by reviewing Caron's problems to date:

- Adult Respiratory Distress Syndrome: If vocal cord problems persisted, an ENT specialist would be consulted.
- Bilateral chest tubes out January 31 (that's the one Caron *pulled* out) and February 4.
- Maxillary Sinusitis: For this, she had been put on ampicillin for four weeks, beginning February 20.
- Pancreatic edema, laparotomy, and splenectomy January 28.
- Pneumovax January 28: Ah, so *this* was the vaccination Caron would need to have on a regular basis.
- Dissection of the internal left carotid artery: He explained that this was a gap between the inner and outer linings of the artery, initially about two centimeters long (but in the second arteriogram, performed February 10, it was seen to be somewhat larger) and two centimeters above where the internal carotid artery branches off from the main artery. He felt that there was no compromise to the blood flow, and he believed that the most likely occurrence would be spontaneous healing, although he did acknowledge other possibilities: "thrombosis of the segment" (clotting off) or carotid surgery (bypassing the dissection with a Gortex or Dacron graft). Of course, he cautioned that carotid surgery risks stroke. For now, the treatment continued to be antiplatelet therapy—which consisted of two aspirins per day. The next arteriogram had already been scheduled for March 6.

- Diplopia (double vision): No intervention would take place before six to twelve months. For now, contact patches (opaque or occluder contacts) would be ordered.

Next, Dr. Perlman continued with information in Caron's favor:

- She was out of post-traumatic amnesia in less than a month, so prognosis was good for 100 percent *physical* recovery. (Post-traumatic amnesia, or PTA, is the interval between the injury and the recovery of ongoing memory for recent events. When a patient begins to remember things on a day-to-day basis, from one day to the next, it can be said that the patient is out of post-traumatic amnesia.)
- She had had "a lot of gains in a short time, with little evidence of plateaus," so ultimate *cognitive* changes "may be subtle."
- On the Rancho Los Amigos Hospital Scale of Cognitive Functioning, she was at level 6: "confused-appropriate."
- Six-hour passes would be available for the upcoming Saturday and Sunday, any six hours of our choice between 9:00 a.m. and 6:00 p.m.
- He anticipated four more weeks of inpatient therapy, with outpatient therapy to continue after Caron was discharged from the hospital.
- Easter vacation with relatives in South Carolina would *probably* be approved; but a school-sponsored trip to Washington, D.C., the following week, in which Caron was still hoping to take part, probably would *not* be okayed.

Each of the therapists gave a short report: Sue reported three physical areas in need of work: weakness in legs, balance, and endurance.

Laura's tests indicated a moderate memory deficit. On the WRAT math test, when timed, Caron had scored at the fourth-grade level; but when given unlimited time to complete the test, she had demonstrated skills exceeding the twelfth-grade level. Concepts and perception were still okay, but she needed to work on details and timing.

Yvonne stated that Caron had difficulties with word retrieval and that cognition was a problem inasmuch as Caron was not adequately attentive to meaning. She especially needed work on attention to detail.

The neuropsychologist summarized that Caron still had some orientation problems, as well as difficulties with attention and concentration, problem solving, and memory. She stated that she would be administering neuropsychological tests the following week, to determine more specific information about Caron's areas of weakness.

When we returned to Caron's room, she jumped us with "When do I get out of here?" Well, let's see, I thought: Dr. Perlman had reported anticipating four more weeks of inpatient therapy. That would put discharge at Thursday, March 23 . . . before Easter.

"Before Easter!" I replied, expecting reciprocal excitement from Caron. But I'd neglected to think about all of the information one would have to have at one's disposal in order to interpret that reply. Caron's face fell, as the only answer she wanted to hear, and in her childlike mind had convinced herself that she *would* hear, was "Today!"

"When is Easter?" she whined. But of course: less than two weeks ago, she couldn't remember what Valentine's Day was and kept calling it Thanksgiving. How could I have expected her to be knowledgeable about Easter? In fact, later I would read in her black notebook that she and Yvonne had talked about months and holidays just that afternoon in her speech therapy session. But Caron was still only touching on the surface of meaning in conversation, never any underlying meaning. Also, she wasn't internalizing much information yet. Most topics didn't make an impact on her. Stubbornly, she was obsessed with "When do I get out of here?"

In working with kindergarteners and first graders, I've learned that "today" is a time concept easily grasped. "Yesterday" and "tomorrow" are concepts we endeavor to teach five-and six-year-olds. "A month from now" is difficult to impossible for children of this age to comprehend due to inadequate experiential background. In other words, they haven't been around long enough yet to be able to have internalized the meaning of the concept "month." And emotionally, Caron probably had not yet attained even the age of five. For her, being at home for good at Easter wasn't going to cut it. I'd have to try a different approach if my goal was to help Caron feel positive. "Tomorrow," I began, "we'll take down all these Valentine's Day decorations and hang Easter ones. Your room will be so pretty! And the day after that you can come home for a visit . . ."

"Oh, goody!" she exclaimed, clapping her hands together in the same manner I remembered her doing when she was two.

"But for now," I continued, capitalizing on her being distracted, "let's have a listen to this tape you received from France today."

Caron and her brother had participated in the French-American exchange together, corresponding during their sixth-grade school year with the families who would host them, and especially with the child in that family who was their age and who would spend three weeks with us first. While Caron was matched with the Dalsace family, Matt was matched with a family named

Longerinas. Coincidentally, the mothers of these two families were best of friends, and Camille Dalsace and Arnaud Longerinas were best of friends as well, so the families did many activities together during the three weeks that my children were in France, and both families came to know both of my children.

The tape Caron had received from France today was from the Longerinas family, and first to speak was Martine, the mother. Caron recognized her voice almost instantly, and while I struggled over the opening line, *"Je ne peux te parler qu'en français,"* Caron was quick to grasp that Martine was explaining that she could only speak in French. In a condescending tone, she translated to me and was impatient to get on to the next part. Touché! Here was an area—*finally*, she may have thought—where she could "star"! And in fact, in the weeks to follow, she played this tape, and one from the Dalsace family, over and over again, sometimes not really listening to them, but playing them all the same—because they boosted her ego. None of the nurses or doctors or other hospital personnel knew French (or, at least, none admitted to it), and most were verbal about how impressed they were to hear Caron listening to French. Many would ask her what was being said, and she would delight in translating. Her primary nurse, Betty, whom Caron had come to adore, was especially perceptive about Caron's need to feel good about herself and how these tapes helped to achieve that. The nurses' station was just outside Caron's door; and when Betty heard one of the French tapes being played, if she had some time to spare, she would come in and sit, listening in awe for as long as fifteen minutes, much to Caron's satisfaction!

CHAPTER 14

"I HATE IT HERE!
I HATE THESE PEOPLE!"

It was now February 24, but the Valentine's Day decorations were still hanging in rehab. Room 1179. Very young children are often mystified by preparations before a holiday, since they barely remember that holiday from the year before, if at all; and so they have no basis of relating to what's going on. For this reason, the best time to help them internalize feelings and facts about a holiday is *after* it has passed. If there are young children in the house, or in the classroom, it's helpful not to remove the holiday décor for a week or two after the celebration. Clearly, Caron had not remembered Valentine's Day prior to the day itself this year. But the day was a memorable one for her, and a good opportunity to assist in her day-to-day memory. With the decorations as constant reminders, she had talked about Valentine's Day every day since. There were still so many things here to help her remember. The cut flowers were on their last legs, but the helium balloons were still perky. The chocolates were gone, but the heart-shaped containers sat about hoping to be refilled. And several new stuffed animals had joined the collection: white ones boasting pink bows or holding red satin hearts. Caron's favorite was the one her friends had brought the night of the pizza party, and she kept it close to her.

Ten days was long enough. Now I stood on a chair, releasing the paper hearts and flowers suspended from the ceiling, and replacing them with paper baskets and colored eggs and cute little bunnies—and a big sign that read, "I'll be home at Easter!" I'd brought Caron a calendar showing the days between now and then and showed her how to cross them off as they passed. She pouted at the rows and rows of little squares separating her from home, but she was soon distracted by her interest in the new decorations being hung. Also, the Longerinas family tape was playing. We were excited by how well Arnaud was speaking English. He had only begun to learn it five years before, when he came to us during that first French-American exchange in our town. Although the French class had arrived in March, we had staged trick-or-treating around our neighborhood and a Halloween party afterward, as this is a holiday foreign to children in France. Now here was Arnaud's voice, much deeper than it had been then, recounting his fond memories of that evening and other good times we'd enjoyed together. On the tape, each member of his family shared memories in one language or the other, in efforts to facilitate Caron's memory. Martine's French was enunciated clearly, and after a few times listening to it, even I could discern the meaning. She started from the very beginning, explaining that Matt had stayed with them and that Caron had stayed with the Dalsace family but that all of them had gone together to the seaside and to a museum and to the opera house. She remembered out loud the things that particularly interested Caron; and I prayed that Caron, assisted by this tape, would remember too in time.

While memory for day-to-day events was improving, for some time now Caron had been exhibiting perseveration, another characteristic of head-injured patients. Perseveration is a frequent and often meaningless repetition of speech or activity, or repetition of an answer that is unrelated to successive questions asked. In a sense, the patient utilizes it to compensate for lost memory: the patient latches on to some particular vocabulary or phrase, using it over and over and over again, thereby relieving the frustration of searching for other words to fill the gap. However, while it served to relax Caron from fear of conversational stuttering, we could see that it also got in the way of restoring her memory. Quite by accident, an incentive system was put into play, to help her focus on this excess reiteration of particular phrases and to make attempts to reduce the number of repetitions.

The night before, a most welcomed visitor had come to see Caron. For years, she had admired a young man whose family attended the same church that we did. She was still a scrawny little kid going through puberty when he graduated from high school, so the infatuation had gone unnoticed, and she made other male friends nearer her age . . . but she never stopped secretly admiring Jim. And now, there he was on the phone, asking if he could stop by the hospital to visit that evening. When she had placed the telephone receiver back on the cradle, she looked at me, glassy-eyed, and whispered, as if to speak out loud would shatter the dream, "That was Jim! He's coming to see me! Tonight!" Then into the bathroom she went. It had only taken one phone call to jog her memory about the existence of such items as nail polish, lipstick, and hairspray! While Jim was visiting, Caron punctuated the conversation with frequent "I'm *dying* . . ." sentences, most of them, "I'm *dying* to get out of here!" Before leaving, Jim held out the carrot: "If you can cut that down to *ten* 'dyings' tomorrow, I'll come to see you at home on Saturday. Your mom will count, and I'll call tomorrow night to find out how you did." So here we were, counting. By noon she had only said, "I'm *dying* . . ." three times (that I heard, anyway)—and each time she enunciated it more clearly than ever before, teasingly, aware of what she was saying and confident that she would be able to stop short of ten. It was a pleasure to see her enjoying a bit of cockiness. Midafternoon, she was at a total of five. By dinner, fatigued by the day's therapies and visitors, she was beginning to babble; and out of control, she reached ten quickly. She ceilinged at seventeen, but only because she succumbed to sleep at seven fifteen. Jim called, and I had to tell him she'd lost, but he said he'd call her Saturday between three and three thirty, anyway.

The next morning was Saturday morning, the day of Caron's first six-hour pass. I arrived at ten forty-five to help her curl her hair, hoping to get an early start on our noon-to-six outing, but Caron was still in bed. She said she had had orange juice from her breakfast tray, then decided to take a nap, and she'd asked the nurse to wake her up at ten. This was a new nurse, standing in for the weekend, and I was beginning to understand that I couldn't train all of the nurses in the hospital, so Caron and I just made the best of it. She did just about everything herself. She showered, washed her hair, dried it and curled her bangs, put in her contacts, dressed, brushed her teeth, and was ready by noon. I got instructions from the nurse, verbally as well as on a Therapeutic Trial Visit (TTV) Information and Instruction Sheet, and she handed me the bag of "meds" Caron would need to take at home. After I'd helped Caron curl the sides and back of her hair, as she was too fatigued to lift the brush, we were on our way. Caron was *dying* for McDonald's food. But of course! It had been over four weeks since she had had a McDonald's burger. How does a teenager survive so long without McDonald's? This, in and of itself, was a small miracle!

Home, full of McNuggets, fries, and a shake, Caron was greeted enthusiastically by Judd, our now eight-month-old yellow Lab. Caron had managed the eighteen steps up the hill to the house quite well, but the eleven stairsteps to her bedroom would be more of a challenge, with Judd's "assistance"! First, he planted himself firmly on the bottom step, so that she had to climb over him to advance. Then he charged around her and ahead, to beat her to her room. We had kept her bedroom door closed for the past month—to protect her belongings from Judd—and now that we'd opened the door, he flew through it and made a flying leap onto the bed, as if to say, "Aha! I *thought* I remembered a bed in here!" (He had been trained early that furniture was not for dogs; but kids will be kids, and he'd learned, even faster, that *their* beds were exceptions to the rule!) Caron enjoyed the puppy's playfulness— for a while; but when she decided to sack out in a recliner in the living room, she had no tolerance for his chewing on her toes. He was unfamiliar with irritability from this family member, but he knew anger when he heard it, and after a few more test nips, just to see if she really meant it, he retreated a few steps and flopped down, resting his head on his paws but keeping his confused and disappointed eyes on this stranger.

Caron was eager to see all of her friends at Uber Drug Store, where she had been working part-time; so when Jim hadn't called by three thirty, we piled into the car for the half-mile jaunt to "Uber's". Ordinarily, we'd have walked, and Judd would have accompanied us, but we were short on time, and Caron still tired easily.

We were only halfway to the back of the store (the pharmacy— where Caron had most enjoyed working) when David McLeod spotted her. Just a couple of days before, Caron had received a pot of beautiful hyacinths from this person whom I didn't know, and I was taken aback by her reaction: disbelief that he had picked them out himself, some annoyed comments about his omnipresence at the store, and some rude remarks about his intelligence. I'd thought her very harsh and was disappointed in her until I shared my experience with some medical personnel, and they all responded, "Oh, that's just 'disinhibition.' It's a normal stage that most closed head injury patients go through." Disinhibition, I would learn, was really pretty much defined in the word itself: the patient becomes less inhibited than (s)he would normally be, saying and doing inappropriate things or responding with tears or laughter without appropriate stimuli.

I hadn't been able to find this young man's address in the phone book; so Caron had brought her thank-you note with her, saying that if he wasn't there today, she could just leave it with somebody, because *everybody* knows David. I felt like somewhat of an outcast, for *I didn't know David!* But here he was now, hurrying in her direction. His focus was entirely on Caron, no one else was within his view. Exuberantly, he grabbed her hand and began pulling her—faster than she was accustomed to moving—toward the pharmacy, announcing, "Look who I got! Look-ee! Look-ee who's here!" He fawned and gushed over her until he was certain that she had been well received and was getting appropriate attention from all the employees and regular customers who had gathered around. Then he surveyed the crowd and determined that I was the only uninvolved bystander. *Aha! An outcast!* He had been clutching the envelope Caron had thrust into his free hand when he grabbed her with the other one, and now he held it out to me with a simple introduction: "I'm David. Will you read this to me?"

"Sure, and I'm glad to meet you, David. I'm Caron's mother." "Oh! Did she like the flowers?"

"She loved them! It was so thoughtful of you. Here, let me read to you what she wrote . . ."

When I'd finished reading, he nodded approval then began interrogating me regarding Caron's well-being, status, and prognosis—probably the most perceptive conversation anyone had tried to carry on with me regarding Caron in the past month. Most people are at a loss for what to say in situations such as this and usually wind up saying something like "She'll be fine." But not David!

"How's she doing?" he began.

"She's making good progress."

"But it'll take a *l-o-o-o-n-n-ng* time."

"Yes."

"How long will she be in the hospital?"

"The doctor says just four more weeks."

"It'll be longer."

"Well, we're hopeful . . ."

"It takes a *long* time. Does the doctor say how she's doing? How *will* she be?"

"Everybody expects she'll be just fine—just like she was before."

"No, she won't be . . . but I'm praying for her."

David *knew* . . . David had *been* there. I made note to find out what had happened, at some later time. Since then, I've come to know David. I pass him often when out walking the dog, or I see him at Uber's. He always says hello and inquires after Caron, but aside from mention of an accident when he was much younger, he's like other head injury victims in that he really doesn't want to talk about it; he just wants to get on with his life.

Jim had been in the store when we arrived, and when Caron began to show signs of fatigue from all the excitement, he took her under wing and escorted her out to our car, to the tune of "It was *so-o-o-o-o* good to see everybody again. I was *dying* to see them. It was *so-o-o-o-o* good . . ."

Caron was pretty bummed about having to return to the hospital, so we had lined up evening guests to entice her back. Karen Herbst's mother brought her and Lauren DiGrande to the hospital with perfect timing—right after Caron had finished the dinner awaiting her upon her return. And Matt had come along with Larry and Caron and me. The kids had a great time razzing

Caron about her psychedelic tennis shoes. Karen delighted in putting them on her friend so that they could all go take a walk up and down the hospital corridors. And by the time we all readied to leave, Caron was quite ready to go to sleep, even though it wasn't at home.

Shoes taking a walk: Karen, Caron, & Lauren.

Shoes returning: Karen, Lauren, & Caron

The next day, Sunday, Caron had another six-hour pass. In response to her complaints about her hair, our longtime hairdresser and friend Carlene had suggested I bring her in for a trim and perm on Sunday so that she wouldn't have to abide the confusion of regular business hours at a beauty salon. This takes real love and dedication—to open one's shop on one's day off to accommodate a customer with special needs! And it worked immeasurably to lift Caron's spirits. Now she could look nice again, even without the use of a curling iron.

We had a nice family meal, albeit not cooked by me. Parents of my first graders had rallied with the ladies of our church, and we were all staying healthy—and putting on weight—while enjoying the scrumptious meals that appeared magically every day. Soon it was time to make the half-hour drive back to the hospital. Again, the return was made easier by Caron's knowing that her good friend Leeann Fu would be coming to the hospital to see her that evening. And Leeann, being Leeann, brought further cheer when she appeared with a basket of origami flowers and an origami frog she'd made herself!

In the week that followed, three more therapies were crowded into Caron's already-busy days: Cognition (Cog) Group, Speech Study Group, and Recreational Therapy (RT), so that, except for an hour for lunch, therapies were pretty much back to back from 8:30 a.m. until 4:30 p.m. Even though this was fatiguing for her, the heavier load was a positive sign, I'd been told: the higher the expectations for the patient, the more rigorous the therapy schedule.

While the groups had been added on Yvonne's recommendation, I was responsible for the RT, having heard about it at one of the Wednesday night meetings and thinking it really sounded like something Caron would enjoy. She was furious with me for being so forward and for arranging this "extra class" for her—especially since it would be one more half hour after what could have been the end of her working day. Fortunately, on the first day of all the added therapies, one of her teachers from school stopped in at four, just as we were headed for RT. He accompanied us down the corridor; and Nancy, the therapist, welcomed us both to stay and watch, if we'd like. With her teacher present, Caron put forth her best effort to be cooperative, and before long she was enjoying herself! Given her choice of several wood-painting projects, she selected one with three teddy bears, below which were three dowels from which to hang things. For years to follow, this first project graced one of her bedroom walls; and from the dowels hung her favorite religious story, "Footprints," and an assortment of bracelets and necklaces. She looked forward to this let-your-hair-down type of activity for the duration of her hospital stay, and the ornamentation throughout our house attests to this!

The group sessions weren't such a big hit. While unable to comprehend or to accept that she herself had deficits, she could see clearly the deficits of the others in the groups, and she didn't want to be any part of them. She was not at all tolerant of others, and especially not of the implication (for why else would they have placed her in these groups?) that she was perceived as being *like* them. Later in the week, when it was time for Cog Group, Caron groaned, "I hate it! It's so dumb!" But she was in better spirits when I met up with her after the group. (To protect all patients' privacy, observers are not allowed to attend groups). They had made pizza, and she exclaimed, "I ate a half a pizza!" Ah, yes, I was willing to wager that she was no longer that nice 128 pounds she had been so thrilled about a couple of weeks before. But at least she had decided that if they made goodies in Cog Group from time to time, then this was a group she didn't want to risk missing; and I wouldn't hear too much whining in the future about not wanting to go. Complaints *afterward*, yes—when they didn't make pizza or some other delectable—but no balking about *going* to this therapy!

Replacing Cog Group as a despicable entity would be arteriograms. She hadn't remembered the first two, as they fell within the time period that she was still in post-traumatic amnesia. She would remember the one done this week, however, and would be fearful about all subsequent arteriograms.

It had been scheduled for 1:00 p.m., so Caron had been NPO for breakfast and lunch: no food. I knew she'd be starved after the arteriogram, which would take but an hour, so I'd come prepared with plastic baggies and twist ties to wrap up the corned beef sandwich and Oreo cookies she'd ordered special from the deli for this day's lunch. (All meal requisitions are done on Fridays for the following week, and at the time we hadn't known that an arteriogram had been scheduled for Wednesday.)

It was one o'clock before a nurse we'd never seen before came in with IV apparatus. She said out loud that she couldn't find any veins in Caron's wrist, but she made a stab of it anyway! By the time she'd fumbled several attempts and decided not to try again, Caron was extremely agitated.

Certainly, unproductive stabs in one's wrist would upset anyone, but head-injured patients rise to unreasonable levels of agitation even without such stimuli. It's natural, I suppose, to feel angry when you're aware that you've lost capabilities that were once second nature to you, or when family roles have reversed, and they surely had in our family. Caron was six when she last allowed me to do her hair. Now, at sixteen, she needed to ask for this kind of help again. Prior to her accident, she had been the family caretaker, reminding us all about commitments and appointments, and the needs to wear our seat belts, go to church, and mind our manners around her friends. Now, we had to remind *her* where to be and when—and to mind her manners around her friends!

Whereas once she had taken it upon herself to be her brother's conscience, nagging him about homework and his language, now he was helping her with her homework and being shocked by some of the things *she* said! Her disinhibition could be embarrassing for us all, at times, and her pretty constant state of agitation was disconcerting too, but we were "assured" by nurses and doctors that these stages were indicative of patient recovery. Initially, head-injured patients have "flat" personalities and speech, so the ability to show anger is an "improvement." However, Caron's agitation today was out of control, and ominous of events to come. When the day was finally over, I'd wish I had spoken up about conditions not being ideal—and refused consent for the procedure to take place on that day.

Two more nurses entered, the first of whom whipped a rubber tourniquet around Caron's arm and began searching for veins. Caron was crying and shaking by this time; and at last, the nurse said she'd leave this task to the people upstairs, after they'd sedated her.

It was nearly one thirty before a transporter arrived with a gurney to take Caron to radiation. She was wheeled into the OR almost immediately, but it was two o'clock before the doctor brought a consent form for me to sign and spoke with me about sedation, which had not been needed for the previous arteriograms. At two thirty a nurse came out to tell me, "She's pretty groggy now. If she'd *let* herself, she'd sleep, but she's frightened."

By three thirty I was quite concerned. The last time we had come up here, for the second arteriogram, she was in and out within an hour. Today it had been two hours already.

Finally, at three thirty-five, Caron was wheeled out into the corridor. She was crying and moaning, "I want to go back to my room! I'm uncomfortable! My hands hurt!" I lifted the sheet to take her hands, and I was horrified at what I saw. Her hands were contorted demonically, almost at ninety-degree angles to her wrists, and at the hand-finger joints, her fingers were bent back close to ninety-degree angles from the backs of her hands, and both knuckles of every finger were bent and rigid. They looked very much like the talons of a hawk when closing in on its prey. Instinctively, I held them, trying to warm them, while talking to her, trying to relax her. There was no change. I couldn't force them back into a comfortable position, either.

When the transporter arrived to take her back to her room, I called his attention to Caron's hands, and he ran immediately to get the doctor. The doctor came sauntering down the hall, but when Caron's hands came into his view, his eyes widened, and he sprang into action, trying, as I had, to relax them. "Have you seen her like this before?" he asked me.

"Never."

"Caron, do you know where you are?"

"I don't care where I am!" she snapped. "Just let me go back to my room."

"Caron," I reprimanded, "you *must* cooperate with this doctor. *He* needs to know if you know where you are. Where are you?" "I'm in the hospital! Now let me go back to my room!"

Instead, the doctor wheeled her back into the OR "to take her blood pressure and . . ." And *what?*

Not too many minutes later, Dr. Farhat—the neurosurgeon with the sixth sense—happened by. I grabbed him, briefed him, and implored him to check on "what's going on in there?" And he did. When he came out five minutes later, the doctor who had done the arteriogram was right behind him, explaining that there was nothing wrong but that Caron's reaction—muscle spasms in the hands alone—had been "highly unusual." And he relayed to me that Dr. Farhat had said there'd have been cause for concern if her legs were also having muscle spasms, if she were arching her back, if she were disoriented, if her vital signs were abnormal, and . . . but I was concerned, anyway: what if, next time, the spasms were not limited to her hands alone? What did it mean? I never did find out what the implications might be; but somehow convinced that all of this was caused by her extreme agitation in the beginning, I did vow that I would never again consent to a surgical procedure when she was in that state of mind.

Now a new concern pierced the air: "I need to go to the bathroom! I need to go *bad!*"

Because of the way an arteriogram is done, the incision being made where the leg bends at the trunk, the patient isn't permitted to bend that leg for four to six hours. So a bedpan was fetched, and the young male attendant struggled to place it under Caron's buttocks, but she was mortified. Here she was, surrounded by a male doctor, a male transporter, and her mother, in the middle of a busy hospital corridor, and there was no way on God's earth that she was going to pee! She resisted the placement of the bedpan, but the attendant won the battle. Then she demanded that it be removed, but still yelled that she had to go to the bathroom.

Back in room 1179, the demands continued, and a noisy nurse arrived with another bedpan. This woman talked incessantly and had no intentions of leaving the room while the patient relieved herself; so Caron, again, refused. Then in came Betty, smooth-talking Southern Betty, who could talk Caron into anything. She just about had her in the palm of her hand when in walked yet another nurse, with a catheter in one hand, and an ultimatum on her lips. This broke the spell, and Caron refused both methods. In the end, they catheterized her. I stepped out into the hall, where Larry and Matt had been waiting with a fabulous meal, home-cooked someplace in Brighton. The intent was that we warm it in the Great Room microwave and we all eat together, but since Caron now had to be prone until nine o'clock or so, I sent them back to the Great Room to eat without her.

Caron came off the catheter screaming, "I *hate* it here! I *hate* these people! They're all so mean to me! They're mean, *mean, mean!* And I *still* have to go to the bathroom. That mean old nurse didn't do a good job!" She kept trying to sit up and had to be forced back down. Obviously, Larry and I weren't going to be going to the Family Education meeting in the Great Room together. We'd have to take turns, and the *lucky* one would be the parent at the meeting!

When it was my turn to go to the meeting, the physical therapist, Rob Bertoni, who was the speaker this evening, was in the middle of an explanation about hypertonicity (spasticity), hypotonicity (flaccidity), and ataxia (clumsiness of gait pattern). I half-listened, my mind someplace else. But my attention was called back when he began speaking of his experiences with patients in comas. "They may never remember hearing you," he began, "but for that instant in time, while you are speaking to them—yes, they may hear and understand you. There've been many occasions where I've been doing bedside therapy with a patient in a coma, and a loved one would enter and say, 'Hi . . . ,' and the patient's whole demeanor would change: he'd be more receptive or responsive or relaxed." Then this speaker was in agreement with the stand we had taken, with Laurie and Cathy and others in SICU. At least indirectly, by keeping her emotionally receptive, our bombardment with familiar stimuli had been to her advantage. Also, Caron hadn't been assigned a therapist at that point, but all of the members of her family instinctively exercised her limbs whenever we were in the room and talking to her or playing a tape of familiar voices or music. And we didn't encounter resistance while we rhythmically flexed arms and legs, rotated ankles and wrists, and wiggled fingers and toes. Perhaps it was because of the familiarity of the sounds, of which Rob spoke. In any event, when Caron had finally reached rehab and Rob's wife, Sue, was assigned to be her therapist, Sue was surprised that her muscle tone was so good after all the time she'd spent prone. So this was helpful too. We had taken the position that if it felt right to us and no one told us not to do it, then we would do it; and it had paid off.

This was a week of medical frustrations, the arteriogram fiasco being the peak. On Monday morning, a lab technician had drawn blood from Caron's left arm and had done no more than the standard procedure of putting a Band-Aid on the puncture. When I arrived a little later, there was a flapjack-sized bloodstain on the left arm of her sweatshirt. She had bled through the Band-Aid, a turtleneck shirt, and the sweatshirt. *Did the right hand know what the left was doing in this place?* I grumbled to myself. It would seem that if a patient was on anticoagulant therapy, the first people to know about it should be those who draw blood!

Also on Monday, with three therapies added to her schedule, and having had to be on her best behavior for the last hour, due to an unexpected visit from one of her teachers from school, Caron dropped onto her bed when she returned to her room. I endeavored to keep her awake, because it was almost five o'clock, when she was scheduled for a dose of ampicillin. She could get in a full hour's nap before dinner if she waited until after taking her medication. Foiled! It didn't come until five twenty. Then on Tuesday, she was given a break at ten fifty and returned to her room to collapse. I overheard her tell the nurse at the nursing station that she planned to sleep until lunch, but at precisely eleven o'clock that same nurse entered the room and awakened Caron to give her her ampicillin. I asked, "What is so sacred about eleven that couldn't have been done at ten fifty? And especially when, just yesterday, five had been rounded off to five twenty?"

Fortunately, this was a very friendly nurse, who was willing not only to tolerate an exhausted, irritated parent, but to try to appease her too! She checked the meds schedule and noticed that Caron was listed for ampicillin at 7:00 a.m., 11:00 a.m., and 5:00 p.m., which didn't space this medication equally over the twenty-four-hour day; so she changed it to 7:00 a.m., 3:00 p.m., and bedtime, none of which times would interfere with Caron's need for rest. Henceforth, she would take the afternoon capsule with her and be entrusted to remember to take it between Cog Group and Speech. An added dividend: increased responsibility.

My own aggravation rose and fell with Caron's. If she was content (relatively speaking), then I was easygoing; but if she was irritable, I was irritable too. And this was a tough week for her. In addition to the heavier load of therapies, her old standby therapies and therapists were tougher on her. Laura put her on a computer. She hated computers. Sue tried to get her to skip rope. She had *never* been adroit at skipping rope. (Larry and I chuckled as we watched her try to learn a new trick!) And Yvonne made her write a story based on a strip of outer-space pictures that didn't make any sense to me, let alone to her. She picked up on the Martians being "bald" and centered her story around people moving from planet to planet but their hairpieces not always arriving with them! Yvonne chuckled over her misinterpreting the flying saucers to be "hair caps." But then, Yvonne made her do it over again. By the end of the week, I'm sure that Caron could identify with Alexander in Judith Viorst's book, *Alexander and the Terrible, Horrible, No Good, Very Bad Day.* Like Alexander, I know I was ready to "move to

Australia"—or, at least, to enjoy a weekend at home. Fortunately for us, Dr. Perlman was Caron's physiatrist, and the wish would be granted: the weekend at home, of course, not a trip to Australia!

CHAPTER 15

"I'M TIRED. I'M ALWAYS TIRED. I'M SO TIRED OF BEING TIRED."

I had been told a number of times that if I wanted to talk with a doctor, all I had to do was tell a nurse and she'd page him to come at his earliest convenience. Valuing their time, I hadn't yet taken advantage of this system. Instead, I waited to ask my questions when they came in to see Caron. Now, however, I had a whole battery of questions, beginning with *Why had the arteriogram been rescheduled from March 6 to today?* (A nurse had called to notify me of it at eleven thirty the night before!) So I asked a nurse if she would ask Dr. Perlman to stop in. When he came, he didn't stand in the doorway shifting his weight from foot to foot and looking harassed, as some doctors might have. Nor did he flinch when I pulled out my long list of questions. Rather, he settled himself comfortably in the easy chair in Caron's room and thanked me for being so organized. He didn't know why the arteriogram had been changed; he hadn't ordered it. But he was very helpful with regard to all of my other questions, which centered around the upcoming weekend. Also, Caron's ophthalmologist had expressed concern about possible epithelial breakdown of her corneas due to her contacts having been in for that entire first week that she was in SICU, and I wanted to get her in to her orthodontist too, but weekends . . . He understood and said he'd write day passes for weekdays, as well as a pass to cover the upcoming weekend, from Saturday morning through Sunday evening.

Both the ophthalmologist and the orthodontist were very accommodating, essentially opening their doors whenever would be convenient for us. The orthodontist needed some time between two appointments to make new bite guards from impressions he would take at the first one. So we scheduled with Dr. Summers at the end of his day on Thursday, and again on Friday morning, after an early morning appointment with Dr. Heinze. And Dr. Perlman wrote an overnight pass for Thursday, as well as for the weekend.

Caron was happy to be at home that night. Together, we put her most recent mail in her scrapbooks, as well as some new photos. To the members of her quintet, for their "1" at the solo and ensemble festival, she wrote notes of congratulations on the backs of pictures I'd taken of them. And we listened to recordings done for her by friends when she had been in SICU. It hadn't occurred to me that we hadn't listened to these since she had been out of post-traumatic amnesia, so it came as a surprise when she claimed that she'd never heard them before. She listened intently to her friends jammin' on tapes for her, and the excitement on her face verified that she really did not remember having heard these—many, many times before. Mr. K stopped by for a few minutes while the Honors Band tape happened to be playing. And Jim came over to help her do her homework.

Hospital personnel had been concerned about Caron's bedroom being upstairs, for one can never know what new traits people will have after a head injury. If she were suddenly to begin sleepwalking, this could be a problem. So Larry had improvised a plywood door hinged to the post at the top of the stair landing railing. Matt could swing it and lock it into position from his side so that he could get to the bathroom or down the stairs, but from Caron's side, she could only get as far as the bathroom.

Caron was tickled to wake up on her own Friday morning— at 6:50 a.m.! She got in and out of the shower before anyone else was up, so she got away with something: in the hospital, she was required to sit in the shower, and her occupational therapist wanted follow-through on that at home too, so she had sent an orthopedic chair home with us for use in the shower. But when I went upstairs to dismantle the barricade at the top, I noticed that the orthopedic chair was bone dry.

Her hair still wet, Caron came downstairs with a loud "What's for breakfast?" I guess she expected hospital service and was disconcerted about having to pour her own cereal and juice and put her own bagel in the microwave—just like before. But she wasn't the only one disillusioned. Because she had arisen, showered, and dressed on her own, I assumed that she remembered her ophthalmology appointment this morning. I had told her we would have to leave by eight fifteen. However, as the clock raced on and Caron ambled through her breakfast, then reached for another bagel, it became apparent to me that the six-fifty rising was purely accidental.

"Caron, are you planning to dry your hair *and* curl it before we go?" I asked. I had noticed that she had plugged in the curling iron.

"Yeah." Nonchalantly.

"Then you'd better hop to it. We're supposed to leave by eight fifteen."

"You never told me we had to leave at eight fifteen." A most popular phrase of late: "You never told me . . ." (Translated, although she wouldn't admit to it: "I forgot.") But she was in no hurry. She continued eating, then went to find Judd, who seemed to have acquired a new name, "Juddy Puddy," in the brief time she had been home this time. They were having a great time romping together in the living room (another "no, no"), so Caron was quite put out with me for breaking it up and sending her upstairs to finish getting ready.

Gadzooks! I had never had to shepherd *this* kid before! I sure hoped this new irresponsibility was temporary!

Though we were late, we were well received at the ophthalmologist's office, and Dr. Heinze got right to work with Caron. He seemed to know a lot about head injuries and was excellent with her. He did extensive testing to determine that there was no third nerve damage and explained to me that the third nerve controls pupil dilation, among other things. Then he measured all of the boundaries of the sixth nerve trauma: left, right, up, down, and distance. Again, he explained as he proceeded: the sixth nerve affects the outside of the eye, causing it to pull in. For close-up work, this isn't so bad, because the closer the visual stimulus, the closer the eyes do center. But the farther away the object is, the farther the eyes must turn outward; and because one of Caron's eyes still resisted this, she was still experiencing double vision beyond book distance. He determined that she was now able to read and write with single vision. This had not been the case two and three weeks before, when she would squint her left eye closed to read cards people had sent her or wear the dreaded eye patch to facilitate writing notes herself. So the sixth nerve was mending! And Dr. Heinze said that as it mended she would be able to see farther and farther without double vision. He talked her out of the occluder contact she thought we'd be picking up on that day, explaining that it would necessitate her changing contacts throughout each day: the occluder for physical therapy, the regular contact for speech and language activities and some occupational therapy exercises, back to the occluder for walking to the cafeteria and for afternoon physical therapy, and so on. He gave her some patches that tie on, as she objected to the elastic bands on the hospital ones, and he suggested she paint one of them to be more interesting for people to look at, such as an eye winking.

Dr. Heinze did find a refraction change in her left eye only: she was seeing with 20/40 vision through her current prescription. No wonder it was always her left eye she had squinted shut, and no wonder she had complained of fuzzy vision! He changed the left contact prescription so that when she walked out of his office, she could see equally well with each eye. But having missed the meaning of Dr. Heinze's explanations, on the way out to the car she complained to me, "But I *still* see *double!*" After picking up her new bite plates, which Dr. Summers had finished, and they fit perfectly, it was only ten forty-five, and I told her she could rest and have lunch at home, as she wasn't expected back until her one-fifteen therapy. She surprised me in saying, "No. We can just go back." I guess it wasn't any big deal, since she'd be coming home again the next morning.

Caron's father had called her the week before, to say he'd be bringing his family to Michigan for their Arizona school system's spring break, beginning the first weekend in March. Larry and I stayed at the hospital until the Schreer family arrived at 8:20 p.m., told Caron when I'd pick her up the next morning, and reminded Ron to call me early in the afternoon to let me know which two or three hours he planned to visit with Caron that afternoon. I explained to him that she fatigued easily and usually needed a nap after two or three hours of activity but that I'd be sure she napped before he saw her so she'd be "up" for it!

When I had picked her up for her first day pass out of the hospital on the previous weekend, Caron had been indignant that I didn't bring her nice new herringbone wool coat for her to wear—and more indignant yet when I explained that I couldn't have brought it because it had been cut off her at the scene of the accident. "Cut?! Why didn't they just take it off me?" I tried to explain that she was unconscious and that they couldn't know where she might be hurt, so they certainly didn't want to take any chances by bending her arm back to pull it out of a sleeve. "But it was a brand-new coat!" she protested. "Couldn't they see that it was a brand-new coat?"

"Caron, it probably had blood all over it. I'm sure no one would have cared about whether or not it was a new coat, anyway."

"Well, they should have! And it could have been cleaned! Where is it? Can we sew it back together again?"

This subject had come up again and again throughout the week, and finally it had sunk in that the coat was no more. It shouldn't have surprised me that when I picked her up on Saturday morning, Caron would say she wanted to go straight to the store where that coat had been purchased, because she wanted to buy another one. And no amount of reason would convince her that by this time of the year they'd be selling bathing suits instead of coats. She was determined, so we passed by Brighton and headed on toward Novi, where we had lunch at Red Lobster, and then proceeded on to the Twelve Oaks Mall to check out Gantos. Caron, disappointed, conceded that they were in fact selling bathing suits, not coats, and she refused to be cheered by offers to buy something else while we were there.

As luck would have it, the car wouldn't start when we returned to it. If I had to transport Caron to outpatient therapies all summer long, I was going to need more reliable transportation. I couldn't reach Larry by phone, as March is the big birthday month in his family and he was out shopping. I tried several friends, with no luck; no one seemed to be at home. But as it turned out, that was fortunate for us, for I ran into one of them in the parking lot on the way back to the car! Caron, tuckered from her one-stop trip into the mall, had fallen asleep in the car; and it didn't disturb her sleep in the least that Peter was out there banging and scraping the corrosion off the battery terminals so that we could get home. At home, she trudged up the twenty-nine steps from street level to the house and then to her bedroom and flopped into bed without removing her shoes. Well, she'd have revived again in a couple of hours to go see her father and his family.

Meanwhile, the phone had been ringing off the hook with friends of Caron's who had found out she was home for the weekend and wanted to come over for a visit. We'd been fending them off for days, pending her father's schedule, as he's not in the state often.

While Caron slept, I went downtown to take care of a little project she and I had discussed. She had wanted to do something to thank the nice people she had met on the 6000 unit, and because she so loved the story "Footprints," she thought a framed poster of this would be nice. She couldn't personally remember anyone on the SICU ward, but liked what she'd been told about them and agreed that a framed poster would be nice for them too. So I went in search of posters, found a couple of nice ones, and took them to a frame shop in town to pick out framing.

When I got home it was nearly 4:00 p.m., and Matt was primping. He was growing so fast that he and I had gone shopping Monday, a school holiday, to buy him a couple of pairs of new pants. As I watched him, I cringed to think of my father turning over in his grave if he could see Matt now and know that the $25 savings bond which he had purchased for this kid back in 1973 had matured to $56 and had been spent in its entirety *toward* the jeans the kid was now wearing. Matt and I had reached an agreement when he first started earning money: I'd pay a reasonable price for each necessary item of clothing, and he'd pay whatever extra was needed in order to satiate his desire to have name brands. Of course, my idea of what was a reasonable price always differed from his. He did approve of the deals this past Monday: one pair of jeans mostly from Grandpa Frank, and I bought the other pair because he'd been so good about Caron's needs. Well, he certainly did look handsome, I thought, in his new light blue jeans, with his pink shirt and pink socks (with little polo players embroidered on them), Timberline shoes—polished, even . . . but *wait a minute! Where was he going?*

"Dad's picking me up to take me to a movie."

"What?!" Based on telephone conversations I had had earlier, he was coming to pick up Caron late in the afternoon. "Is Caron going?"

"Naw, just us guys. He's going to see her tomorrow."

The next time the phone rang, it was Jim. I invited him to "come on over," then went upstairs to arouse Caron.

Larry had picked up pizza for dinner, so while we were eating I broke it to Caron that her father would see her tomorrow instead of today. I thought this would upset her, so I added quickly, "But Jim's coming over in a little bit."

"Oh, that's right!" she exclaimed, as though suddenly remembering something. "I haven't seen Dad since Christmas. Well, it'll be good to see Jim again! I like Jim. It's always good to see Jim."

"Wait a minute, Caron. Run this by me again. Think! When did you last see your dad?"

"At Christmas." Then, reading the shock on my face, she added, "Oh, I know you told me he came to see me while I was in intensive care, but I don't remember that, so the last time I saw *him* was at Christmas."

"And when was the last time you saw Jim?" "Thursday night."

Whew! Talk about selective memory! We did, of course, refresh her memory about the visit with her father and his family in the Great Room just the night before. "Oh my gosh!" she gasped. "I forgot that they were there last night!"

Yes, Caron still needed work on her memory! While Jim was visiting that evening, she abruptly left us at one point, trudged up the stairs, paused briefly, then clomped back down the stairs and returned to the living room. He asked why she'd gone upstairs, and she shrugged. "I don't know. I forgot."

The verbal perseverance persisted. She now designated less usage to "dying," but "hate" had replaced it, being constantly replayed. Currently, her favorite words were "adorable" and "cute," which, while preferable to "dying" and "hate," were becoming tedious too—especially in combination with the familiar low-pitched monotone drawl, "so-o-o-o-o": "Juddly is *so-o-o-o-o* cute!" and "He's *so-o-o-o-o* adorable!"

The word-retrieval problem lingered, particularly when she was tired, when she would say such things as "My feet are cold. Where are my ducks?" meaning her slippers, which were plain blue terrycloth slip-on slippers, bearing no resemblance to ducks. One night she said, "I'm tired. I'm going to go lie down on my hamburger." While these types of mistakes weren't made often at home, where she was less stressed, they still happened often in the hospital. In the late afternoon and evening, she seldom caught the mistakes herself; but in the mornings, when she was most refreshed, she often realized after the word rolled off her lips that it wasn't correct. Usually, she would search for the correct word, and most of these times she was eventually able to find it.

It helped me to remember Dr. Perlman's analogy of the brain as a large file cabinet, the contents of which had somehow been dumped. When they were replaced, they had not been put back in the original order, so it now took longer to find things. I could visualize Caron's brain, once very efficient, now going to the place where it used to find the word "bed," but finding the word "hamburger," instead. So it would serve up the word "hamburger" to the speech center of the brain; and with no interference that word would complete the spoken sentence, "I'm going to go lie down on my . . ." Then, of course, the brain's auditory center would become active and realize that something was not right—

whereupon, if Caron were alert enough, she'd will her brain to go back and take another look for the right word. Sometimes she had to repeat this process several times. In the hamburger case, the next response retrieved was "hot dog," which, of course, didn't satisfy her, either. Whenever she was at her peak of alertness (which still didn't compare favorably with her pre-accident peak of alertness), she could usually find the right word eventually; but when she was tired, she either wouldn't recognize the mistake or she would become frustrated before finding it. This latter was the case with the word "bed," and she appealed to us for help.

It served Caron's memory better if our help was in the form of guidance that led her to find the word herself. As had been discovered by Yvonne, Caron's speech therapist, phonics cues were especially helpful to her: "You want to lie down on your b . . ." But sometimes she was too weary to tolerate this and would whine, "Just tell me!" or would turn angrily away from us and refuse to participate. Such was the case on the hamburger/hot dog night, and she was almost instantaneously asleep.

Sunday morning, we all got our first full-blown blast of the rigidity that head-injured patients usually exhibit. Certainly, we had experienced Caron's rigidity already—as, when she insisted on returning to Gantos to buy a replacement for the coat that had been cut off her at the scene of the accident. In such instances, we had viewed her actions as stubborn ones, childish demands, indicative of a return to a much earlier stage of her emotional development. Now, however, we learned the true meaning of rigidity—as well as the ensuing ramifications within the patient's family.

Saturday night, having experienced Caron's irreverence for time on Friday morning (as I'd tried to hurry her to ready for her appointment with her ophthalmologist), I set my alarm for an hour earlier than I normally would for a Sunday morning, and I readied for church quickly so as to allow extra time for Caron to get going. I didn't have the difficulty in getting her *up* that her nurses had reported having. However, once she *was* up, it became obvious that, to her, every effort presented a potential obstacle, and every encountered obstacle was insurmountable. The first snag was due to our not having laid out her clothing the previous night. She wanted to wear a particular cotton skirt and blouse, both of which needed to be ironed—and she refused to proceed to something else until all of her clothes were ready and assembled. She wanted to iron her clothes herself—an improvement over Friday morning, when she'd expected someone else to prepare her breakfast. Time didn't allow for her to do this domestic chore in addition to all of the self-care ritual she deemed necessary, but she could not subscribe to some part of the logic involved in time being saved if I ironed her clothes while she showered. Eventually, I nagged long enough that she slammed the iron down and stomped upstairs to the bathroom and banged the door shut. When I was content that the shower was running, I returned to the ironing board but found it in use by another Schreer, irritably claiming squatter's rights. This one, who had not suffered a head injury but was truly headstrong, refused to succumb to the logic that Caron was not going to come out of the bathroom until she was fully dressed. (It was part of her ritual, established many years before and, unfortunately, not lost to her as a result of her accident.) But why should he? It really wasn't logical at all, for on Thursday night she had been so exhausted that, while Matt and I were still in her room, she had begun pulling off her jeans and underwear in readiness for bed. If she'd been so immodest Thursday evening, what should keep her from coming out of the bathroom in just her slip now?

Sure enough, as Matt completed ironing his shirt and pants, Caron began yelling for her skirt and blouse. Then Matt started storming about because Caron wouldn't let him in the bathroom to take his shower until I brought her the rest of her clothes. I ironed as fast as I could, ignoring stubborn wrinkles, and steaming myself over no time having been saved.

The dressing dilemma could not be hurdled until she had her contacts in, but already upset by our dispute and now further upset by Matt's tirade, she couldn't get her contacts in, and she refused to leave the bathroom until successful. I suggested she come have breakfast or dry her hair first; but she persisted for what seemed like forever with those contacts, crying, cursing, yelling. Finally, defeated, she opened the door and asked for help—which, in this case, I really couldn't give. I had no idea how to insert contacts. Eventually, she consented to dry her hair while I got Larry up, because he would be able to help with the contacts. I got her downstairs and placed the hairdryer in her hand, whereupon she proceeded, distractedly, to dry the air all around her head.

Now she was hungry; and having forgotten about the contacts, she made her way to the kitchen, her hair still dripping. As she ate, she wanted me to curl her hair, but of course, she didn't like the way I did it, and besides, I pulled too hard. It's awfully hard using a curling iron on damp hair, but whenever I tried to return to hair-drying, she became agitated: she'd already *done* that! Obviously, most of my efforts were in vain. The wet locks simply fell limp again after the curling treatment, and Caron cursed me for my lack of finesse. But in time she became cranky about all of us holding her up. *She* wanted to go to church, so she dismissed her hair as "done." In bad temper, on the way out to the car, she chastised Larry for the ice in the driveway (which persisted despite his having salted it); but at least we were on our way.

Church went well. As per my request upon learning that Caron would be able to accompany us to church on Sunday, the pastor seemed to have shortened his sermon to accommodate her short attention span. It was, possibly, the shortest sermon he'd ever delivered in our church, and it wasn't really even a sermon, as one thinks of them. Rather, it was two related stories, one Biblical and one allegorical. Though Caron may not have derived the meaning of these, her interest was captured for the duration, and her face glowed throughout, for she was, once again, back in church. Afterward, she gathered quite a crowd. Everyone was relieved to see her back on her feet, and she was thrilled to see everyone.

She slept soundly for three hours after church, and we awoke her just in time for some dinner before her father was scheduled to pick her up. He arrived an hour later than anticipated, and in that time she had already slowed down. When he came to the door, she greeted him with "I'm tired. I'm always tired. I'm so tired of being tired." Such a greeting, and hello to you too!

They went to the house of her stepmother's sister and brother-in-law, where they and their children greeted her, as well as a new grandchild and Caron's stepsisters and a stepbrother and her half brother. Lots of excitement! With Caron and Matt and their father and stepmother joining the group, there were over a dozen people in that one house that afternoon, and Caron would do her best to be sociable, as this is what she has always done best. Later, she would again be frustrated and angry that what she most enjoyed was so fatiguing for her.

Again, to assuage any added remorse over having to return to the hospital, we had also lined up a visitor there for Caron. Her friend Britt brought gifts and chatted fairly comfortably with her for a while but afterward asked me to come out in the hall with her, where she expressed concern about Caron's being so "childlike." "Will she lose this?" she worried out loud. Good question—and one that plagued us all. We could better have enjoyed her childlike qualities had we had a guarantee that she would grow through and out of them. Unfortunately, with head injuries, there are no guarantees. Nothing is for sure except that every patient is different from every other one. There is not a norm, or status quo, of head injuries.

Caron didn't have any hallucinations about big mice or anything else that night, she didn't voice any concerns about not being awakened in the morning, and she didn't plead with us not to leave her at the hospital. She would have preferred to crawl into her bed as she was, but already half asleep, she readied for bed obediently when Betty asked her to—and was asleep in the time it took us to don our own coats!

On our drive home, we chatted happily about only having to return Caron to the hospital two more Sundays before she'd be home for good, commuting to the hospital only on weekdays for outpatient therapies. We'd all get more rest then. Our nerves were pretty frazzled now, mine by my commitment to Caron's needs and by taking no time for myself; and Larry, I don't know how he managed to teach all day—swim practices before school and practices or meets after school—and then come to the hospital almost every evening. But in two weeks our lives would become easier.

CHAPTER 16

"COGNITIVELY, YOU'RE NOT DOING SO WELL."

hart rounds were coming up Wednesday morning concerning Caron. These, I'd been told, were professional team meetings held biweekly for each patient in St. Jo's rehabilitation unit. Parents are not included in the chart rounds, but their input can be introduced by the hospital social worker assigned to the case. For this reason, I was expected to meet with our social worker a day or two before each of Caron's chart rounds. In meeting with her now, I reminded her that we looked forward to learning Caron's precise discharge date, which was one of the topics I understood to be pertinent to chart rounds. She responded that it was too soon to be bringing this up. I was confused, for on February 23 Dr. Perlman had said discharge would probably be in about four weeks, but the *next* chart rounds wouldn't be until March 22, the end of that four weeks. She thanked me for bringing this to her attention and promised to bring it up on Wednesday. We also discussed plans for Easter vacation, which would commence concurrent to Caron's release from the hospital. And I asked her to confirm for us whether Caron's participation in the school trip to Washington, D.C., was to be rejected or permitted, in whole or in part, the week following Easter vacation week.

Wednesday morning, Caron's associate nurse greeted me with a new "three-point program" for Caron: she was to put her own dirty clothes in a hamper brought from home, she was to return her own breakfast tray to the food cart in the corridor, and she was to make her own bed. It's interesting how the hospital atmosphere tends to convince one, and one's family, that one is somehow incapable of certain tasks. I hadn't thought about this phenomenon before, but here it was, boldly and clearly presented. Hospital personnel thought, no doubt, that this patient needed to be retrained to clean up after herself and that, furthermore, it was their job to do it, and that after their doing so, there would be carryover into real-life situations; that is, then she would clean up after herself at home, thanks to their expert training. Unbeknownst to them, Caron had naturally resumed not only the clothes-in-the-hamper routine when she came home on the weekends, but she had also already done a load of her own laundry, hand-washed some delicate items, and commenced an ironing task. She not only cleared her own place at the table, but she had also resumed her place in the family with regard to taking her turn at doing the dishes. And she had spontaneously made her own bed after getting up each morning she had slept at home. But in the hospital, a nurse or patient-care assistant had always come in to retrieve the food trays after each meal; and while Caron was in therapies in the morning, housekeeping had come in and made her bed. As for my part in perpetuating irresponsibility, I had always just taken home with me each day the clothes that Caron had worn that day, as I stayed until she was ready for bed, anyway. As far as I knew, Caron had been hanging her own pajamas on a hook in the bathroom after taking her shower in the morning, but maybe not; maybe housekeeping had been picking up after her.

This new three-point program reminded me of a structured nursery school style and method in which children use specially made materials to learn skills which are supposedly then generalized to real-life situations. That this carryover actually takes place is controversial, but the program is popular and has survived many years. Now, similarly, I was being instructed in a structured program designed to help my daughter learn skills I already knew she had. No matter, I thought: it is a matter of courtesy to clean up after oneself, no matter where one is, and it wasn't going to hurt her a bit. Further, it would enhance her regaining independence. I had been put in a good mood by this nurse, who concluded her three-point program explanation with the comment "Of course, she won't be around here much longer to *do* these things!"—a reminder that chart rounds were to be that day and that discharge was close at hand!

After lunch, however, it was this same nurse's job to break it to us that the team had decided that Caron should stay in the hospital another four to six weeks. Caron, devastated, immediately protested, "Six weeks is an eternity!" And then she spent the next hour staring at the wall.

I was more concerned with the choice of words used to explain *why* the team had made this decision. "Well, Caron," the nurse continued, "you're doing so well physically that I just thought you'd be leaving soon; but cognitively you're not doing so well." What did she mean by "cognitively . . . not doing so well"?

Dr. Perlman appeared an hour later, and I respected him too much to question the decision that she stay four to six weeks more. We would simply adjust to it. But I did want to ascertain that Easter vacation wasn't also out, and of course, I wanted to get the good doctor's interpretation of the nurse's statement. Easter vacation was out, he confirmed. Florida was too far, and ten days was too long. (In fact, the time frame itself was prohibited by a clause in the auto insurance coverage that defined therapeutic visits outside the hospital.) He suggested that the family proceed to Florida, anyway, without Caron; there was no reason we couldn't enjoy our planned vacation. "That would be pretty depressing for Caron!" I responded.

Caron's thoughts were transparent. Throughout this conversation, she had continued to stare at the wall. This had never been *our* vacation. It had been planned by, with, and for Caron; and she was despondent now to learn that it had been canceled. The former pastor of our church, whom Caron adored, now lived in Florida; and looking forward to seeing him and attending his church there was incentive for her, helping her get through the difficult days between now and then. The visit itself promised to be therapeutic. When her condition had been critical, Pastor Dave had called me almost daily for reports on her status; and when she became well enough to talk on the phone, he called to talk with her. Following the February 23 team meeting in which we'd learned that Caron would be out of the hospital before Easter, we had talked about a trip, and she had voiced preference for the trip that would culminate in her seeing Pastor Dave. He was like family to us all, but Caron was especially endeared to him. The next time he called her, she remembered to tell him we were coming at Easter time, and she remembered to tell me that he had called and that she had told him we were coming. At a time when she was not yet very reliable about remembering things, the memory and reporting in and of themselves were indicative of the importance of that impending visit.

Well, if Caron had to be on inpatient status through mid-April, insurance rules would obviously prohibit our taking the trip all the way to Florida, but a large part of the excitement for Caron had also been the prospects of seeing family again in South Carolina. She hadn't been there since my sister's wedding nearly a year and a half before, and she so loved her aunt Susie and her uncles Bobby and Billy and my stepmother, Ruth. Could we take an extended Easter weekend to drive there? It would be a consolation to Caron, and just to look at her one knew she could stand some cheering. He granted us the time from Thursday morning until Sunday night. She had to be back in her hospital bed Easter evening. He didn't prohibit travel by car, but he recommended air travel, if possible.

I set aside the question about Caron's cognition. For now, it was important to reorient her to an altered Easter incentive so that she could get on with the important stuff of concentrating in her afternoon therapies and progressing and getting better—improving her cognition.

On Monday of that week, Caron's physical therapist had decided to put Caron to the test of getting to all of her own therapies independently, without a transport. This decision wasn't premature, for the favorite transporter, Michael, had reported coming to get Caron several times the week before, only to find that she had already left and had ambulated successfully to her therapies without assistance. So Sue showed Caron where to find and how to use the machine for stamping charge sheets for each of her therapies. Until now, transporters had been responsible for this means of documenting charges accruing for the insurance companies. Also, Sue instructed Caron to check at the nurses' station a couple of times daily to see if there had been any scheduling changes in the day.

Unfortunately, in the first two days of her new independence, several hours of neuropscych tests had been scheduled, which overrode the therapy schedule and really confused her. I was told that she had slipped up on some of her morning therapies. (I had begun not coming in until noon, to allow Caron the independence of getting through the mornings without family support.) In the afternoons, I was still sitting in on her second PT, second OT, and second speech therapy of the day. Following Sue's giving Caron increased responsibility, I continued to attend the therapies, but I didn't go with her when she left so that she could be responsible for getting to them on her own. I'd give some excuse about something I wanted to finish up first, or an errand I needed to run. Then I would slip into the therapy a few minutes late.

With regard to the neuropsych tests, Caron reported that they "went bad. I didn't know anything she asked me. And then when I didn't know something, she asked me five thousand times about it. I was really kind of ticked with her." These tests were important to Caron, as they would determine her base level of competencies and deficiencies, upon which progress would be determined. She would have to take the full battery of tests every six months until two years after the date of her accident. Neuropscych tests aren't given when a patient is still in post-traumatic amnesia. Caron had begun the tests soon after Dr. Perlman announced that she was no longer in post-traumatic amnesia, and they were completed this week. No doubt, the results of these tests played a large part in Wednesday's decision that she should remain on inpatient status longer than originally projected. The parents were not yet privy to the results.

Throughout the day on Wednesday, I had received messages from various nurses and therapists that our social worker wanted to talk with me. Late in the afternoon, she arrived, with Caron's neuropsychologist. The two of them wanted to talk to me. I wasn't pleased by this prospect. I had not yet had sufficient contact with the social worker to have established a trust relationship with her, and although realizing that I was upset and probably not judging her fairly, my first impressions of her were that she was the kind of person who made mountains out of molehills and shifted sand dunes to other terrain. As I'd shared my concerns with her on Monday, I'd wondered how they would be interpreted when she voiced them in the chart rounds.

Caron held a very strong aversion to the neuropsychologist. Now seeing her with the social worker intensified my uneasiness. The grounds of credence seemed to shake beneath them both. However, I hadn't much choice except to listen as, alternating as speaker and supporter, they launched into the first part of what they'd established to be a twofold task. Part One was to explain the delay in date of discharge. One of them began by saying that Dr. Perlman didn't usually engage in predictions and that it was unfortunate that he had, for it was obvious to see that it had caused disappointment. Neither of them seemed to listen as I explained that I was thankful for Dr. Perlman's prediction, for both Caron and I are goal-oriented, and both of us uncomfortable with the unknown. We had enjoyed two weeks of projecting comfortably toward a March 23 discharge date. Sure, we were disappointed today—but we would both be fine by tomorrow. It's much better to have one bad day once in a while than to have to live in constant limbo about the future. By tomorrow we'd have adjusted to a new target date, and we'd be fine.

They didn't comprehend. Nor did they ever successfully explain what was so different at this point as to cause the team to push discharge to four to six weeks instead of two. One of them eventually said, "There's nothing wrong . . . ," but she couldn't say what was right, either, nor why two to four more inpatient weeks had been added. Perhaps the nurse had been right in her choice of words: "Cognitively, [Caron's] not doing so well."

Since they were failing so miserably at making explanation, I tried an interpretation of my own, asking, "Is it that every head injury progresses at its own rate? That each patient has his own timepiece within him? And that two weeks ago it was thought that Caron's was ticking faster than it really was?"

"Yes, something like that, if you want to use those words," answered the neuropsychologist. So! Still no answers. Had Caron slowed down? But even at four to six more weeks in the hospital,

Caron was going to be discharged within the two-month period that a nurse had originally told me was considered a short stay in rehab.

The social worker changed the topic with "We have another issue." Aha! Part Two! And *this* one was "an issue." In this portion of their twofold task, they suggested that I not come to the hospital a couple of days each week, rather than continuing to attend "all" of the therapies. Not three weeks before, this same person had given me an information sheet that outlined the team philosophy in these words: "The team strongly encourages family members to attend the patient's therapies on a regular basis. We feel that this is a very important part of our therapy program. Your participation in the therapy day will increase your understanding of the difficulties which your family member is currently facing, will teach you some therapy tasks you can do with your family member to reinforce the team's work, and will teach you the skills you will need to assist your family member . . ." But now she was, in effect, telling me to back off. And I already had. Few parents value independence in their children to the extent that I had always made it a priority for mine. Now, in an effort to reinstate that independence in my daughter, I had been staying home mornings to let her try her wings.

Stay home a couple of days a week? "I'm already doing better than that," I said and then explained, "I arrive at noon and only observe the afternoon therapies. Further, I've told all of the therapists that if it's ever not appropriate for me to sit in on a particular session, all they need to do is tell me and I'll be out the door, no offense taken. I expect only that they be up front with me." The therapies were for Caron, not for me. I was only there to learn so that I could follow through with the therapists' methodologies. When my being there would interfere with Caron's learning, however, I had made it quite clear to all of Caron's therapists that I wouldn't want to be there.

"Do you feel mistrust toward the team?" I was asked.

"No, I haven't, up until now. Larry and I are thrilled with Yvonne and Laura. And that Caron describes Sue as 'awesome' is good enough for us. But yes, things have happened in the hospital within the past couple of weeks which have been cause for concern." I briefed them on the arteriogram and blood test fiascos of the previous week, then continued, "And now you're telling me that 'the team' has asked that I attend fewer therapies. Where did that idea originate?"

"From the team."

"A whole team doesn't originate an idea. An idea can be accepted and adopted by a team, but it originates with one person's suggestion. Why didn't that person simply ask me to attend fewer of her therapies?"

My question was ignored, and the topic again changed: "Do you feel you *need* to be here?"

"Yes, I do."

"I was afraid of that. So for your own well-being, you should be in the hospital every day."

No, it wasn't for *my* well-being that I felt I needed to be here, but never mind that. I was more interested in the second part of the statement, " . . . you should be in the hospital every day." Was this her unsolicited psychological assessment of my well-being? Or was it permission? I'll never know—or care. I decided to accept it as permission. If I read their body language correctly, the meeting could be over at this point. So I said nothing, and they both got up and left.

Tuesday of that week, I hadn't arrived at the hospital until 3:00 p.m. Larry, unable to visit Monday and Tuesday nights, due to parent-teacher conferences at his school, had taken the day off to be with Caron and attend therapies with her. I used the opportunity to run a half a dozen errands that had been piling up, including driving a new car Larry thought might interest me, getting Matt to the dentist, visiting the school nurse for an update re: Caron's eventual school re-entry, catching up on some correspondence, and stopping in at the state office of the Michigan Head Injury Alliance, which I had learned was in Brighton—our town!

I arrived back at the hospital in time for the second speech therapy of the day. Caron had done well the day before, and it seemed to me that on the Rancho Los Amigos Hospital Scale of Cognitive Functioning, she had been at level 7—automatic appropriate—for a while and was now trying to move on to level 8—purposeful appropriate. She did well again today, but as was often the case in Speech, another misconception surfaced which needed to be corrected, and Yvonne would handle it with finesse, as always—but this time she'd be unable to keep a straight face.

Yvonne had asked if her father had been to the hospital to see her that week, and Caron had responded in the negative, explaining that he had gone to Traverse City "for a . . . for a . . . for a . . ." She couldn't remember the words. After a bit of an internal struggle, she settled for the phrase "for a memorial service"—for Buddy. Buddy was her stepmother's father, she continued, and he had died.

"Does the word you're looking for begin with an 'f'?" prompted Yvonne.

"No." Caron was quick to comprehend which word Yvonne thought she meant. "Buddy died a couple of *months* ago. His body was already cremated—and Grandma Jean has the cream."

On Monday, the day that Sue had designated increased responsibility to Caron, in charging her with getting to all of her therapies herself, Yvonne had changed Caron's morning speech session from eleven thirty to nine, explaining that she had a new patient who wouldn't be able to be up and around so early but that Caron could handle it. This squeezed Speech into the half hour between her eight-thirty self-care OT in her room and her nine-thirty clinic OT. Due to this schedule change, as well as the neuropsych tests which changed her schedule, Caron was disoriented on Tuesday and didn't remember to go to her morning speech without a reminder from Laura. But she adjusted quickly after that.

Following Caron's 3:00 p.m. speech therapy on Wednesday, I asked Yvonne if the real reason she had moved the morning therapy to the earlier time was to preclude my coming when I happened to arrive at the hospital a little before noon. No, she assured me, that was not the case; I was welcome at Speech anytime. Yvonne had always been candid with me, never afraid to voice her opinion, and I trusted her. Later in the week, still concerned about the words, "Cognitively, [she's] not doing so well," I'd get clarification from Yvonne: It wasn't that Caron was moving slower, nor that she had suffered any setbacks. Rather, in the initial assessments done, she had appeared—deceptively—to have fewer problems than what later surfaced. Now this I could understand, because this was the Caron I knew, my "overachiever." She had always been highly motivated, but while she was indeed a bright young lady, she had also always appeared to understand more than what she actually did understand, because she worked so hard to achieve beyond her comfortable comprehension level.

Yvonne assured me that while the cognitive difficulties were greater than originally thought, there was nothing that couldn't be tackled and improved upon through therapies—which meant more time than originally expected. Prognosis, she summarized, was no less optimistic; it would simply take longer.

It's difficult to get a prognosis out of most hospital staff members, so I was thankful for Yvonne's explanation. She knew that I understood there were no guarantees. I thought of that now: that despite any conjectured prognosis, head injuries were really not predictable. They were all different. No matter how positive or rapid or consistent a patient's progress, the progress could come to an abrupt halt at any time. Some head-injured patients reach a ceiling—the limit to their capacity to improve to any significant degree. That idea always choked me up. It was hard to envision Caron not returning to all that she was before, not achieving the potential she had to do anything she wanted to do, be anything she wanted to be.

Yvonne read my mind, or the tears running down my cheeks, and was quick to say, "I didn't realize that this was a worry of yours! We have *no* reason to believe that Caron won't continue progressing to her full potential. It'll take time, but we expect it to happen." And she reassured me again that Caron's naive, childlike quality would pass too.

Before I left her office, she shed some light on perseveration, also, validating my suspicions that Caron was getting maximum mileage out of words such as dying, hate, adorable, cute, and the latest addition, "ravishing," *because of* her word retrieval problem. Her insecurity about retrieving correct words lent itself easily to her persevering with tried and true words: if they *work*, stick with 'em!

I smiled, reflecting on a Monday perseveration episode. As tedious as "cute" and "adorable" and "ravishing" had become, I'd have taken a thousand of them gladly, in exchange for the embarrassment of Monday. With the change in her Speech schedule, Caron now had a very long lunch break; and along with Sue's new physical independence program, Caron had been granted the use of cafeteria passes for lunches, whenever I could be there to accompany her. She was excited about this new liberation, and bubbling all over with new confidence in herself—confidence that was not totally supported by actual capabilities, so it manifested itself in criticism of others. This criticism wasn't new to us. It had begun as a defense mechanism: when Caron couldn't validate that she was okay, it somehow appeased her to assess others as being "not okay"—so she had made vicious attacks on the neuropsychologist (not within her earshot, fortunately) and then on the neuropsych test administrator, who she complained to us was fat.

To Caron's way of thinking, "fat" must have been a good word, easily recognized, irrefutable. How could she go wrong with a word like that? After we had enjoyed lunch in the hospital cafeteria— and were greeted enthusiastically by old friends such as Laurie Kadish, Caron's primary nurse on SICU—we started our walk back down the long main corridor of the hospital toward rehab. Far down the corridor, Caron spotted a very hefty woman coming in our direction. Truly, the woman was huge, but with Caron's double vision, she must have appeared to be colossal! She brought the woman to my attention, saying, "Look at that fat woman!"

The woman was way too far away to hear our conversation, regardless of volume; other noises in the corridor would cover our own. But it was an unkind thing to say, and how was Caron to learn appropriate behavior if those of us who loved her didn't teach her? Too often, families of head-injured patients dismiss rude comments by saying, "(S)he doesn't know any better." But guess what the patient learns when allowed to get away with rudeness time and time again! I told Caron to shush; that wasn't kind.

"But it's true!" she protested. "That lady *is* fat!" I continued to try to quiet her, but the more I tried, the more insistent she became to be heard, and the louder she voiced her opinions: "I *hate* it when people get so fat! Why don't fat people go on a diet?" Meanwhile, the woman continued to advance in our direction, and we also were closing the gap between us. She was coming within hearing distance as Caron persevered, "When people get fat like that, they look gross! Fat people should go on a diet!" The woman was passing us now, with Caron looking right at her and lecturing, "She's *really* fat! She *really* should go on a diet!" *Really*, I couldn't remember a time when I'd been so mortified!

I was not at all displeased that Larry would be taking Caron to lunch in the hospital cafeteria the next day! And according to what he reported, she might be on the other side of that fat fence before long. Now that she had unlimited choices for lunch, she was choosing all the things she loved without regard for what was wise. Larry was afraid she'd create a scene if he said no, so for lunch on Tuesday, she had a large Mountain Dew, French fries, Polish sausage, and a big piece of cake with lots of frosting.

The weekend was a struggle. It was Caron's first full weekend at home, from Friday after therapies until Sunday evening. She had many plans, including listening to the Brighton High School Wind Ensemble perform at the district band festival Saturday afternoon, watching some friends acting in a high school play Saturday evening, and attending church Sunday morning. Caron had always been a planner. I think it must have been hereditary. She got it from her mother, who got it from her mother. But Caron had always done much better than her mother and her grandmother: she had actually followed through in carrying out the plans. Now, she had not lost the ability to plan, and she hadn't lost the deep sense of disappointment with herself whenever her plans didn't materialize; but she was lacking the middle step: the capacity to carry out the plan independently. This put me in the position I had recommended to Matt just a few Wednesdays before, the Tom Landry philosophy of getting someone to do something they didn't want to do in order to achieve something they wanted to achieve. At risk of earning a black eye for my efforts, I practically dragged Caron out of bed Saturday at noon, to get her ready for the band competition. She protested that she didn't want to go, after all; but when she got there, she was greeted with a hundred hugs from band friends who hadn't seen her since before her accident, and she witnessed her band taking "1" ratings all the way, including the sight-reading portion. "I'm *so-o-o-o-o* glad I could be here," she murmured.

She napped when she got home, and I had to fight with her again to get her to the play *Snoopy*, where she was reunited with many more friends and again was "*so-o-o-o-o* glad" to have come. Also, had she not gone, she would have been sound asleep in bed when her father and his family dropped by at nine thirty to say good-bye; they were on their way back to Arizona.

Sunday morning was another battle. She didn't want to go to church, after all—translated, "I don't want to have to get *up!*" I told her that next time she "didn't want to do something"—*really* didn't want to do it—all she had to do was let me know the day before, or at least before lying down, and I would take her at her word. But today she was going to church, and she was glad once she got there, of course . . . "*so-o-o-o-o* glad"!

The weekend ended on a positive note, Caron and I laughing 'til our sides ached while both Jim and Larry worked with poor little Judd, trying to get him to leave a dog biscuit on his nose until told "okay!" He caught onto the "okay" part very quickly but practically had to be held in a vise for all that preceded that part! Caron was now a lot like that too, I mused: eager to accept the rewards, but not too cooperative about doing the work which must precede the rewards.

CHAPTER 17

DENIAL

A t last, the picture frame shop completed the frames for the "Footprints" posters, and they were ready to be delivered. I wrote a note to accompany the SICU poster, because Caron didn't remember any of the people or her experiences there, but she wrote the one to the people on the 6000 unit, whom she remembered fondly:

> Dear 6000 Unit Staff,
> "Footprints" is my favorite contemporary religious story. God certainly has been carrying me through my recovery. You folks helped too! Remember "Footprints" if you ever have a difficult journey to travel!
> Thanks, and love, Caron Schreer

In two separate trips, on different days, so that Caron wouldn't become overtired, we went upstairs to deliver the framed posters and some homemade cookies. The staff on each unit was happy to see how well Caron was progressing; and when we returned at a later date, we would see these framed posters proudly displayed, along with Caron's junior school picture and, on the 6000 unit, her note.

This was Caron's seventh week in the hospital, and her fourth full week of therapies. In PT she was up to eight minutes on the stationary bike (sightseeing pace), two minutes jogging on the treadmill, and five sequenced legwork activities on the mat. Balance work was part of her program too (including use of a balance beam and a rocking balancing board), and such eye-hand coordination exercises as bouncing and catching a ball and dribbling a ball. Her endurance was noticeably improving, but she still had considerable difficulty with the balance and coordination activities—and Sue had not given up on getting Caron to jump rope!

In OT, Caron was playing lots of games, including concentration and memory games on the computer and rummy with Laura, after which she was required to write down the rules of the game and results of the day's play. She was accompanying Laura on practical missions too, such as a trip to the library to look up some information, and then to make a copy of an article found, using a copy machine. Such outings were specifically planned to help Caron relearn and/or practice skills she would need when she returned to school, but to remove any possibility of Caron perceiving this as demeaning, Laura always presented them as tasks she had to do, and would Caron like to come along?

In Speech, Yvonne capitalized on a fabulous book of photos that one very perceptive Uber's employee had put together to help Caron's memory with regard to the store and all of its employees. There were pictures here of every employee, using every inch of the store as background. Yvonne spent days pumping Caron with questions, then turning the page and asking her to remember details from a photo on the previous page. At first she was as obvious as "Study the person on this page," and then, in turning the page, asking, "What was Michelle wearing?" Later, she moved into questioning which appeared to center on the employee(s) in the picture, but she would occasionally slip in a question that seemed incidental: "And what kind of candies are these on the counter?" Ultimately, she would turn the page and ask Caron to name six of the seven kinds of candies that sat in the plastic bins next to the cash register.

In RT, Caron continued to enjoy her crafts. During this particular week, she completed the teddy bear wall hanging for herself and went on to a plaster and tile trivet, and then a small wooden box (to sand and stain) with an inlay portion on its lid, for which she had chosen heart shapes and created a nice design. She gave both of these projects to me and chose for the following week's project a teddy bear clothes rack for a young cousin's upcoming birthday. During all of her RT sessions, which had stretched to an hour, Nancy chatted informally with her, asking about her weekends, following up on discussions which Caron had previously initiated about personal relationships—or which Nancy had learned about from one of Caron's other therapists.

Caron's young cousin, Kelly, seems content
with the teddy bear rack Caron made for her.

I was moved by how well all of the therapists internalized each patient's life and remembered to ask all the right questions to help the patients remember things from day to day. I knew that they talked among themselves, also, sharing patients' accomplishments and insights, as well as information shared with them by family members. This gave them "ammunition" against the days when patients might be reticent to talk! I never found any therapist to be lacking in a supply of questions that could ultimately evoke a response from even the most cantankerous of patients. They really worked together beautifully!

Caron relaxed in the informal, no-pressure setting of RT, and she really admired Nancy, so I stopped attending RT, to better allow the one-on-one social relationship for which the setting and mutual respect was so conducive. I continued to attend the afternoon sessions of PT, OT, and Speech, which were truly work sessions, and where I could continue, through observation, to learn techniques for helping Caron grow in skills and independence when she was not in therapies.

One afternoon the week before, Nancy had taken Caron on an extended outing outside the hospital. They had dinner together at Big Boy, and they shopped for a purse that Caron had said she needed. I had given her money for it, but she returned to the hospital empty-handed, reporting in her black notebook, "I didn't quite see the perfect one." On the basis of that trip, Nancy told me she felt Caron could benefit from joining in community re-entry activities with other TBI (traumatic brain injury) patients. These activities took place a couple of evenings each week in the Great Room and sometimes also included afternoon group outings in the TBI-owned van. So independent of each other, we both set about working on Caron to persuade her to participate in these socialization activities with other patients. Neither of us was successful, so we worked out a cooperative plan which we felt would be foolproof: One evening I initiated a walk at precisely the time I knew that tie-dyeing and puff painting would be in full swing in the Great Room. We took the shortcut through the Great Room (as we usually did to get to the main hospital corridor, which is otherwise reached only by a circuitous route past the charge desk)—and surprise! Look what they're doing here! Caron looked intrigued by the projects, and Nancy called out to her to welcome her and encourage her to take part, but Caron surveyed the other participants and urged me to get her out of there fast.

While Caron had been in group therapies which I couldn't attend, or in RT, which I no longer attended, and even as I sat observing her working out in PT, I had come to know and have compassion for many of these other TBI patients and their families. Here was Katherine, who was still incoherent four months after her accident and unaware that she was six months pregnant; Shana, still here after a half a year; Joe, whose children were all grown and on their own, and he had begun to prepare for retirement and travel just before his car was crushed by a truck. Here were two more young people, April and Mary, drooling into their laps as they sat in their wheelchairs, and someone else actually did their projects for them. April was a victim of poisoning. Mary's vehicular accident had been a year and a half before. Kevin, who was Caron's age, was a high school student from a neighboring town, who'd been in an accident just a couple of weeks before her. I already knew them all as individuals, and I prayed for their recovery just as I prayed for Caron's. But she was seeing them clearly now for the first time, and so many of them all at once, all in one place. She was tugging at me, impatient to leave. My first reaction was to want to throttle her: did she think she was somehow better than all of them?

I held myself in check long enough to analyze a bit more of what may have been going on. Caron was still in a state of denial. She remembered her pre-accident self and just wanted to pick up from there and move on. She really believed she could, but reality kept nipping at her. Here were all these medical people, and therapists, and even her parents, insisting that she remain in the hospital, that she needed help. She resisted this reality. She willed herself to believe this was somehow all a nasty nightmare and that she'd wake up and find that she was right about herself, that she was "okay." She couldn't look at herself objectively. But she could see these other patients clearly. Clearly, *they* had problems—the kind of problems that her doctors and nurses and therapists and parents seemed to feel that *she* had. This must have been frighteningly threatening to her own definition of what was real. She couldn't face them. She couldn't face the reality of who she might really be.

After Caron refused to go to a movie (a movie she really wanted to see!) with the group, we decided to try a new approach. Two of her close friends were coming to visit: the Kathy and Kellie who Caron had said "go together" when she was planning her Valentine's Day pizza party. On the night of their visit, wood projects were being offered in the Great Room, and they agreed to exert peer pressure to get their friend to participate. It worked! They were so relentless in their demands for flawlessness in the finished sanded product that Caron had worked hard, oblivious to her surroundings. It took her an hour to meet the quality control standards of Kath's and Kell's inspections. Then they had to leave so as to be able to complete their own homework that evening. Her friends gone, Caron's motivation went downhill fast, but she did manage to complete the minor chore of staining her little bookrack before quitting. There sure is something to be said about peer pressure! We repeated this scenario a couple more times with the assistance of other school friends, and once in the habit of attending the group activities, it was no longer difficult to get Caron to participate on her own. In a couple of weeks she would even consent to going to a movie with Nancy, Kevin, and another boy their age.

Thursday night was a particularly distressing night on Caron's wing in rehab. We had come to expect the status quo to include increasing moans and protests and occasional shrill screams from up and down the corridor as the evening advanced. During the hours that they could be used, Caron's tape recorder, television, and VCR usually camouflaged all but the screams, especially as we were able to keep the door closed while we were visiting. During quiet hours, however, other patients' suffering—or perceived sufferings—were known to all up and down the corridor, and closed doors were not acceptable during the night hours, when the patients were the responsibility solely of the nurses.

On this particular night, the patient in a room next door was especially agitated. Shrill wails and screams pierced the air at regular intervals, and the wall between the two rooms shook when objects were shoved or thrown against it. We did all we could to create distractions for Caron. Nothing worked. The riot next door could not be ignored. Later, as we were leaving, I would learn that the patient had had a messy bowel movement in her chair and her sister had summoned help in cleaning it up. The cleanup perturbed the patient, who protested vocally as well as physically, hurling objects at the intruders, missing and hitting the walls. When there were no more objects within reach, she began hurling her excrement at them. No one who'd come to help escaped clean, and nothing in the room was missed, either. The patient had to be sedated while the entire room was disinfected. I comforted the sister, who was shaken and in tears. How easily our positions might have been reversed. We were all so vulnerable, it was easy to empathize with others here, even complete strangers.

That night, Caron's "big mice" returned, I was told by a nurse the next day. Caron had received her first full weekend pass, so I had told her I'd pick her up after all of her Friday therapies, instead of coming at noon to join her in them. When I arrived, she was crying, because "I didn't know where you were!" So here was a little setback in self-confidence and/or her day-to-day memory. Perhaps it had been initiated by the disturbance of the night before, but regardless, the task at hand was to help her relearn self-assurance so that, among other things, she could effectively combat environmental disturbances that had nothing to do with her. I handed her a St. Patrick's Day card that had arrived in the mail from her father. Of German ancestry himself, he'd added a little note acknowledging another branch of Caron's lineage, "That Hathaway blood is sturdy stuff, isn't it?" She didn't understand, so we talked about the meaning, especially as it pertained to her now, and she agreed that she could probably ignore the mice, and she'd try to remember, and not be upset about, deviations in my arrival times in the future. (This was a good concept to establish, because in snow and ice conditions, it's impossible to guarantee a precise arrival time every day, anyway; and one day previously in the week, she had been upset that I'd arrived at 12:05 p.m. when I'd told her I'd be there at noon!)

In any event, we didn't need to be concerned about big mice or a five-minute tardiness for the next few days. Caron was checking out until Sunday evening. After taking little green baskets of goodies to my first graders, I had spent the rest of the day cleaning and decorating the house (with green crepe paper and shamrocks, of course!) and setting the dining room table with St. Patrick's Day paper products: table covering, napkins, and plates, and a leprechaun centerpiece. When I'd left for the hospital, the corned beef was already simmering on the stove, and the vegetables were cleaned and cut, ready to throw in at 5:00 p.m.

Judd had come along for the ride and to greet Caron for her first full weekend at home. It took longer than usual to check Caron out, as the nurse who usually prepared the on-pass meds and instruction sheet wasn't here, and the nurse in charge today was inexperienced in the procedure. I was worried now about what Judd might be disassembling in the car! But when we finally joined him there, I praised him: he'd maintained his patience longer than usual and had just begun to bite into the one-serving samples of cereal which I'd plucked out of the mailbox on the way out of the driveway. In his excitement upon seeing Caron, Judd didn't notice my removing this intriguing treat from his reach.

Nor did Caron seem to notice all the St. Patrick's Day decorations around the house. When we sat down to corned beef and cabbage at the kitchen table instead of at the decorative dining room table, even then she didn't ask any questions. And when at 7:00 p.m., Lisa Darby arrived looking like the cutest little leprechaun you ever did see in breeches, suspenders, bow tie, and Irish tam (truly *not* her usual garb!), Caron merely greeted her with "Thanks for dropping by." It took the arrival of a few more friends—Kath and Kell were next, and Leeann and Amy hot on their heels—before Caron began to suspect that something was up! Cindy Swinehart arrived soon afterward, then Karen and Lauren, and, finally, Britt.

Left to right: 'Darbs', 'Kell', Leeanne, Caron,
'Kath', Karen, Cindy, Amy, and Lauren

The surprise St. Patrick's Day party was a big success. Lots of girlish chatter filled our house once again. All had come in Irish garb, but although Karen campaigned in her own behalf, touting herself as the closest in stature to true leprechaun height, Darbs was voted the best-dressed leprechaun and won a gift certificate to the girls' favorite hot fudge sundae hangout in town. But everyone got to partake in an enchanting bakery cake with "Happy St. Patrick's Day, Caron!" on the top. This was accompanied by green ice cream, homemade by a parent of one of my first graders, and by a green sherbet/carbonated drink concoction. Such fun! Everybody noted Caron's progress in memory and spatial orientation since the Valentine's Day party. Tonight, people moved about freely, and she wasn't confused by their changing places. And as was expected, the evening came to a close with "It was *so-o-o-o-o* good to see everyone again!" But did I detect a note of vocal inflection? Yvonne and Caron had been working hard to eradicate the flatness of her vocalizations; but it was, once again, the peer group that effected the actual change.

Saturday Caron and I drove to Frankenmuth, best known for a year-round Christmas store, but the fudge and candy shops accommodate all of the holidays, and we were in search of a chocolate basket for Yvonne, whom Caron had determined was a chocoholic. We found the basket, and she also picked out a chocolate teddy bear for Nancy and "You are special" chocolate bars for Sue and Laura. I bought a chocolate radio for Matt's basket and a chocolate telephone for Caron's. She saved me from wondering what she might like to have in her basket: she picked out all of the rest of the basket fillings herself! By Easter Sunday, a week away, she'd have forgotten about it and would be surprised. There was some small humorous compensation for this upheaval in our lives!

Sunday after church, Caron brought me the homework Yvonne had assigned for the weekend. I was surprised that she had already completed most of the assignment on her own and was only asking for help on the items which had stumped her. For most of these, she ventured a guess at the answer, and it was correct; she merely needed validation. In addition to her doing her homework independently (Saturday night? Sunday morning?), she had done all of her own laundry and also attacked the clutter that had accumulated on her desk and dresser since her accident. When we left to return to the hospital, she left behind a clean room, and she brought with her the clothes she herself had washed and ironed.

My little girl was growing up again, and when I prepared to leave her at the hospital now that the weekend was over, she wasn't the penchant child she had been on previous returns. Rather, she was truly sad. I hated leaving her like that. How I wished she were home with us.

In the week that followed, Sue succeeded in teaching Caron to jump rope! Yvonne repeated the word-naming test given over a month before, and Caron demonstrated memory of acorns as being the nuts from oak trees; but she still couldn't remember the names of such objects as harmonica, hammock, trellis, sphinx, pyramid, compass, protractor, pelican, or igloo. Nancy persuaded her to join Kevin and Jeff in a game of Pictionary; and in two evening group sessions, Caron made a layered sand candle and a leather loop belt—although she said, of the latter, "This'll probably be a collar for Judd, 'cause nobody I know would want a belt like *this!*" Most challenging that week were her OT exercises. She did word searches, studied and interpreted want ads, and followed a written recipe to make chocolate chip cookies—but most difficult of all were the yellow pages of the telephone book. Her task was to identify a category that would remedy a given problem, then look up and write down a number to call for help. One example was "There are ants in the kitchen. What company would you call to help?" No matter how hard she tried, she couldn't find "exterminators" or "pest control" in her personal memory bank of words. It's overwhelming to realize how many everyday living areas are affected by a loss of vocabulary. Without the ability to identify a category, a person would never be able to use the yellow pages to seek help needed—for anything!

Caron's vocabulary was still limited, but her miscues were becoming closer to the correct words. One of the weekend nights, we had had chicken divan for dinner. One of Caron's exercises in remembering details was to report to her speech therapist everything she'd consumed the day or weekend before. On Monday, she would tell Yvonne she had eaten "chicken divine." When she and Yvonne went on an errand to fetch some tape, she called it an "error"! She described a new necklace as being made of wooden beans, instead of beads. She told Nancy that the trivet had been "touch" (tough) work. She was proud of her "stores" (scores) in computer games she was playing. And over Easter weekend, when she got behind in writing in her black notebook, she would say she'd have to "scrabble" to catch up.

It had been two weeks since Sue had decided Caron should get to all of her therapies independently, stamping her own charge sheets in advance and requesting that the therapists sign them. I noticed that this responsibility had not impacted on Caron, but it was between Sue and Caron, so I stayed out of it. Reminders and responsibility aren't usually compatible, so I didn't say anything to Caron about it. I knew that Sue would, in due time. The time she chose was the day before the four-day Easter weekend. In her quiet voice, she told Caron that she hadn't been fulfilling her responsibility with regard to the charge slips, so she'd show her again how to do it. She paused then, searching for a time in her schedule when she could do this. I had observed the first instruction and now had plenty of time on my hands, so I asked Sue if she preferred to do this herself or if it would help if I did it. She seemed appreciative for the reprieve, so when PT was over, Caron led me to the room where the charge slips were done. She was absolutely out of practice but was able to figure everything out without instruction. Then she calculated how many she would need for the remainder of that day, as well as for the next morning, and she stamped them all.

The March 22 chart rounds came and went. I saw Dr. Perlman afterward, but all he said was that our social worker and Caron's neuropsychologist would talk with me after the Easter weekend regarding the neuropsych test results.

As per instructions following the chart rounds two weeks prior to this time, we had investigated airlines for the Easter weekend trip. There were only two flights with openings at that time. One would have cost $2,000 for the four of us, and the departure time of 6:30 a.m. was prohibitive in itself, as we'd never be able to get Caron moving so early. The other available flight not only had a two-hour layover in Chicago, but also, it didn't fly to Greenville, so Ruth would have to pick us up in Charlotte, North Carolina, a round trip of four hours for her. The two hour layover would bring our total trip time to ten hours—but we could drive it in less than twelve, and for a small fraction of the price of airfare. We decided to drive.

Larry had readied our old van, a '70s vintage, homemade camper conversion. Jim had agreed to stay at our house; so we didn't have to worry about securing the house, notifying the police of our absence, or kenneling Judd. We all met at the hospital Thursday before noon. We were on the road by noon, planning to arrive before midnight.

I drove the first leg of the trip, and everyone else slept. I was proud to get us through Ohio without a speeding ticket. (Ohio must have an abundance of policemen—or else the ones the state hires are exceptionally zealous about their jobs. We always consider it a major accomplishment to get through Ohio without a ticket.) Just inside Kentucky, I turned the keys over to Larry, who noticed steam rising from the hood and assumed that I'd been speeding. Here began a chain of stops to let the engine cool and to add more water—lots more water. Dinnertime provided a natural break for the engine to cool down, but we had to make many additional stops, searching gas stations and K-Marts for leak-stopping solutions. None of them proved effective. Six hours after discovering a problem, we called Ruth from Knoxville to report that we'd have to spend the night in a motel and look for a place in the morning that could find and fix the problem. We'd call her at noon Good Friday regarding our estimated arrival time.

Meanwhile, the kids had apparently already settled in for the night: they were snuggled up in sleeping bags on the bed in the back of the van. Both were sleeping soundly. Larry decided to push on. Not far down the road, we were forced to stop again to allow the engine to cool. The start after that didn't get us far, either, before the poor van began sputtering and dying. Larry nursed it to a rest area, from which he called a tow truck. (He was lucky to find something open at 1:00 a.m.!) But the tow truck driver was confident that he knew what the problem was, so instead of towing us to the nearest town, he did a temporary fix: one of the hoses had a big hole in it, and he didn't have the right replacement part, but he improvised with what he had, and it did, in fact, get us to Greenville—just barely. (The next morning, when Larry took the van to be repaired, the makeshift hose blew before he'd gone a mile!)

As per our telephone call from Knoxville, Ruth wasn't expecting us until the next afternoon sometime, so we didn't bang on the door when we pulled in her driveway at 5:30 a.m. Caron and Matt hadn't stirred, so Larry and I stretched out on the floor until Ruth let the cat out at eight thirty. After twenty hours in the van, it surely was good to enjoy a cup of coffee and some good old Southern hospitality!

Caron had had plenty of sound sleep, and when she finally rolled out of her sleeping bag sometime later, she couldn't believe we were there *already!* Our two-day, two-night stay proved invigorating for her. She loves all of her relatives, but especially my sister Susie. She was ecstatic to get to spend "so much time" with her: dinner at Susie and Pete's, a movie with Susie and Pete, wallpaper shopping with Susie ... and when Susie and Pete brought their teeny little dog, Nibble, over to antagonize my stepmother's cat Smokey, Caron thought this was the best show ever! Then my brother Bob showed up with his cocker spaniel puppy, and the three animals provided even better entertainment than the two had!

The trip back to Michigan was uneventful—hallelujah! Caron had many memories to share with Yvonne the next day, and she didn't begrudge us leaving her at the hospital that Sunday night. Once again in her life, she had news for "Show and Tell"! I was relieved that the trip had, after all, been a success—even though Caron really *was* surprised by all of the things in her Easter basket.

CHAPTER 18

"I DON'T CARE!"

It was our first day back after the Easter weekend; and as Dr. Perlman had promised, Caron's neuropsychologist and our social worker had set a time, that very afternoon, to share the early March neuropsych test results. After my last meeting with this twosome, I dreaded another one alone. I called Larry at school, and he said he'd make arrangements to be at the meeting at 2:30 p.m.

Larry's presence was comforting, but the more encounters I had with the neuropsychologist, the more discomforting her demeanor became to me. Yes, I could certainly see why this woman annoyed Caron. The social worker, by contrast, was beginning to appear to be a fairly regular person who just didn't have a knack for warmth in an introductory meeting and then lost footing from there by association with this "doctor." Be that as it may, this meeting was for the purpose of the neuropsychologist sharing her field of expertise, so the social worker said nothing, unless a question was specifically directed at her. Her presence was for support. Whose support? I'd thought that her responsibility was to serve as the family's interpreter of hospital policy, but even the physical arrangement of this meeting belied her function as a family support person: she sat in the chair next to the neuropsychologist, across the table from us.

The neuropsychologist launched into her interpretation of the test results, throwing out percentile scores and seeming to take great pride and pleasure in interpreting what they meant: "Caron scored fifth percentile in this area: that's very low . . . fiftieth percentile here: that's average.

Anything from the twenty-fifth to the fiftieth percentile is average." Average for *whom?* My daughter had never seen standardized test results so low and would never have accepted the fiftieth percentile as average, not for herself!

By her prolific interpretations, it was obvious that this NP person had not shown us the courtesy of finding out anything about us before this meeting. Between us, Larry and I had over forty years of teaching experience, in addition to four degrees, which had included coursework in statistics and test measures; we certainly did not need to have percentiles defined and spelled out to us. All of this would have been evident to any professional person who took the time to glance at the conscientiously completed Personal and Family Biography Sheet which I'd been asked to prepare, when Caron was admitted to rehab, for the benefit of hospital personnel working here. I had been told at the time that this would be placed in the black notebook that Caron had to carry everywhere she went in the hospital. To date, it had not appeared in Caron's notebook, and she complained incessantly about people asking her the same questions over and over again, questions to which the answers were spelled out plainly on the Personal and Family Biography Sheet. Toward the end of this meeting, when I asked the social worker why a copy of this had not yet been placed in the black notebook, the neuropsychologist flipped to the back of her own folder and found her copy of it. Her comments indicated that, indeed, she had never before looked at this; yet it had been available to her for over six weeks.

Percentiles are often confusing to parents of school-age children; and because standardized tests most often use this statistic in reporting, school systems owe parents an education in interpreting percentiles if, in fact, they report these scores to the parents. No doubt, neuropsychologists should do the same for patients' family members, unless they are professionals in a field, such as education, where it could be expected that they would need little or no explanation. Uninformed parents often equate percentiles with percentages, which is inaccurate. If a student scores 50 percent on a test, and every item was weighted the same as any other, then it is correct to assume that the student got half of the items on that test right and half of them wrong. Percentiles are not so simple, because they don't report the student's own score; rather, they offer a comparison of one student's score to the scores of all of the other students who are taking or could be expected to take the test. Fiftieth percentile does not mean that the student got half of the items right and half wrong. Depending upon the group with which the student is being compared, it could even mean (s)he got most all of them right, or most all of them wrong. For example, if the student were a high school senior taking a test in calculus and being compared with the scores of university math professors, fiftieth percentile might be a very high score for that student! But if the comparison group consisted of fifth graders, then fiftieth percentile would be very low for our high school senior. Such comparisons aren't realistic but are given as extreme examples to illustrate the obscurity of percentile scores if one doesn't know the composite of the comparison group.

Percentiles report the number of scores above and below them. A score of fiftieth percentile means that half of the other test takers had lower scores and half had higher scores. Similarly, twenty-fifth percentile indicates that a quarter of the tested population scored lower and three-quarters scored higher.

We were accustomed to Caron scoring in the eightieth and ninetieth percentiles on tests established to accurately evaluate college preparatory students. When compared to *all* students her own age, we would have expected to see Caron scoring in the ninety-sixth to ninety-eighth percentiles. Before her accident, her academic standing was eighth in a class of nearly four hundred students—that is, in the top 2% of her class academically . . . or the ninety-eighth percentile.

That was two months ago. Now the neuropsychologist was reporting that, in comparison to *same-age peers* (*all* sixteen-year-olds, not just the ones bound for college), Caron was at the fiftieth percentile in attention and concentration, forty-fifth percentile in visual memory, and third percentile in overall verbal memory. *Ninety-seven sixteen-year-olds out of one hundred could remember what was said to them with more reliability than Caron could.* Some percentiles weren't given to us; rather, it was simply reported that in information processing speed, both written and oral, and in executive functioning—including planning, organizing, and solving problems—she was "severely impaired at this time" (in the lowest couple of percentiles). The severe impairment in executive functioning was demonstrated by rigidity, or inflexibility, in thinking, which resulted in an inability to generate alternative solutions.

With regard to fine motor control, Caron was "slow, more so on the right side than on the left, due to the left hemisphere damage." Academically, her reading comprehension was at a sixth-grade level. Math was at an eighth-grade level when timed but increased to a twelfth-grade level when given unlimited time to complete. (In other words, it was the severe impairment in information processing speed that was handicapping her in math, more so than any significant physical damage to the portions of her brain responsible for math concepts and calculations.) It was not even particularly encouraging that her spelling was at a twelfth-grade level, as she had always been a great speller, scoring a 12.6 grade equivalent in spelling way back in elementary school; twelfth-grade spelling level at *this* time indicated a loss.

The biggest blow came last: Caron's full-scale IQ at this time was 85. This was a loss of thirty to forty intelligence quotient points from her pre-accident IQ. Reassessment was recommended for August, as well as continuing speech and language therapies, and scheduling an IEPC (Individual Educational Planning Committee) meeting through our local school system. The Brighton High School nurse would be contacted the next day. I knew the IEPC meeting wouldn't be difficult to schedule, as Kay Kroth and I had already processed all of the paperwork necessary to expedite Caron's receiving special services, if needed, and both our local school district and the countywide intermediate school district through which special services come were ready and waiting for Caron.

There was to be a team meeting the next day which we were told was for the purpose of therapists' sharing with us specific examples which support the results of the neuropsych tests we'd just received. But for today, I was already exhausted. Lunch in the cafeteria with Caron was important for her, but never fun for whomever accompanied her. She always took the opportunity to gripe about anything and everything, at length, with one gripe leading into another. Today it began with not having had enough time that morning to curl her hair, and it was driving her crazy. When I suggested that she might have done it during the long morning break she had now that Yvonne had moved morning speech from eleven to nine, she launched into Laura having added in another half hour of computer work (and she *hated* computers!), and she'd begun yet another new group that morning, as an assistant to the therapist—and "they're all so *dumb!* They don't even know what *month* it is!" (Hm-m-m . . . it seemed that Caron needed to be educated about where *she* had been—and, especially, about such qualities as empathy and compassion!)

For my part, I missed my daughter! I missed my laughing, cheerful, positive daughter. I prayed that *this* daughter, this angry, haughty, negative daughter, was merely passing through a phase and that this would not be a permanent personality change resulting from the head injury.

Earlier, Caron had been excited about her father having called that morning, but now when I suggested that she set her alarm for a bit earlier in the morning to accommodate hair-curling, she shouted, "NO! If I get up at seven thirty, I have enough time to get ready—if people didn't bother me on the telephone!" So what had previously been happy news was now ammunition for her grump! Her moods were so unpredictable, and for some reason, mood swings were most pronounced over lunch.

I noticed that the pocket of her black notebook was stuffed with charge slips, and I wondered if she'd actually remembered to submit them to her therapists Wednesday afternoon and Thursday morning before Easter weekend, and then stamped new ones this morning for today—or if these were left over from last week and lots of forgetting. I didn't ask. The neuropsych test results had brought me down even further, and after dinner I asked Caron if she'd mind if I left a little early. Over Easter weekend, she had begun to perseverate a new sentence: "I'm not going to want to drive again for a *l-o-n-g* time." Her rationale was that she didn't want to take a chance on being in the hospital ever again. This must have been on her mind, for when I told her I was tired and asked if I could leave a little early, she voiced a new concern: "What if you fall asleep while you're driving?" But all I had to do was remind her how hard it was for me to fall asleep *any* time, and she quickly resolved, "That's true. I guess that's one I never have to worry about then."

On the next day, during Caron's afternoon's PT, I asked Sue how Caron had been doing with her charge slips, and Sue's response was "When I remember to remind her ..." So the ones in her notebook had probably been the ones she'd stamped last week, after all.

Caron's Cog Group followed PT, so I had a half hour free before the team meeting would convene. I lingered behind in the physical therapy room, as I'd been conversing with Mary's mother, Evelyn, and there was no need for me to leave. What a strong person Evelyn was; I wondered if I'd have had her fortitude if Caron had been injured so severely as her daughter. Mary had had multiple internal injuries as well as massive brain damage. The blow to her head had rendered her left side paralyzed, and the medical consensus was that she would never again walk, except perhaps to bear her own weight to move from her wheelchair to an easy chair or into bed. Together, Evelyn and I watched as, prompted by her therapist, Mary struggled to stabilize her body in a standing position, holding a pole in front of her. Though her accident had been eighteen months before, she was still disoriented as to where center was. "But," offered Evelyn, positively, "they said she'd never be continent, either, and she is now—all day, and often through the night.

"They also said she'd never be able to talk. But she understands the language and responds. She gives no response if her answer is no, and she holds up one finger for yes: the higher the finger, the more emphatic the yes!" Clearly, this mother still held hope for her daughter. Although "home" was seventy-some miles north of the hospital, she or her husband, and sometimes both of them, had made the trip every day, for a year and a half, to be with their daughter in therapies.

Evelyn also knew that if she weren't there to stick up for Mary, she couldn't be confident that anyone else would, either. "When Mary learned how to let us know that she had to go to the bathroom, I was so encouraged," she told me. "Then one day I was in the room when she gave this sign to a nurse, and the nurse told me that she didn't have to go, because she just went an hour ago. 'Do you have children?' I asked her. 'And is this the way you potty-trained them—telling them they didn't have to go just because they went an hour ago?'" Ah, yes—the struggles we parents have to go through to convince some of the nurses that our children are human beings worthy of consideration, in spite of the fact that they've suffered a head injury.

＊＊＊＊＊＊

It was almost 2:30 p.m.; so I excused myself from the PT room, found Larry in the corridor, and walked the short distance down the hall to the pavilion conference room which had been indicated as the meeting place for this special team gathering. The neuropsychologist was at the board, writing on it the team's overall goals (toward Caron's independence). They were these executive skills:

- Initiation
- Decision-making
- Follow-through
- Response time

Then, contrary to what she'd told us the day before regarding the purpose of today's meeting, she directed her attention to us, asking that we give examples of what we'd seen of Caron's deficits in these areas. Not only was this a blatant reversal of the stated intent of the meeting, but also, it was highly unfair. This woman always came to meetings with prolific notes and tended to read them. I doubted that she could speak extemporaneously and without a written page to hide behind. She always knew when she would be called upon to make a presentation. She'd made a lasting impression on me when, on February 22, she had come into Caron's room to talk with her, "alone," for ten or fifteen minutes "because I have to give a report on her at the team meeting tomorrow." In just ten or fifteen minutes she planned to meet a new person and get to know her well enough to give a report on her the next day! And she would arrive at that February 23 meeting with sufficient notes to instill in all of the other team members a belief that she knew this patient quite well. Yet now she expected one or both of us to speak without preparation, without notes, and without any forewarning that we would be asked to do this. And when I did begin, no doubt after much stammering, she had the audacity to interrupt me with "We were hoping you'd be more specific."

Of course, *she* had specifics—all written down in the longhand notes before her. To improve upon her initiation, decision-making, and follow-through (the first three of four executive skills targeted by the team):

1.   Caron should pick out her own clothes.
2.   Caron should fill out her own menus.
3.   Caron should do her own laundry.
4.   Caron will prepare a meal in the hospital.
5.   I shouldn't remind Caron about her charge slips. "She should be allowed to fall flat on her face."

Caron had been picking out her own clothes for over three weeks. She had been doing her own hospital menus, independent of anyone's help, for two weeks. She was doing her own laundry at home, unprompted. She prepared her own breakfasts and lunches on the weekends. Given that these were the objectives for Caron's increasing independence, I knew that she wasn't going to be given the opportunity *here* to "fall flat on her face"! Yes, I wanted her to regain her independence, and I'm a believer in allowing children to learn from their own mistakes. But all of the goals these people had established for my daughter's "recovery" were, in fact, blatant proof that they truly were not observant and had not gotten to know Caron—or could it be that they believed I was laying out her clothes, ordering her meals, doing her laundry, and reminding her to remember her charge slips?

Now the neuropsychologist asked the speech therapist to comment on the fourth executive skill: response time. Yvonne began by saying that Caron needed to be allowed more response time. As an educator, I'm well versed in the value of response time. In educational circles, we call it "wait time." Test yourself next time you ask someone a question: how long do you feel comfortable waiting for an answer before the silence unnerves you and you either rephrase the question or suggest a possible answer or in some other way break that uncomfortable silence? As a teacher, I've learned not to interrupt the silence for at least fifteen seconds. It's a very long time to wait, but some children need that much time to formulate a response. And if normal children might need fifteen seconds, consider the time needed by some brain-injured patients! I was gratified that the team recognized Caron's need for more "wait time" and that they were targeting this area, themselves, for some attention.

Sometimes, during speech therapy, Yvonne directed questions at me to verify what Caron was telling her. At these times I spoke. At all other times, from my position behind Caron so that she couldn't see me, I listened only, seldom even making eye contact with Yvonne. I busied myself taking the notes that have ultimately woven themselves into the sentences on the pages of this book. Had I been invited in advance to make a presentation at this meeting, I could have drawn from hundreds of pages of notes.

I was exhausted, and yesterday's neuropsych results had added to a despondence uncharacteristic of me. I had most assuredly taken a side trip into a bit of wallowing in self-pity. Surely, I felt Caron's frustration in her bemoaning, "I'm tired. I'm always tired.

I'm so tired of being tired." Now I did a double take: Was this new list of "team goals" merely another misguided directive that I back off? Did this team view my presence as inhibiting Caron's independence building? I knew that this wasn't so, and in fact, it was often independence enhancing. Just the night before, Caron had completed her dinner and left her dinner tray on the tray table while she went into the bathroom. At that time, a PCA entered the room and matter-of-factly began to pick up the tray. No, no, no, I shook my head, explaining that it was Caron's job to remember to return the tray herself.

After each therapist had had her turn to input, Larry and I returned to Caron's room to discuss the implications of the meeting and what, if anything, we would try to change. I was noticeably upset, and Betty came in to see what was the matter. She listened then reassured me that she, at least, had noticed our relinquishing responsibilities to Caron as she became ready, and she thought we were "right on!" She knew, for example, that Caron had done all of her own laundry at home the past weekend; and she had wondered why Laura had proposed that she help Caron do her laundry here at the hospital, instead. I added to what she knew, saying, "I never once went downstairs to check up on her. If she forgot to add soap, who cares? She wouldn't die from the filth! And what if she left the clothes sit in the dryer? She could live with a few wrinkles until she decided to do something about it!"

"You're all right." Betty smiled, as she put her arm around me. Whew! I needed that!

Larry and I decided that we weren't going to change anything that we were doing but that I should try to eradicate some of my sensitivity. Worrying about what hospital personnel thought was depleting my energy level and counterproductive to Caron's needs. I shouldn't need someone else to tell me that I was all right, any more than I needed someone to tell me that what we were doing with Caron was helping, not hindering, her progress.

Caron returned from her afternoon therapies, and we talked seriously with her for over an hour, until dinner arrived, about initiation and decision-making. "But," she argued, with regard to making decisions, "I *don't* care! That's the way I am!"

We encouraged her to practice making decisions, anyway. "Every time you're given a choice," Larry instructed, "we want you to make a choice—whether you care about that choice or not. Do it for practice."

At 7:00 p.m., we left her, primed to make a decision in the evening recreational therapy, which would offer various wood projects. She decided to make a basket with chickens on each end. But Nancy handed her a cat basket kit instead. Said Caron the next day, "I didn't want to argue about it."

On this third day of this week, I saw that Caron's name was on chart rounds, but she'd just been on it last week. I learned soon enough that it was for purposes of setting a discharge date: April 13! Caron was so excited, she couldn't wait to tell Larry. Discharge was just fifteen days away!

Yvonne sought me out during her lunch break. She had heard about my meltdown the day before; and she wanted to apologize for poor examples and implications, and for not extending credit where credit was due, for all of the support Larry and I had given, not only to Caron but also to the team. She only wanted to be sure that we understood the intent: teamwork, for Caron's best interests. We're with you all the way, I assured her.

Kevin, Caron's age, had been hanging around Caron's door just before dinnertime each night; and whenever we asked him how he was, he'd respond, "I'm still here!" Kevin was persevering too: he'd found a response that worked, so he used it every time that question was asked.

"Now, Kevin," I said, "I can *see* that you're still here. I'm going to ask you that question again, and this time you're going to answer, 'I'm great!' Have you got that? Now, here goes: 'Kevin, how are you?'"

"I'm good." He grinned. I hugged him.

The following day, I'd ask him how he was; and he'd respond, "I'm still here!" But after I knit my brows and glared teasingly at him, he'd amend to "I'm great!"

That next day, Thursday, I'd see some blatant examples of Caron's rigidity, in Speech. Yvonne had told me over two weeks before that there were five areas of weakness on which they were especially concentrating in speech therapy:

1. Sustained attention: concentration.
2. Auditory processing, especially speed.
3. Reasoning and problem solving: Caron was showing insecurity and much inflexibility, or rigidity, in these areas.
4. Organization of thoughts: This weakness reduces language skills—speaking, reading, and writing.
5. Memory: Her general memory wasn't bad, but she was still having considerable difficulty recalling specific details. (It was toward the goal of improving memory for specifics that Yvonne had utilized the book of photos from Uber's Drug Store.)

Thursday, I decided to attend morning therapies instead of the afternoon ones. Yvonne was specifically working on problem solving. Given three written clues, Caron's task was to name what was being described. There were forty items to be done that day, and Caron groaned when Yvonne promised, "I have *more* of these!" She had difficulty with most all of the day's forty, but some which were particularly troublesome were these:

- "Rolls in an alley, is heavy and has holes, can be rolled in a gutter." The first word, "rolls," brought to Caron's mind a barrel, and she couldn't wipe that thought out of her mind, so the second and third clues didn't impact on her. After a discussion of the day's planned recreational therapy outing, bowling, Caron was prompted to read this item again. Then she was able to give the correct response, but she was very insecure in doing so: "All I can think of is a bowling ball."
- "Holds clothing, is metal or wooden, has a triangular portion with a hook on top." Again, she got hung up in the beginning. Having decided that a closet holds clothing, she was unable to generate any other ideas. The last clue confused her, but she held fast to her closet idea.
- "We carry many of these, should make duplicates, opens things that are secured." This time, it was the last word that captured her attention; and once she'd defined "secured" in her mind as "something to do with a bank," she wasn't able to derive any other meanings for the word.
- "Fingers hit them, black and white, make sounds." This one was really tough for her. The first clue brought to mind a typewriter, but "black and white" prompted an association with television (I don't know why: she's always had the advantage of color TV), and the final clue didn't do anything for her until she was prompted to think of *musical* sounds, at which time she thought of an oboe. Then she was unable to let go of any of those ideas to pull together one idea.
- "You put money in it, it times you, it expires." If you put money in it, she decided, it must be a bank account. No matter that bank accounts don't time you or expire.

- Of the forty items, there were only nine for which Caron was able to give the correct answer, but she was timid and insecure about each of them.

After Speech, Caron had her computer group with the therapist Carol. I was welcome to attend this group, because there was only one other patient and focus was on computer use rather than on group dynamics. At this particular session, Carol had Don at the computer and had assigned Caron the job of taking notes. The task was for the two of them to jointly operate a hot dog stand for a season of football games. Their goal was to earn $1,200 by the end of the season. There were many variables to be considered, including the weather, the type of game (as preseason vs. homecoming), the time and date of the game, and so on. The stadium held one thousand, but it was only packed on beautiful days or for important games. Based on their decisions about each of these factors, Caron and Don needed to decide how many hot dogs, buns, chips, cans of pop, and courtesy packs (catsup, mustard, and napkins) to order for each game. There were choices within choices too (such as regular, higher, or highest quality hot dogs; and the pop and chips were cheaper in large quantity).

This activity was clearly for the purposes of promoting initiation, decision-making, and follow-through. Don had no difficulties with these: he jumped right into it. Caron held back. I knew she was weak in these areas. I also wondered if some of her reticence might have been due to her having been assigned the job of note taker: did she think it was his job to make all the decisions and all she had to do was write them down? *Whatever* she thought, she didn't care enough about computers to ask any questions or clarify any misconceptions. She ventured ideas only when Carol specifically asked her to. And Don was motivated enough for the two of them: he'd have been happy to do the assignment alone.

Later, I asked Caron what had caused her to remain silent except when prompted. She said she didn't want to say anything because she felt guilty that he might give in and change the way he was doing things—and she really didn't even care. I couldn't make her care, but in talking it over, I was at least able to plant a seed for the concept of compromise: Don had wanted to charge 75¢ for pop. When forced to venture an idea about price, Caron had suggested 50¢. And he had *not* given in. Instead, he had *compromised* with "How about 65¢?" There was much that head-injured patients could learn from each other! If only we could instill in her some empathy and compassion so that she could set a good example for the patients in the group in which she was assisting, as this young man had done for her.

She went into OT in a grump. Laura's agenda was to get Caron to decide on a menu for a lunch she would prepare next week. Several times, Caron objected, "I don't want to do this!" She didn't want to prepare lunch, and she didn't want to have to make any decisions about it, either. Decision-making was hard! When Laura broached the subject of who would be invited, Caron began her protest, "I don't even *want* to do it!" but then brightened as she thought out loud, "I could invite Yvonne!"

"It'll mean one more sandwich," Laura warned. But for Yvonne, that was no problem! Enthusiasm took over, and the menu unfolded! Invitations were written for lunch at 12:15 p.m. Thursday, April 6.

Another mood swing after OT: Caron began to rant about an 11:00 a.m. neuropsych appointment that had just that morning been scheduled: "I hate that lady! She doesn't even know me, and she asks all these really nosey questions, but she's not going to get to know me in half an hour a week, and she doesn't care, anyway . . ." and so on. Then she switched to a new concern: at 11:00 a.m. she was supposed to help Sandy with her beginning speech group, so she had to let her know that she couldn't be there today, but how was she going to do it? It was ten forty-five now, but she couldn't be there at eleven because she had to be with that dreadful doctor at eleven, but she could only see Sandy on the hour or on the half hour, because "she's probably got someone in there with her now." (Rant. Rave.) Indeed, she did. "So how am I going to tell her without bothering her?"

"Can *you* think of a way to do it without disturbing her?" I threw the question back at her.

"I could write a note." "Good idea!"

"But I don't have any paper." "Where could you get some paper?"

"Do you have a piece of paper I could have?"

"Sure." I tore a sheet of paper from my notebook, and she wrote a nice note.

"*Now* how do I *get* it to her without bothering her?"

At this point we were running short on time, so I suggested the "long reach, quick exit" move. I explained that Sandy would understand that she didn't intend to intrude or interrupt, so she'd be able to proceed undisturbed—or choose to break and talk with Caron, which was her right of choice. Caron worked up a sweat before finally accomplishing this move, but she finally did, and then scurried back to her room for her 11:00 a.m. appointment, whereupon the neuropsychologist showed up just long enough to say she'd cancelled the appointment but she would see Caron "tomorrow," at a time she couldn't yet name.

PT was a fabulous experience that morning. It must have been exhilarating for all of the therapists, for everybody was making terrific progress. Caron smiled at me a lot while using the hand bike, rickshaw, and treadmill. In response to "How are you?" Kevin exclaimed, "I'm great!" A new stroke patient, Barb, was able to get out of her wheelchair with only her therapist's support in front; she didn't need the usual assistance of a second therapist's push from behind. And later she began using a walker for the first time. Katherine, with her husband and therapist cheering her on, also was up using a walker. She was in great spirits, smiling, laughing, even clowning around. When she and her husband and two therapists played catch with a squoosh ball, she occasionally tired of it and placed the thing on her head and laughed! Even Mary was "walking": Two therapists had her leaning on a rolling patient tray table and were prompting her, "Step with your left! Now shift your weight! Step with your left! Now shift your weight!" Her beautiful face glowed as she inched forward; who would know that her right side was paralyzed?

Caron had, on her own initiative, made charge slips that morning for two days and obtained her own lunch pass. Now, as we walked toward the cafeteria at a fast clip, she grinned and asked, "Did I used to walk slower than this?" Yes, by golly, she did! And when had that changed? I remembered well the tedium of the snail's pace, but I'd never identified it as having disappeared; yet it had! It must have been gradual, but today it had been sprung on me all at once. What a welcome surprise! Caron was improving all the time, sometimes before our eyes and sometimes so gradually that we weren't aware of it. This was a realization that guaranteed that this would not be one of those days Dr. Farhat had compared to the sun passing behind a cloud. Despite the deficits we knew Caron still had, this was, indeed, a bright, sunshiny day!

CHAPTER 19

DOUBTS

wo weekends and two sets of inpatient weekdays were all
that stood between Caron and discharge. She regained
some of her inherent enthusiasm in anticipating and
planning for this long-awaited event. In actuality, Caron's stay in
rehab, which would be eight weeks and three days by April 13, was
considered a short stay, the shortest of stays, in rehab. Six months,
I had been told, was average. Many patients stayed much longer or
were readmitted after their discharge, as Mary had been.

Caron's planning seemed to be prompted by some fear that
the powers that be might change their minds. The first of her final
two weekend visits at home, when I arrived to pick her up, she had
readied all of her plants and stuffed animals to make the trip with
us, and most of the banners, posters, balloons, signs, pictures, and
cards which had covered the walls. She seemed to be acting upon
a theory that she might somehow prevent a change in plans by
moving everything out well in advance of the target date. Perhaps
she felt that if all physical reminders of her were absent from the
room, then they would simply cease to think of her as an entity, a
patient, and she could just slip unobtrusively away!

Whatever she may have thought, her goal of going home had inspired her to make decisions, initiate behavior, and follow through—the very executive skills which the team had this past week spelled out as its immediate goals for Caron. As she headed off to speech study skills that Friday, she instructed me, "Get those medicines and sign that paper so we can go home when I'm done with this group." Hey, now that was good memory, planning, and initiation!

I found Vickie, the nurse who had taken Betty's place at the team meeting three days before, and shared with her my observations about Caron's progress in initiation and organization. She didn't dampen my enthusiasm when she replied that meds wouldn't arrive until at least a half hour from then. Since Caron was no longer taking medications to counter acidic secretions in her stomach or middle ear fluid or stuffiness or hard stools, all that remained of her meds was her anticoagulant therapy: aspirin. I suggested that we could supply the aspirin ourselves this weekend, but she misinterpreted my ardor as impatience and retorted, "She can just wait. It's a good learning experience for her." So what had happened to the team's goals? Obviously, there was a weak link on the team, a member who either had no commitment to follow through or was oblivious to the concept of reinforcing desired behaviors. Ah well, only two more weeks of her. When I'd initially found her, she had been sauntering aimlessly down the hall, with the demeanor of one who had no mission, nothing to do—so now I persisted by asking if I could at least sign the TTV (checkout) form. She snapped, "Do you think I could just get myself organized?" Well, since she phrased it that way, no, I doubted that she could; but I forced myself to merely nod then retreat to Caron's room to wait. Fortunately, by the time Caron had returned and was ready to leave, the meds had arrived; and Vickie, TTV form in hand, was feigning congeniality.

At home, Caron was beginning to function independent of reminders, taking the initiative in resuming her pre-accident role as a member of our family. Finding out that Matt was working pretty steadily all weekend, she teased, "You'd think he'd take time off to see me while I'm home!"

And one of us shot back, "He'll have his fill of you in a couple of weeks!" Not long before, she would not have been able to tolerate this type of remark, but now she was able to laugh. Yes, they did squabble! It's all part of the fun of having siblings, isn't it?

Caron went about her homework independently. Yvonne had given her a number of divergent thinking exercises, including a few crossword puzzles. While she busied herself with those, I drafted a thank-you letter to the seventy-five district teachers and counselors who had donated leave days for my use in assisting Caron. It was obvious now that I was going to have to be out of school for the remainder of the school year. Once Caron left the hospital, she would need to be transported to and from the high school at irregular hours and to her daily outpatient therapies at St. Jo's in Ann Arbor. What a blessing it was to me to have so many kind-hearted colleagues who were willing to ensure that my status as taxi driver and home-school tutor, among other roles, didn't have to put a crunch on the family budget!

It was harder to write the letters to the parents of the children in my class and, especially, to my first graders. Until now, they had had a substitute teacher, and expectations that I would return. I had been greeted with warm hugs when I attended their spring music program early in March, and they demanded to know when I'd be back! The last time I saw them all was the morning of St. Patrick's Day, when I'd visited to tell them an Irish story, teach them an Irish song, and give them little green and white paper baskets filled with green candies. (When Caron's occupational therapist had seen me weaving the tiny baskets, she had decided that this would be a good project for Caron's eye-hand coordination, so a very adamantly protesting Caron got roped into helping. Other patients were intrigued and joined in willingly so that at the end of that session, two-thirds of the baskets were completed.) By March 17, I had still expected to return, and the parents and children expected me to return to teaching. It was a difficult task, but I completed the letters this weekend, while Caron worked on her homework.

That afternoon, we went to a very large craft fair to pick out parting gifts for therapists Yvonne, Laura, Sue, Nancy—and, continued Caron, let us not forget Sandy, Ann, Carol, another Sandy, and another Sue! It turned out to be an expensive exercise in providing opportunities for her decision-making, but a joyful excursion, nonetheless! Later that evening, Larry took her on a more practical decision-making venture: grocery shopping. She made choices for the next day's meals and followed through in finding the items needed and adding them to the cart.

No reminders were needed on Sunday morning: she readied for church without incident. Perhaps she was inspired by the new clothes she had acquired at the craft fair shopping spree the day before. She got through church okay and even elected to attend a youth group meeting afterward. But when that was finished and she perused the bulletin board in the fellowship room, she was indignant to see a sign advertising need of a regular church nursery manager and attendant. "*I* do that!" she protested.

"But you haven't been here," I reminded her.

"I *will* be! Can I start next week?"

We talked with the pastor about it, and with Ramona, the church secretary, one of whose many duties was staffing. She had had a rough two months. Some of Caron's friends had volunteered to help out until her return, but none of them were willing to be so regular as she had been, and there'd been some slipups due to misunderstandings about whose turn it was. Ramona was pleased that Caron was coming back. I would assist, as Caron was truly not yet up to taking responsibility for babies and toddlers.

The following weekend, her last one where as an inpatient she had to check out, we attended the 8:30 a.m. church service, as usual, and Caron joined the high school students' dialogue group, as she always had before, and then we managed the nursery during the 11:00 a.m. church service. She was "glad to be back," as she told each parent who entrusted a preschool child or two to our care, but her tolerance level was decidedly not high enough to have done this job alone. When the baby she was holding began to whimper, she thrust him disgustedly at me. As long as they were good, she played well with them, but she couldn't cope with this maternal part of the job. She was barely moving into responsibility for herself so she was ill-prepared to be responsible for someone else. Church nursery would turn out to be an outpatient therapy of sorts for her. And I enjoyed it! It had been a long time since I'd had the opportunity to hold and soothe a chubby, fuzzy-headed, powder-scented infant. Even the crying ones were not an unwelcome challenge, and quieting them was rewarding. But in the weeks that followed, I would need to relinquish this joy to Caron, in small steps, so that she could resume sole responsibility for this nursery, as she had before.

That Sunday afternoon, Caron was inducted into the National Honor Society with her friends. She had earned the honor before her accident, and the consensus in the school was that she deserved this recognition. If she were unable to uphold the standards of the NHS upon her return to school, then that would be an issue to be dealt with at that time. For now, she could be recognized as an exemplary student. She needed guidance during the rehearsal, and there was no shortage of friends volunteering assistance. Even so, this was a difficult afternoon for Caron. Double vision was still a problem for her; so even mounting the stairs to the stage and maintaining her position there, looking out at an audience which appeared twice as big as it actually was, was frightening. She worried that she'd forget the sequence of events and do something stupid. She was quite disoriented, and her memory was truly not yet very dependable, but she managed herself nicely and was relieved when it was over. It had been an afternoon for pride—but, for Caron, also no small amount of doubt: could she really maintain honor-student status? Determined, motivated, she *knew* that she could . . . but she *doubted* that she could. "What if 's" kept cropping up, confusing her confidence.

Although encouraged that this was the last time I'd have to return my daughter to a bed in the hospital, I was still sad to leave her there this final Sunday evening. The late morning in the nursery and the afternoon with friends at the high school auditorium had magnified many of the problems that Caron would face consistently in her struggle to re-enter the real world, but this was the therapy she most longed to have: the opportunity to resume her life, in the world with which she was familiar. She was terrified of what the consequences might be, but determined to face them and get it over with.

Comforted by her friends' acceptance of her, she wanted more than anything to be back with them and to fit in. Nevertheless, being in the spotlight when with them was tension building; and whenever she returned home, she had to let off steam. It wouldn't be pleasant for us to be the brunt of her anxieties as she moved back into her social and academic world, but we would learn to cope with it.

Now, as I left her at the hospital for this last time, I reflected upon Saturday night, when she had gone to a friend's very large birthday party. She was exhilarated upon her return home, bubbling over with things to tell us, but intolerant of any interruptions. This was *her* account, sometimes rambling and unintelligible—it was late—but we were not to ask questions! When we tried, she barked at us. She was incapable of "conversation" when she had a lot of news to impart. It broke her concentration, messed up her memory, and irritated her. I realized that we would be the object of her frustration and anger again and again in the days, weeks, months to follow; but I somehow felt that I could cope better with that than with her institutionalized behaviors when she was in the hospital, where she didn't want to be. She cared not at all for what was going on there, and except that she loved her therapists, I doubted that she'd have been able to learn much more there, regardless of the fine program. *Her* goals were to go home and to get back to school; she was methodically walking through hospital routines, playing along, until she could be released so as to really *begin.*

In her last couple of weeks as an inpatient, responsibility was delegated to Caron for her own physical therapy: she was given written instructions concerning how many repetitions or how much time, as regarded each of her activities, and she proceeded through her paces on her own. This was good for her and freed up Sue, as well, to a new patient during those time slots. Caron was delighted to have been granted this independence, and she carried out her physical therapy assignments conscientiously.

Her April 6 luncheon also came off well, despite her initial reluctance. With Yvonne and me as guests, Laura and Caron made four. Caron prepared potato salad, corned beef sandwiches on croissants, with Swiss cheese, lettuce, tomatoes, and mustard available. She had set out a bowl of fruit for dessert. We all enjoyed ourselves, even Caron. After this obligation was completed, she would have to return to using the yellow pages, brushing up on her typing skills, and retaking the WRAT (test). She might find herself wishing she could plan and prepare another lunch, instead!

Divergent thinking was the focus of speech therapy in these last two weeks. Caron was having a terrible time with even the concept of synonyms. Before her accident, she had had excellent

English language training, such that she was always seeking new and different ways to say the same thing. To say something twice, using the same words, was unforgivable on an English paper; and Caron had generalized this rule to all of her writing. But now she couldn't cough up a synonym, due to her rigidity. Once she heard one word, she was stuck on it. She could not think of another way to say policeman or purse or happy or understanding. And if the list had been composed of the words "patrolman," "handbag," "joyful," and "comprehension," she wouldn't have been able to give a synonym for those, either. Compounding the problem were her perseverance and her intolerance: *why* did she have to think of another word when the one at hand worked perfectly well? Yvonne was patient—Yvonne was always patient—enticing her to think divergently through use of games such as 21 Questions, other games that she had on hand, and a couple of divergent thinking types of games I'd purchased. She thought Caron would enjoy crossword puzzles too, and this is an excellent exercise in divergent thinking. Caron hates crossword puzzles, but she worked on them dutifully—but only because it was Yvonne who assigned them.

Convergent thinking, or generalizing, was difficult for Caron only in that generalizations should accurately sum up a larger set of facts or statements. Caron felt she could generalize just fine (so, of course, she was extremely resistant to anyone's suggesting that she couldn't and that she needed to practice this skill); but then, she didn't realize how inaccurate her generalizations were. As was the problem with divergent thinking, she would become stuck on the first piece of information given. Thus, the rest of the information fell by the wayside; and she concluded by restating or, at best, paraphrasing, the first statement. Cleverly, Yvonne introduced her to a computer program where she had to follow a path by trial and error then make a generalization about what the rules of movement must have been. The word "generalization" was never uttered, and Caron thought this was just a fun little game.

The therapists all worked together, and at about the same time that Yvonne had Caron practicing generalizations, Sandy (in whose group Caron assisted) asked Caron to watch the news on television each night and report one current events item to the group each day, "to help them become aware of what's going on in the world." Of course, the exercise was to Caron's advantage, not only in becoming aware of what was going on in the world but also in making a decision (about which event to report), paying attention to details, and generalizing a whole news report to a few statements for her report to the group. Thus began Caron's first experiences in watching the news. She started learning about such news items as the eleven-million-gallon oil spill off the coast of Alaska, a 300,000-strong antiabortion march in our nation's capital, and Steve Fisher's appointment to the position of head coach of the University of Michigan basketball team. Her decision-making and attention-to-detail skills improved immensely with this ongoing assignment, although her report conclusions tended to be trite; but through the perseveration of the word "definitely," it was obvious to all who listened that Caron was, indeed, writing her own reports: "The oil spill has *definitely* caused many problems," "The controversy over abortion is *definitely* an important issue," and "Steve Fisher is *definitely* a coach that people believe has the spark."

The cognition group played games such as Uno, which requires that players think of at least two things simultaneously—the color and the number of the card on the draw pile—and then make a generalization about the cards in their hands: Could they play? Or must they draw?

Caron went on several group outings in her last two weeks, dinner and a movie among them. And in her private recreational therapy she completed her last project, another wooden one with dowels from which to hang things. She had shown a preference for these wood projects to paint, and this final one was a rainbow with the sun peeking over it. It promptly gained a spot in her bedroom next to the three bears project that had been her first. And from one of the dowels hangs a poem about the beauty of each day ... *if the beholder has a positive approach to life.*

The problem right now was that being in the hospital was a clear message to Caron that she must not be all right. She questioned the validity of her hopes and dreams. She couldn't wake up smiling. It was difficult to see the rainbows for the rain. It took all of her time and energy to help herself, and she couldn't reach out to others as she had always done before the accident. She was being restrained from living the life in which she believed, and she simply could not see this hospital as a beautiful place. Until her accident she had constructed her life for the fulfillment of hopes and dreams—hers and others'. Being a pleasant "morning person" had never been her forté, but only because she was so goal-oriented: she had always prepared a to-do list before going to bed, and when she awoke in the morning, always early, she set to work ambitiously striving to check off every item on the list during that day. The smile was in her heart. She embraced every day as a new beginning. This poem had once been her but was no more. Would it be again, someday?

CHAPTER 20

"JUST GIVE ME A CHANCE, PLEASE!"

There was a necessary surgery to be performed before Caron's discharge from the hospital: a left myringotomy and ventilation/tube placement, which is to say, an incision in the left eardrum for purposes of extracting fluid and placing a tube there for future drainage. Stuffiness in her left ear, which had sustained the blow in the accident, had diminished neither spontaneously nor with medication; so surgery was the next step.

Caron was irritable. Surgeries were not in her bag of favorite things. Nor was NPO after midnight, the print on the sign on her door that prevented the nice people with the food trays from entering.

By noon, the surgery had been completed, all had gone well, and Caron was back in her room complaining loudly about the cotton ball in her ear, "How long do I have to wear it?"

"Probably at least three days," I answered, as Dr. Ho had prescribed eardrops for three times per day for three days.

"I don't want to wear this for three years!" she wailed. Obviously, one doesn't hear well with cotton in one's ear! "And I'm starved!"

But Caron was still NPO. She also had to have another arteriogram before leaving the hospital, and it had been scheduled for the same day so that she would miss only one day of therapies due to surgical procedures, rather than two. At twelve thirty Gary Catskan, which the jovial transporter called himself, arrived with a gurney. Back up to the second floor we went!

The arteriogram was the procedure that most worried me, due to the horrible experience we'd endured the last time. Caron was obsessed with thoughts of resuming her oboe playing. If this arteriogram showed the tear in the interior arterial wall to be repaired or improving, then it wouldn't be long before she could be making music again. Preoccupied with this goal, she didn't think to fret about the procedure itself. Sally, the surgical nurse we'd met here on all previous trips to radiology, appeared just minutes after Caron had been wheeled into the surgical room to say, "She's asking questions. That's a good sign!"

This eased my mind, and in the next half hour, while the procedure was performed, I chuckled in remembering the conversation Caron had carried on out here in the corridor with Dr. Knake, our favorite radiologist, who was performing the arteriogram now. "Do you have to put a Band-Aid on?" she had asked him.

"Well, yes, we'll put one on, as we make an incision . . . ," he began. Caron cut him off with a tirade: "I *hate* that! The Band-Aid from *last* time didn't come off until the day before yesterday!" *That would have been thirty-two days after the last arteriogram! Silly goose! Why didn't she just pull it off?* I asked her that, and she lectured me (with "Boy, are you stupid" body language), "Because it *hurts* to pull off a Band-Aid!" So every day she had showered—she was doing that independently now—and hoped it would just fall off!

One would think that by now she would know the true meaning of the word "hurt" and never again complain about the short-lived pain of a Band-Aid's removal. But no, the nature of a head injury is such that patients almost always suffer post-traumatic amnesia. She would never remember that pain. God's plan, no doubt, and a good one; but I couldn't help but smile that she would gripe about a Band-Aid!

Caron was already in Speech when I arrived the next day. Her face was puffy, blotched, tear-stained, and still wet. She had been told that morning that oboe playing was out, pending the results of the *next* arteriogram, which would be scheduled in three to six months. The person who told her, not her doctor, was a technician who didn't know Caron well and couldn't have known how important this was to her. Caron, on the other hand, couldn't understand how he could *not* have understood, for music was her life! Shouldn't everybody know that? She blamed the informant: how could he be so mean?

Always the good teacher, Yvonne abandoned the day's planned material and zeroed in on the problem at hand. Much progress could be made by encouraging Caron to think divergently about this very real problem: Why do you suppose that decision was made? And what are the alternatives? During the majority of the half hour, she let Caron spill out her woes, only occasionally trying to redirect her thinking; but Caron was on one track and was not about to be tricked into switching to another! In the last five or ten minutes, Yvonne drew a diagram of the problem and assured Caron that she had nothing to worry about, because her condition was stable and because her treatment was designed to keep it that way. But if she commenced playing the oboe, Yvonne went on, it might cause the tear to balloon out, disrupt blood flow to the brain, and even possibly cause a stroke and maybe paralysis. She kept reassuring Caron that she understood how important playing the oboe was to her, but perhaps there was something more important, after all. No, even Yvonne was not going to talk her out of her stance. Caron couldn't *see* "quality of life." *It* wasn't her concern. Playing the oboe *was*, and that was all that she could see.

She was in no frame of mind to see "that lady" after Speech, but this was the day of her weekly visit with her neuropsychologist. She returned to the room afterward, sputtering, "I hate her! She says, 'Caron, I hear you're upset about not being able to play the oboe. Would you like to talk about it?' And I said, 'No!' So what does she do? She spends the whole half hour talking about it anyway! She's so dumb. She doesn't even *know* me, and I'm *not* going to share my problems with somebody who doesn't even care about me enough to try to get to know me! And then she says that *she's* coming to the meeting next week at Brighton High School. Why does *she* have to go? It's none of her business! She doesn't know anything about me, and *she* says she doesn't think I'll be able to handle more than one high school class! Yvonne's going too, and I'm going to tell *her* to tell 'em that I can handle at least two!"

But Yvonne was not so malleable as Caron had hoped she would be. She was accustomed to Yvonne's empathetic understanding of her complaints and was positive that Yvonne would join ranks with her to crusade against this injustice. She was doubly devastated, then, when Yvonne not only supported the "one class" decision but went a step further, saying she should only sit in on the class—monitor or audit it, but not take it for credit.

"Why *else* would I take it?" Caron gasped. "I need the credits to graduate! I don't want to waste my time just sitting around in a class and then have to take it all over again this summer!"

Yvonne suggested that Caron's memory might not be good enough to ensure the type of success (that is, an A) that Caron was accustomed to and would demand of herself. Caron implored her, "Give me a *chance!* If I can't handle it, I'll drop one of the classes! And if I can't do well in either one, I'll drop the credit opportunity. Just give me a chance, *please!*"

This brought to my mind what had been said in the previous Wednesday's Family Education meeting: There was a patient who had *insisted* that he was ready to go back to work. Hospital personnel knew that he was not ready, but they allowed him to give it a try, for he had to find out for himself that he couldn't do it; he was not going to believe *them.* Couldn't these people see that this was where Caron was coming from too? She had really been putting forth effort—taking initiative, making decisions, formulating her thoughts better and better, following through, showing responsibility—but they were holding her back, frustrating her. She needed a new challenge. She really needed, and *now,* that opportunity to fall flat on her face. The team meeting called the week before seemed to be for the purpose of educating us to that concept, and we were made to believe that we were being asked to cooperate with the team in this endeavor. Now it appeared that only Larry and I were to let her have opportunities to fail, and the team was determined to protect her from failure at all cost. They didn't know her as I did, to know that if she weren't made to feel that her own efforts were being rewarded, and soon, she might well simply give up.

Caron's discharge meeting was scheduled for the morning of Wednesday, April 12, with the LISD (Livingston Intermediate School District) IEPC to follow in the afternoon. Dr. Perlman opened with introductions: Caron's primary four therapists were in attendance, as well as her neuropsychologist and also Dr. Seigerman, the neuropsychologist who was the director of the TBI unit, where Caron would come for her outpatient therapies. Our social worker was here, and also Carol Pearlman, the new social worker (who worked out of TBI) to whom we were being assigned. Reliably, Barbara Zukowski was also here to expedite financial resolutions, as regarded the responsibilities of Caron's auto insurance company. Dr. Perlman said a few words about the implications of the most recent arteriogram: no oboe, no downhill skiing or water skiing, and no high-velocity amusement park or carnival rides. Then he turned the meeting over to those who would represent the hospital team at the IEPC.

"That lady" spoke first, stating that Caron had shown significant improvement in information processing speed and verbal memory but was still impaired in these areas. Given another test in memory, she had scored only at the first to third percentile. Recommendations for work within her high school included the following:

1. help with reading comprehension and speed,
2. minimal distractions in the environment,
3. slower pace,
4. one hour in the Resource Room, working one-to-one with the instructor, but not for credit, and
5. mainstreaming into one not-too-demanding academic class, again not for credit.

Caron had made some progress with her appeals: she had been granted approval of two hours in school, albeit not for credit and only one of which would afford integration with friends.

Dr. Seigerman addressed the credit issue, explaining that the hospital had no vested interest in Caron's earning credit: the school system might decide to give her credit, anyway. The unspoken message was that this was beyond the hospital's control. The door had not been closed firmly on Caron's wishes.

Laura gave her occupational therapy report, recommending that Caron continue with the word processing program begun in the hospital and that she be encouraged to participate in such functional tasks as planning for meals, grocery shopping, preparing meals, and other such organizational activities.

Sue stated, "Physically, Caron is, I think, back up to par." She did warn that supervision should always be provided for any potentially dangerous activity in which Caron might participate again for the first time since her accident because, following a head injury, we never know what skills a patient might have lost until the patient tries them. She cited swimming as an example, with the potential of drowning if swimming was a skill Caron had lost.

Dr. Perlman added to his list of no-no's: "No diving."

Yvonne passed, as she had kept me well informed of Caron's progress and in which areas she needed continued work. She had secured as the TBI speech therapist a person whom she told Caron, "I reserve for only my favorite patients." This had made Caron feel good and gave her someone to look forward to meeting at TBI: Jennifer, by association with Yvonne, would be wonderful, she had already decided!

Nancy, the recreational therapist on rehab, reported that Caron had increased in self-confidence and sociability on out trips, that she had moved into a leadership position in group decision-making, and that she had enjoyed the individual projects so much that Nancy was going to give Caron some catalogs so that she could order materials and supplies to further her hobby interests.

Barbara Zukowski was brief as the final speaker, informing Larry and me that we would be reimbursed per mile for all trips we made to get Caron to and from TBI. We had simply to document dates of trips and mileage, and the insurance company would verify dates with therapies TBI would report that she actually attended.

✦ ✦ ✦ ✦ ✦

Caron's neuropsychologist and Yvonne were overwhelmed by the turnout at the IEPC in Brighton that afternoon. Ron Misiak, special education coordinator from the LISD (Livingston Intermediate School District), was here, as he was at all IEPC's

(Individual Educational Programming Committee); and he was accompanied by LISD psychologist Barbara Wilson, and Chris West, LISD teacher of POHI students (Physically or Otherwise Handicapped). Sheila Bradley, special education teacher at Brighton High School, had been selected as the Resource Room person who would help Caron; she was here, as well as Caron's counselor, Marty Lindberg, the school nurse, Kay Kroth, and the assistant principal, Dian Kolis. All but one of Caron's current (junior year, second semester) academic teachers were in attendance: Eric Dahlberg (Advanced Placement Biology), Bill Nuber (French 4), Max Sherman (Government), and Pat Rogers-Wilson (Health), and of course, Carl Klopshinske (Wind Ensemble). While her Analysis with Trigonometry teacher was not in attendance, another math teacher, Art Steele, was present. We had already determined that math would not be one of the subjects Caron would complete this semester, and Art had volunteered to tutor her in Analysis with Trig during the summer. There were other interested teachers here too: teachers who knew Caron as one of their past students, cared a lot about her, and had volunteered to help in any way that they could. Diana Rose, who had instructed Caron in several English courses, was one of these. Caron and Larry and I had been seated at the long table early. Caron was initially nervous, but greeted by each arriving teacher, she was soon full of glee and forgot her fears. She was among friends. As more and more people arrived, more chairs had to be provided and crowded into all of the remaining floor space of this room which really only comfortably accommodated one long table and the eight chairs that fit around it.

The hospital professionals were first on the agenda, as they had most recently worked with Caron and knew her as she now was. The high school staff strained to hear. They were genuinely interested in the current status of this young lady they all loved. The neuropsychologist, noticeably unnerved by this large attendance of unfamiliar faces, rattled on even faster than she usually did; but Ron Misiak was quick to interrupt her and ask for specifics, and "slower, please." Eventually, everyone came to understand that, while there was a discrepancy in results between two respected batteries of tests, Caron was in truth impaired from her pre-accident abilities. In math, she was at the twenty-seventh to the seventieth percentile, depending on which test's results were used and whether or not the test was timed. Her spelling, which had been extraordinary before, was now between sixty-first and seventieth percentile. And reading, at eleventh to forty-seventh percentile, was as low as sixth-grade level, tenth grade at best. The teachers voiced concerns: would her previous abilities come back? Oh, how I wished that Dr. Perlman might have been here, for he would have relieved everyone's minds with his "There's no reason to believe that she won't . . ." But *this* woman ("that lady") responded with percentiles and statistics, leaving the questions unanswered.

Yvonne spoke next, conveying to this group all of the information she had previously given to me regarding Caron's speech and language deficits. Yvonne too was nervous in the face of this huge crowd, and she stumbled over her words. Looking around the room, I could see that this speech/language specialist whom Caron and I adored was not establishing credibility with this group of school professionals. How could a person who couldn't pull the language together herself possibly know anything about someone else's capabilities and weaknesses? I could see the resolve of a new challenge on the faces of most of the teachers in this room, and I knew that my daughter was going to get her chance to fall flat on her face. But Larry and I were placing our bets on Caron: her determination had always taken her beyond her inherent abilities, and she hadn't lost any of that determination in the accident. The accident had added stubbornness and intolerance to her repertoire, and while we didn't generally support these traits, we did have to concede that they fueled her determination!

Yvonne's final words imparted the hospital team's feelings about Caron's return to school. They didn't feel that her memory was sufficiently reliable to ensure any acceptable degree of success in school. As such, their honest recommendation would be that she not return to school at this time. However, taking into account Caron's desires, as well as her need to re-enter her previous social world, they could support her sitting in on one class, not for credit, as well as spending one hour per day in the Resource Room, for help in such areas as concentration, reading comprehension, auditory processing, reasoning and problem solving, organization of thoughts, and memory, with special attention to detail.

Sheila Bradley was taking prolific notes. But some of the other teachers were noticeably tuning out the hospital's recommendations.

Ron asked for Caron's input, and her flat monotone but indignant reply was "I'm a 'student'! That means I go to school!" A smile spread over the face of every teacher in the room. In no more words than one can count on the fingers of one's hands, she had won them over.

Each person in the room was given an opportunity to give input. Most of the teachers stated that they would leave the choice of classes to the special education experts but expressed that if theirs was a class chosen, they would do everything suggested, *anything* they could to help Caron. Diana Rose presented a specific proposal. While Caron wasn't currently enrolled in one of her classes, she felt that, as an English/speech teacher, she was probably the teacher most needed at this time, because Caron's deficits appeared to be most pronounced in areas of speech and language. Further rationale given was that in her senior year Caron would be required to elect two semesters of English, anyway; Diana proposed that one of these semesters be taken now, leaving one hour of the second semester of her senior year open for completing her AP Biology course, which was most likely to be dropped for the time being, as it was a college-level course and Caron had already missed eleven weeks of it. Diana was offering to give up her prep hour, which was second hour, to tutor Caron one-to-one in speech! The heads of every district and county specialist in the room were nodding enthusiastic approval of this course substitution.

Earlier in the day, at the hospital, it had been suggested that health be the one course Caron resume, and Yvonne brought this up now. She seemed satisfied when I explained that during the lunch hour I had found out that health was being offered in the Howell Community Schools' summer school program and that the Brighton Community Education program was also considering offering it. Because it would be available in the summer, it now seemed most prudent that this course be put on hold. This made sense to Yvonne, and she graciously voiced that Diana Rose's proposal was a generous one and should be in Caron's best interests.

Sheila Bradley spoke next, stating that her tutoring hour was fifth hour, too far removed from second hour, which all present had agreed would find Caron receiving speech instruction with Mrs. Rose. Therefore, Sheila offered to see Caron during *her* preparatory period, first hour. This would afford Caron one-to-one attention, whereas in the tutoring hour she would have shared Sheila's attention with five or six other students with dissimilar handicaps. Sheila was very positive, checking the notes she had taken while Yvonne was speaking, and saying she was sure it would work out just fine. She was the only teacher I hadn't already known for years, and I was instantly inspired by her. Caron would be in good hands with Sheila first hour and Diana second hour! The representatives from the hospital were also amenable to the outcome of this meeting. The schedule that seemed acceptable to all of the school team seemed to be precisely what the hospital team would have put together for Caron.

Then Bill Nuber spoke up. I had kept him apprised of Caron's apparent retention of her French, as evidenced by her understanding of the tapes from the Dalsace and Longerinas families in France. He had also listened intently to the hospital input and now recognized fatigue as an important factor in Caron's learning or not learning. His only French 4 course was fourth hour, which was split into two half hours, with lunch sandwiched in between. He suggested that Caron be given a place to rest for the first half of *third* hour and that she report to him for the second half of that class. This was a first year French class for him, so the structure of the class period was normally instruction in the first half hour and student follow-through exercises with teacher support in the second half hour. During this second half hour, he felt that he could provide Caron with tapes, videotapes, and one-to-one instruction in some of the skills she had missed in her absence. Then she could stay for the first half hour of her French 4 class and leave when they broke for lunch.

"It's too much," objected one of the hospital duo, but Larry was quick to point out that without this, Caron would be totally segregated from social contact with peers, and this would defeat the hospital's own goal of community reintegration. All heads around them nodded approval, and the duo from St. Jo's resigned themselves to accepting that which they could not condone. But they did express discontent with Mr. Nuber's alluding to Caron's possible completion of all second semester requirements. I interceded on the hospital's behalf, explaining that the object wasn't necessarily for Caron to complete all course requirements and receive a grade by June; rather, it was expected that she would probably receive a grade of Incomplete in the course and have to complete assignments during the summer or even at some later time.

"Just let her do what she can do, and don't pressure her to do makeup work," I finished. It appeased the hospital team representatives, and they visibly relaxed. Bill and I exchanged a knowing glance: the Caron *we* knew would probably *pressure him* for makeup assignments!

After the meeting, Caron and her teachers reversed roles—*they* standing in line to get to talk with *her!* This tickled her to no end! And Marty Lindberg really made her day by informing us that she would not only get credit for Speech and French, but also for Tutorial with Mrs. Bradley. When everyone had finally departed, Caron and Larry and I left too, Caron prattling on and on about getting to attend not one, not two, but *"three* 'classes,' *and lunch!"* No one had said anything about lunch at school. It was a *generalization* she had made herself: after all, she would be there at the time lunch hour began, anyway, and she *did* have to eat lunch! I could see that being back in her element was at least going to speed improvements in her ability to make reasonable generalizations! She was also figuring out loud that if her therapies at St. Jo's didn't begin before 1:00 p.m., then she'd have time to go to the after-lunch half hour of French 4, also! And "probably therapies *wouldn't* start until one because people at TBI have to eat lunch too!" What a conniver she could be!

Back at St. Jo's, Caron got a tour of the Joyce M. Massey Traumatic Brain Injury Day Treatment Service (no wonder they refer to it as TBI!), a new-to-us portion of the Catherine McAuley Health Center, of which St. Joseph Mercy Hospital was but one part. Rehab had been an addition to the far northeast corner of the health center complex, so to get anywhere from rehab meant a long walk through many long hospital-scented corridors. As Caron became more physically fit and mentally more alert, our walks in the hospital had repulsed her, increasingly more so by the sights and smells than by the exercise itself. It appealed to her that the TBI wing was an addition to the west side of the center of the hospital, right off the main parking lot: she could be dropped off at the door and avoid all hospital scenery, proceeding directly to

TBI. Also, as expected—having been set up by Yvonne, who surely told *all* of her patients that she reserved whichever therapist to whom they were assigned for her "favorite patients"—Caron loved Jennifer immediately. It wasn't going to be such a struggle getting her to report here daily, after all.

That evening, Larry and I attended our final Family Education Night meeting. This was actually the first meeting of a new eight-week series, but we had missed this one in our own series, as it had taken place while Caron was still in intensive care. The speaker was Charles Seigerman, PhD, TBI neuropsychologist and team leader; so we were particularly interested at this time. He set everyone at ease with a little humor in the beginning: "I promise there will be ample time for questions—but if the questions are too hard, there'll be no time for answers."

Much of what Dr. Seigerman had to say must have been frightening for the newcomers but was by now very familiar to us. Afterward, when I glanced over my notes, I could identify with most everything that he had said and realized that he had been very thorough. People new to head injuries can only have gleaned an overall picture. But everything that he had to say was so valuable that I found myself wishing that he'd written a book on this subject and that it had been available to me to begin reading almost three months before, when I'd known nothing and had so many questions. His expertise would be ever so much more helpful to you than my untrained impressions, but I'm going to put my notes into sentences here, in hopes that they might inspire readers to fill in the gaps by asking the experts the questions that this overview will surely incite. All of the following information is attributable to Dr. Seigerman, with portions in quotes indicating his exact words in that evening's presentation.

A traumatic brain injury is diffuse: spread out, not concentrated in one particular area. It can happen in a variety of ways, including near drownings, cardiac arrest, gunshot wounds, and a moving object hitting a stationary object, as in the case of automobile accidents. There are five major areas of concern regarding head-injured patients: medical problems, physical problems, cognition problems (including problems of attention, concentration, orientation, perception, memory, thinking, reasoning, problem solving, and judgment), psychological problems, and family issues.

Next, Dr. Seigerman explained that soon after admission to the inpatient component of McAuley's TBI service—that is, what we knew as rehab—an early screening took place to determine whether or not the patient would be able to participate in the full six—to eight-hour evaluation. The initial screening included two portions: the Personal and Family Biography Sheet (which I had filled out and which was finally placed in Caron's black notebook in her last two weeks as an inpatient) and the interview. Aha! Finally, I understood the purpose of the ten to fifteen minutes that Caron's neuropsychologist had requested alone with her on February 22! It was merely for the purposes of ascertaining Caron's perceptions of her abilities and deficits and establishing what she remembered about what had happened to her. This interview might also have determined her retrograde and anterograde amnesia: how far back, before the accident, did she have to go in order to remember something (Dr. Seigerman added, "Only in the movies is this a *long* period of time"), and how far forward could she remember? (What was her capability for remembering new information?) I realized now that Caron's inpatient neuropsychologist was simply following hospital procedure when she conducted her ten-to fifteen-minute interview; but I also knew that Caron might have been more receptive to this interview and to the person who did it, had she taken the time to meet her informally beforehand, just as Yvonne and Laura and Sue had come to her room to meet her on her first day in rehab. Nothing stressful, just "Hi! My name is . . . , and I'm going to be your . . ." I can't help but believe this informal meeting prior to the interview would be beneficial for all patients—a brief introduction, so that the patient is not being interviewed later by a complete stranger.

The full evaluation, which Dr. Seigerman said took from six to eight hours, assessed many aspects of the patient's status quo. The neuropsychological assessment includes the following:

- Orientation: Does the patient know who (s)he is? Where (s)he is? What year it is? The month? The date? The day of the week?
- Language and aphasia screening: Aphasia is a language disorder in which the patient may have difficulty understanding, formulating, and using words.
- Sensory and perceptual screening: Are all the messages getting *in* there?
- Attention: Sustained attention and concentration are difficult for traumatic brain injury patients; distractibility is increased.
- Learning and memory: It takes head-injured patients longer to learn, and it's harder for them to remember.
- Concept formation.
- Verbal skills: These include problem solving, forming an answer, and vocabulary. There are often word-finding problems. "These things become of especial concern when the patient returns to school. Schools are *very language-oriented!*"
- Performance skills: These include the patient's visual-spatial abilities, ability to put things together, and ability to sequence.
- Cognitive flexibility: This is "the ability to change your response as the situation changes; the ability to generate alternative solutions to problems."
- Fine motor control and speed.

- Academics: Among these are reading, writing, spelling, and math.
- Psychological/psychiatric problems: Those which may be present as a direct result of the injury are depression, anxiety, flat affect, agitation, and aggression. Later, reactive problems may surface, in reaction to what has occurred.

Behavioral problems are of the utmost concern "because society does not tolerate these." Behavior problems might include the following:

- Agitation: often caused by an overloading of stimuli, plus the fear of not knowing what's going on.
- Belligerence: caused primarily by the patient not feeling in *control* of what's going on.
- Lability: emotions beyond the normal emotions—up, down—extreme.
- Apathy and indifference: such that the patient won't learn and won't get better unless (s)he is motivated externally.
- Impulsivity and disinhibition: saying and doing things apparently without thought, without inhibitions—things the patient would not normally have done and said.
- Paranoia and suspiciousness: fear that the hospital, and even one's family, is plotting against one.
- Rigidity and inflexibility: strong resistance to change; inability to adapt to unfamiliar situations, change one's mind, or generate alternative solutions or ideas.
- Irritability and decreased frustration tolerance: How very difficult it must be not to be able to do what one has done all of his/her life or to remember something one knows (s)he should be able to remember!

- Age-inappropriate behaviors: a return to the emotions and behaviors of an earlier age.
- Self-centeredness and egocentrism.

But "don't take the behavioral problems personally," Dr. Seigerman warned! (Easier said than done!) "These are a natural result of the head injury."

Upon discharge from the inpatient rehabilitation program, patients may require an extended care facility (nursing care). Some patients go into a transitional living facility. Others go home, but rarely do they go home with a pat on the back and the final dismissal, "You're fine." Most patients can expect to spend some time attending outpatient therapies after their discharge.

A neuropsychological assessment is done again six months after the initial assessment. Said Dr. Seigerman, "I know a problem is permanent when I do a neuropsych testing six months later and the results are the same. Then the person must learn to compensate for the permanent losses." When patients continue to improve, neuropsych tests will indicate this after six months, a year, and two years. Whatever is not regained within two years is not likely to be regained.

Community re-entry is often impeded by long-term psychological problems, including adjustment reactions, personality changes, behavioral problems, psychosocial problems (friends dwindle away), and sometimes psychotic behaviors, although these are rare unless the patient was so inclined before the head injury. Head-injured patients are, however, more vulnerable for substance abuse, because their coping abilities are down and because they have time on their hands. It's best to be *preventative* with them about substance abuse, because intervention is particularly difficult with head-injured patients.

The patient isn't the only one who may suffer long-term psychological problems. Within the family, there are often role reversals: if it is the family breadwinner who has suffered the head injury, someone else may have to assume that role, either temporarily or permanently; a teenager with a head injury may just about have reached maturity and independence but will now be "back in the fold." Family dynamics change. Family members may experience burnout, depression, anger, frustration, and a multitude of other emotions.

Certainly our family was no exception. I know that I had experienced all of the above-mentioned emotions, and many more, sometimes several at a time, confusing each other. Other members of my family were suffering as well. One evening, late, I received a call from a police officer, notifying me that my son had been involved in a malicious destruction of property incident. Here was anger! Four boys, including my own, had headed out to one of the wealthier subdivisions in town in a van, smashing mailboxes with a baseball bat. I don't know what the other boys' excuses were, and certainly mine was not to be excused, either, for this behavior was unacceptable; but I could identify with his anger! And talk about emotions on top of emotions: I was a bulging bottle of anger and helplessness and exhaustion and exasperation from the nightmare I'd been feeling my way through for over two months, and now I was furious with my son for throwing yet one more problem into our lives—but I hurt for him too. He'd always been a bright child, and a creative one, but a "stinker" more so than "naughty." This behavior did not seem to be consistent with his usual range of interests and activities.

No charges were pressed but, of course, the boys were ordered to pay restitution. Matt thought we were way overboard to impose a penalty on top of that. "I *already* have to pay for the mailboxes!" he argued.

"That's not a penalty," we explained. "It's your *responsibility*. It's what you owe: the price you must pay for the form of entertainment you chose. The 6:00 p.m. curfew *is* punishment, for your *irresponsibility*—and a guarantee to us that you're not out smashing mailboxes."

Yes, Caron was coming home; and as earlier predicted, she was going to see a lot of her brother—even more than we'd expected!

CHAPTER 21

"I HATE BEING DUMB!"

When Caron had come home on her last therapeutic trial visit the weekend before her discharge, she had brought with her everything that she wouldn't need in her last four days at the hospital; and every day of that last week she had sent home the day's laundry with me so that on Thursday, April 13, she was ready to walk out of the hospital with only her bag of toiletries and cosmetics in one hand and her black notebook in the other. In the notebook, the last entry made had been dated Tuesday, April 11: "Yvonne doesn't want me to take any classes at all. I'm disappointed."

Several pages back, however, and unbeknownst to me, she had used one of her daily journal pages to make a rough draft of three thank-you letters, one thanking Yvonne for being so helpful and caring (and expressing especial appreciation for the entire session discussing problems which could arise from playing the oboe), a second thanking Laura for all she'd learned and enjoyed with her (including discovering some joy in computer word processing!), and a third thanking Sue for making physical therapy fun ("especially the jump rope!"). What a kid! My daughter was truly making a comeback!

Her comeback was due in large part to who she had been and was fighting hard to become again. We had been able to predict her progress, almost literally, from the writing on the wall. Caron had always kept her social plans and appointments, school assignments' due dates, friends' and relatives' birthdays, and other important events on a large calendar in her bedroom.

Additionally, at the beginning of this year (before her accident), she had written one quote on an open space for each month of 1989. I don't know where she had found these quotes, but they were obviously very important to her or she wouldn't have written them on her calendar. In the days immediately following her accident I discovered them while consulting her calendar to determine if there were any upcoming commitments, financial or otherwise, which I should cover for her. From the moments when she began coming out of the coma, her recovery was almost predictable from the goals she had pre-established for herself:

> In January, she had quoted Michael Gross: "The worst thing in life is to have no . . . goals, because then you have nothing to reach for, nothing to live for."
>
> In February, when she was wrestling to express herself and prove that she could eat real foods, control her own bladder, and walk independently to the bathroom, the handwritten quote on her calendar read, "If we aimed only at what we could reach, we should reach nothing." Julia Wedgewood.
>
> In March, as she battled others' doubts about what she could accomplish, and fought to convince everyone to let her go home and back to school, the words on her calendar encouraged her and us: "Stand tall on the wings of your dreams, and let nothing stand in your way." Anonymous.

And in April, the words she had penned on her calendar had strengthened her resolve to return to school: "You can do what you envision." Anonymous.

During non-therapy hours in those last few days at the hospital, Caron and I busied ourselves wrapping gifts. It looked like Christmas inside her cupboard of shelves, which had previously been filled with clothing. But after all, she had received the best of care here, and there were so many people to whom we owed thanks. Along the way, there had been some small aggravations, as I've noted, but life offers its own aggravations, and this hospital complex was, after all, a slice of life. We would have been unrealistic to expect no problems. But we would also have been foolish and ungrateful not to recognize that this was an outstanding facility, which offered exceptional care and opportunity. Because of the wealth of warmth and patience and expertise we'd found in this place, our daughter was able to walk out of here talking and laughing and eagerly anticipating a return to who she had once been.

Caron enjoyed playing Santa Claus to her nine therapists and some special nurses who had worked with her. And I'd been busy with my camera in those last two weeks, getting pictures of all of the regular RNs, LPNs, and PCAs of C Hall, the rehab wing in which Caron had resided. Now she gave the framed composite to Betty to hang in the hallway for future patients' and families' reference. We didn't forget Jackie, the custodian, who'd been an angel in so many ways to us, nor "that lady" and the social worker who, despite the differences in our personalities, really had done their jobs as they thought best. I probably wasn't among the easiest of family members with whom they'd ever worked, either; but I believe we may have come close, at least, to a spirit of understanding that each of us was doing the best we could, in the only way we knew how to do it.

There really was no way any of us could have thanked Dr. Perlman enough for everything he was for us. Perhaps, in the next few years' periodic checkups, Caron's progress would be one of the rewards for which he so superbly lived this job.

The C Hall physicians' assistant made an appearance in the last few minutes before our departure, thrusting into my hand what appeared to be a half-dozen prescriptions. They weren't actually prescriptions at all but, rather, assignments: Make follow-up appointments with Dr. Perlman (physiatrist), Dr. Farhat (neurosurgeon), Dr. Austad (plastic surgeon), Dr. Ho (otorhinolaryngologist), Dr. Whitehouse (for interpretation of arteriograms)—and make an appointment for another arteriogram in three months. Now why couldn't these have been given to me earlier? All of these doctors had offices in the Reichert Health Building, which was part of this huge complex, and I could easily have set up these appointments in person or with a quick call from Caron's room while I was waiting there during her group therapies. Ah, well, it was but one final parting aggravation. So what? My daughter was coming home!

Soon, we were on our way out of C Hall, to check out! As I stood in line reading the check-out procedures ahead of me on a wall which I'd never before had occasion to meet, I was shocked to find that there was a *charge of nearly $6 per day* for in-room television and telephone! Caron had been here seventy-six days, and except in SICU there had always been a phone and TV in her room. It was going to cost a minor fortune to get out the front door, and the sign confirmed my fear that these charges weren't going to be reimbursed by any insurance company. Fortunately, as I arrived at the front of the line sputtering about never having been told, the clerk asked if we'd initially come through emergency, which, of course, we had. "No problem," she reassured me. "People coming through emergency aren't given this information. Just pay what you think it was worth to you, or nothing at all if you wouldn't have used them." Whew! She suggested $45 (about ten percent) as reasonable, I paid it, and we moved on.

Eventually we really were headed for the main door of this hospital for the last time. Passing through the main lobby, we ran into Dr. Judith, who remembered Caron and was pleased to see the progress she'd made thus far. Caron smiled when "introduced" to this fine young doctor and, of course, didn't remember having once told her "where to go!"

Caron didn't look back as we drove away from the hospital. She would be back daily for therapies, but she really wanted to put this all behind her.

The school schedule to which all had agreed would begin on Monday, after a three-day weekend rest, but Caron was eager to return to the high school on Friday. At the IEPC Wednesday, she had received teachers' permission to sit in on the classes to which she would not be returning; so on Friday she spent most of the day at school, in her bright turquoise and yellow high-top tennis shoes! Karen Herbst had dared her to do it on her first day back and had bet she wouldn't have enough nerve—but Caron, still a bit disinhibited, didn't have any qualms whatsoever about wearing those clunkers to school. And this from a young lady who'd always taken such pride in her appearance that curled hair, makeup, nylons, and dress flats were standard whether a dress or slacks and a sweater came in between. What a shock it must have been to friends to see her for the first time in months wearing *those things!* If they hadn't realized *before* that she would be different, surely one look was enough to give them an instant education!

In wind ensemble, last hour, Caron teased Karen that a deal was a deal; and she was going to wear them the entire day, even to the Birmingham Theatre, to which Karen had invited her that night. Karen knew she was just teasing. But did she? Certainly, Karen knew that the Caron she had always known *before* would not have done such a thing—but, then, she wouldn't have worn them to school, *either*, as *this* girl had.

When the Herbsts pulled into the driveway that evening, Karen jumped out of the car and came bouncing up the steps to get Caron, who stepped out of the house and met her halfway, wearing a new white dress, necklace, earrings, a blue satin dress coat on which was pinned the coming-home corsage her father had sent—and "the tennis shoes."

Karen thought it was a pretty funny joke and kept waiting around for her friend to retreat to the house for a quick change. Her face fell when our Caron waved good-bye to us and proceeded on down the rest of the steps to the Herbst car. Karen lingered behind, certain that there was a punch line here, someplace; but when she turned to me with a shocked question on her face, I could only shrug helplessly. Well, in fact, I couldn't be of any help now. Caron was already in the car. It was her joke, and it would be up to her to remember that her dress flats were in her purse! Would she? I wondered.

Saturday night, we took part in our church's annual road rally: Larry, Jim, Caron, and me. We actually even won it, but without any help from Caron. The clues one encounters in road rallies offer precisely the types of thinking skills at which head-injured people do not excel. We were all patient with her, feeding her near solutions, most of which she still couldn't piece together; but a few very obvious ones came to her lips, and I think she felt that she'd helped. Certainly, all of her OT work with the yellow pages was put to the test, as we had been instructed to bring a telephone book with us.

The whole road rally bunch was very kind and supportive, and I believe Caron slept easily after that evening among friends. But having to watch how very hard she struggled to try to fit in, and being always in the position of observing people's reactions to her, especially among her peers at school and around town, I continued to feel sad for her and to have difficulty sleeping. People didn't intend to be mean, but they couldn't help but stare. This was not the Caron they had known, and they were frightened that this might be the new Caron. Still, without the advantage of all of her previous faculties, she was determined to save face. I surely had to give this kid a lot of credit. She could have chosen to go in the other direction, to be a recluse. She might at least have opted to save herself the humiliation of public mistakes by continuing to mend at home and within outpatient therapies. But no, she was driven to return to school and to tough it out. It was rough on her, but no doubt, it would speed her recovery. She seemed to know what she needed to do.

She resented my assisting at the church nursery on Sunday mornings too; it was *her* job. But at this point in time, much as they all loved her and were cheering her on, probably few among the congregation would have entrusted their infants solely to her care. How do you tell her that? You don't. You just take the verbal abuse.

Speaking of abuse, I wasn't thrilled with her phone conversations, either. From our end, I could hear, "Oh, hi . . . oh, nothing, just scrubbing in the bathroom. My folks lived like pigs while I was in the hospital."

Sometimes it was very difficult to heed Dr. Seigerman's words, "Don't take the behavioral problems personally. These are a natural result of the head injury." But the people to whom our daughter was talking on the phone didn't know that these statements were due to disinhibition, rigidity, egocentrism, and other natural results of head injury!

I tried to reason with Caron about such conversations. For one thing, didn't she realize that we too had lived at the hospital? In truth, except to collapse into bed at night, people hadn't often frequented this house in the seventy-six days that she was hospitalized. But she wasn't at all flexible about this or other issues and continued to spread the word about town that I hadn't been a very tidy housekeeper. Oh, the joys of motherhood!

Sunday afternoon was a Brighton High School concert, and Caron wouldn't hear of *not* going, but *going* turned out to be a strain on her. How difficult it must have been for her to listen to Gina playing all the oboe parts, and even "her" part in "her" quintet, which repeated its "1"-rated performance for the hometown audience that afternoon.

She was sullen when we returned home. Some of this may have been sheer fatigue for, although she didn't like to admit it, she was still winding down by late afternoon, losing attention and focus, gazing but not comprehending, and becoming more susceptible to depression. At dinner, she abruptly left the table at some small thing and fled upstairs to her room. When I joined her there after dinner, she was spilling tears all over her French book. In answer to my question as to what was wrong, she wailed, "I hate being dumb!"

But the time she had spent perusing the French text over the weekend paid off. When I picked her up after her first morning at school, she was fairly bursting with excitement and pride: "I was the only one in French class who knew what was going on!"

Speech was a different story. She had been assigned a speech to be given the next day. It was intended as merely an introduction: "Who am I?" but Caron had turned it into a major production. Nervous, she'd gone right to work on it during her third-hour break, and when I looked at the notes she'd scribbled down, I saw in the making several potential "how-to" speeches: how to play the oboe, how to play the piano, how to be an effective marching band member, how to run a church nursery, and how—to the most minute detail—to be a good employee at Uber's. Oof! Organized she was, yes! But we had a lot of work to do to get her just to understand the nature of the assignment, let alone to *do* the assignment! Eventually, after many retreats upstairs to work, and many returns to the fold for reassurance that she was doing okay, she completed a suitable introduction and conclusion. She resisted Mrs. Rose's instruction not to memorize it. The intent was that she talk it, but she felt too insecure to do that. When I went to bed, she was still wrestling with memorization and hadn't yet decided upon the "meat," or content, of the speech.

The next day, I chanced to run into Mrs. Rose in the school office while I was waiting to pick up Caron, and she reported that Caron's speech "had a nice introduction and a nice conclusion, with some stuff in between." She also mused out loud that the kid hadn't lost her organizational abilities.

Caron's first words as she got into the car were "She didn't tell me what my grade was." She was really agitated about this and refused to try to understand that it was to her advantage not to be given a grade until the end of the semester. In light of the nature of her head injury, Caron was not now in a position to excel in writing and delivering speeches, but she would hopefully improve. Mrs. Rose had, therefore, decided that the only fair way to grade her would be on improvement, rather than on an average of grades on speeches. But Caron didn't know how to work without the external feedback of a grade! Well, that was one more thing she would just have to learn.

The next speech assignment *was* a "how-to" speech. Ah, good, I breathed. She had several starters for a "how-to"! (No doubt, Mrs. Rose already knew that and was capitalizing on it!) Nevertheless, Caron decided, instead, to do "How to Pack for a Trip Abroad." She prepared the initial draft independently but then solicited help. However, her draft had already taken its place in her mind as a final copy; so while she claimed, verbally, to want to know what changes she could make to improve the speech, she actually resisted any changes suggested because "I'd have to erase this whole sentence!" (Horror!) And despairingly, "I might as well start over!" (Yes, very dramatic!) She wouldn't admit to fatigue; and of course, she was *never* "irritable"—but the Caron who used to live here would never have griped about erasing a sentence to improve a product.

In the end, she settled for what she'd originally written: quite a nice paper, but not a very suitable speech. Her vocabulary was prosy, and she'd written most of her sentences in the passive, so the speech didn't have much punch or pizzazz. The next battlefield was rehearsal: she had this speech all written up like a paper and insisted on memorizing it.

Mrs. Rose was very clever in approaching this rigidity of Caron's about memorization: she assigned her a persuasive speech to prepare, memorize, and give whenever she was ready, probably the beginning of June. In the meantime, while she was preparing for that "big one," there would be eight or nine lesser assignments, which wouldn't be assigned far enough in advance to permit memorization, the goal being that they be talked or told, using minimal notes.

Meanwhile, as predicted, Caron was determined to make up all missed assignments in French. She was using her tutorial time to do French assignments, and in addition, Wednesday was her day off from TBI therapies in Ann Arbor, so she remained in school all day working in the media center on French exercises. Again, on the weekend, she worked steadily on French. In the middle of her second week back in school, she felt she was caught up. At this point in her study of French, she was more advanced than I in the spoken language, but I was still in a position to be able to offer her help in the written language. The "completed" assignments she handed me to look over made quite a hefty pile, so it was obvious that she had put much time into this work. The organizational and motivational aspects of her personality seemed to be intact. But as I looked over her work, I discovered that attention to detail, which Yvonne had said was a problem, remained a problem—as well as her overall attentiveness. There were entire exercises where she had either been inattentive to the lesson preceding, or she had missed the point of the exercise, so that every item was wrong. On other assignments, she was making far more errors than she'd ever before made: adjectives and pronouns which didn't agree in number or gender with the nouns they modified or replaced, verb endings which were incorrect for the subject, incorrect verb tenses, misspellings, words copied wrong—careless mistakes that Caron would never before have made in such volume.

She was irritable with me about each exercise I suggested we look over again; but once cued as to the intent of a lesson, she was able to make the corrections independently, and she was grateful to have caught her errors. However, predictably, she would then argue that all of her *other* makeup assignments were correct as they stood, and there was no need to look at *those* again. She simply could not *generalize* that if she'd made mistakes on one assignment it was possible that she may have made mistakes on others. (Or perhaps, here was more example of the "Can I be done?" syndrome.) Once again, the process was repeated: irritability followed by cuing, which prompted an "Aha!" feeling, followed by independent corrections, followed by certainty that all was now finished and correct. She was able to learn well with cuing, but how does one convince an independent, self-motivated teenager that it's essential that she ask for help? And heed the *helper!*

Night after night, we continued to review her written makeup assignments, until she had finally discovered and corrected the major mistakes. I didn't correct typical errors, as students must be accountable for these themselves. Additionally, Caron needed to relearn how to ask teachers for help. The only help that I offered at home was that which addressed difficulties specific to her head injury: inattentiveness or lack of concentration and failure to notice such important details as the *main idea* of a lesson! Without relearning these essential skills, her progress in school could never again be what it once had been.

With Caron reestablishing herself in school, our telephone was once again tied up pretty constantly all evening long, and it was through overhearing some of her conversations that I came to realize the severity of her cognitive impairments, as well as auditory memory difficulties. She was still infatuated by the nice young man, Jim, from our church, and totally unaware that he was really just being a Good Samaritan. He had told me that he was quite interested in someone else, a friend of Caron's, who attended our church, but he was afraid to ask her out, as she seemed pretty serious about another guy. On the telephone one night, Caron's friend told her that she'd *kill* for a date with Jim, he was so "cool." In her very next phone conversation with Jim, she not only told all but also agreed to a conspiracy to assist in setting these two friends up on a date! Later, she would bemoan the fact that Jim no longer called her, but she wouldn't remember that it was due to her own inability to keep a secret.

She was forgetful about so many things I'd always come to take for granted with her. Now she'd go off after school with someone, forgetting to let me know where she was. She'd never before done that; she had always notified me of her whereabouts—usually far in advance, often writing it on my calendar in addition to telling me, and then leaving a reminder note on the kitchen table on the day itself; and when advance notice wasn't possible, she had always called. Naturally, I worried now when she didn't come home. She wasn't simply a forgetful kid, inconsiderate, or a "typical teenager." She was a kid with a head injury, with known impairments and other potential problems as yet unknown. (Seizures, for instance, can result from head injury but may not appear until months after the blow to the head).

In the last week of April, Mr. Nuber imparted end-of-the-year take-home exam information to his French 4 students: they were to prepare a speech and an accompanying advertising pamphlet (in French, of course) for the hypothetical purpose of selling something. He stressed that only one of a kind would be allowed, so students were encouraged to submit their topics to him as soon as they decided upon them. Caron was eager to get started, and that night she decided to design and advertise her own French restaurant. (Oh yes! She made a decision!) She wrote down some ideas, and it looked to be a topic with which she could work easily. The next day I asked if she'd remembered to tell Mr. Nuber her topic. But she had forgotten, as she did again the next day, and the following day, and the day after that. With all the excited telephone chatter I was hearing about her restaurant ideas, I expected that by the time she remembered to notify her instructor of her topic, someone else might have claimed the idea. This would have been a setback for her, as she continued to have extreme difficulty (and irritability with regard to) changing gears. On the other hand, such frustrating experiences inevitably forced small but significant steps toward improvement. In this case, she may better have learned the importance of keeping secrets and being timely. However, her friends were loyal ones, and no one pilfered her topic.

Now she had two long-range assignments for the month of May. She had decided to research animal experimentation for her final speech with Mrs. Rose. At about this same time, Mrs. Rose began to feel that two courses didn't offer enough of a challenge for Caron, that she was being held back from her potential. She suggested that Caron add Government back into her schedule. Caron readily embraced this idea, and Sheila Bradley got the news from both of them, then called me in to see what I thought. Truthfully, having witnessed Caron's struggles every evening, I felt that one more thing would be overwhelming for her. But *we* weren't pushing her. Her teachers were pulling for her because she herself was so motivated. And I certainly didn't want to stand in her way. I told Mrs. Bradley that I'd offer all the support necessary to help her achieve her goals. What did Mr. Sherman have to say about her adding this course so late in the semester?

"Well," began Sheila, "before pursuing this any further, I wanted to be sure that he had room in his third-hour Government class, and do you know? Caron's teachers all *love* her! And I can see why! Mr. Sherman said, 'Room? For Caron Schreer? Of *course*

I have room!' He's willing to give her credit for just the fourth quarter, if she makes up the work she's missed. Or he'll give me work for third quarter too if she wants to try to complete the whole semester. Mr. Nuber is impressed that Caron has already made up all of her third-quarter work, and when I asked how she did on it, he said all was fine, 95.3 percent overall."

Sheila was enthralled with Caron's motivation and told her so. One day after school, Caron announced with genuine naiveté, "Mrs. Bradley says it's my motivation that's brought me so far so fast. Is this true?" A childlike question. Yes, she was still very childlike, but she was improving. Each day the old Caron emerged a bit more. It was a little like watching a slow-motion film of a butterfly emerging from a cocoon: one frame a day.

And on her May calendar, in her early January handwriting, were the words of Theodore Roosevelt: "Far better it is to dare mighty things ... even though checkered by failure, than to rank with those spirits who neither enjoy much nor suffer much, because they live in the grey twilight that knows neither victory nor defeat."

CHAPTER 22

AVOIDANCE TECHNIQUES

D uring the month of May, Caron and I watched French videotapes in the evenings, continuing the learning she'd missed in February, March, and the first half of April. And she launched into preparation for the French final, which was of interest to her and held her attention more readily than more difficult tasks. She poured through cookbooks, selecting recipes that had French names or could be translated into French. These she arranged menu-fashion under the following classifications: *Les Hors d'Hoevres, Les Soupes, Les Salades, Les Entrées, Les Desserts,* and *Les Boissons.* The resulting menu for her restaurant, which she decided to call *Chez Caron,* was a beautiful four pages, expertly laid out (thanks to her OT introduction to computer word processing!) and beautifully printed on a friend's laser printer. It looked very professional. The pamphlet was shaping up nicely too, with written descriptions of her restaurant's "history" and gourmet food choices, photocopies of décor which she had selected for the ambiance of her establishment, and a map showing *Chez Caron* conveniently located where two major expressways crossed in Brighton. Her speech, which she completed early in May, touched on the restaurant history, décor, and a few of the chef's specialties.

Happy to do something at which she was successful, Caron practiced this speech religiously every night, and by the end of May it was smooth and fluent. By then, she had also decided to add to her presentation a sample of the chef's dessert specialty, *Mousse Blanc Chocolat Avec La Sauce Framboise.*

On the day of her presentation, she came home distraught because she'd been asked to save the menu and brochure distribution for a later time, for use with video. Still very inflexible, she'd been unable to effect an impromptu change in the parts of her speech that referred to these props. However, her face lit up when telling about the class's reception of her white chocolate mousse with raspberry sauce. And with all the rehearsals she'd had, the speech couldn't have been so bad as the horrible scenario she relayed to us. The proof came with her final grades in French: quarterly As, exam A, and final average: A!

Ironically, speeches in her native language were stressful for her, even the interim lesser assignments before the big one. For her third, an informative speech, she had a week to prepare and told me early in that week that she planned to use her Uber's job description idea for this one. Throughout the week, she reported working on it; but two nights before the speech she brought me her "work," asking for help on the finishing touches. In effect, she had only notes and "just" wanted me to string them together for her! I agreed to work *with* her, but it was a tedious evening, as she wanted both for me to *do* it for her *and* to have the satisfaction of having done it herself! She was in a particularly uncreative, inflexible, and irritable mode; but when I'd offer a suggestion, she'd either reject it or forget what it was. I tried to elicit ideas from her, and this was about as easy as sweet-talking a pit bull to "give." Then, when she'd finally come up with an idea, I had to be careful not to reject it, no matter how weak I thought it was. This was her speech: the thoughts and mistakes had to come from within her, or she'd never progress to thinking independently. It was difficult for me to allow her the opportunity to fall flat on her face, now that she truly could do just that. Never before had either of my children struggled in school, so it was all too easy for me to preach to other children's parents: "Let the child do it! Let him experience responsibility. Let her learn how to handle her own mistakes. Don't step in and correct everything!" Easily said, when your own children are so successful! Here was a totally new perspective for me: it's *hard* to watch your children flounder and not to bail them out! This experience with Caron was surely going to make me a more insightful teacher!

One of Caron's most serious impediments to her success *now* was her impeccable memory of who she *had been*. She'd been as close to invincible as a teenager could possibly be. She'd been a planner and an organizer who was also capable of last-minute success. She'd plan the time needed to do her homework, and then she'd get everything else done first: working at Uber's, practicing her oboe, eating, doing the dishes and her laundry, straightening her room and belongings, talking with friends on the phone, watching a favorite television show . . . Finally, the hour would arrive when she needed to begin her homework in order to complete it by the time she'd decided to go to bed that night, and she'd settle in to study—and retire on schedule, give or take a few minutes, having accomplished everything. She wanted to pick up now where she'd left off the morning of January 28 and save her homework for last each day. She thought she still could. But she couldn't, and categorically not with speeches.

I had encouraged her to productively use the hour's driving time to and from Ann Arbor each day. Because she couldn't very well be doing any of her non-homework business in the car, she was at least putting in some time studying in the afternoon. But she was always quick to set aside speeches for "later." The afternoon before the morning of the Uber's speech was no exception: "I'll work on the speech later. I think I'll do my French assignment now."

"No, *no, no!* Caron, you cannot keep putting off these speeches until the last minute. That's not how speeches are prepared. And it's certainly not how you can succeed at this point, in any event." I made her get out her speech. Contrary to her promise the night before, she had not touched it since we stopped working on it together. I had gotten her to the point of completing her introduction and formulating an outline for the central part of the speech. She had promised to go to work on the details for the four categories of jobs whose description would comprise the speech. But here she was with still only the introduction and some notes. On the way to TBI, she didn't have any difficulty talking through two of the job descriptions, as well as rehearsing the introduction. On the way home, she practiced the introduction some more and also talked through the other two job descriptions. By the time we got home, she was confident enough to develop the conclusion totally independent of me, and early in the evening she was ready for a listener. She had done well, after all, in pulling together all of the elements of the speech; but her perseverance with "It's important to . . ." was tedious. Initially, she used this as her lead-in for every detail presented, dozens of details. So that night we worked only on developing alternate ways to say, "It's important to . . ." Generating synonyms was still difficult for Caron, but practice was essential, and relieved to have the composition of the speech behind her, she was more willing than usual to cooperate in some home therapy. By the time Larry came home from an evening visit with his sons, Caron was able to deliver for him a good rehearsal of her speech, complete with such phrases as "You must . . . , It's imperative that . . . , You need to . . . , Bob expects . . . , It's essential . . . , You have to . . . , Bob insists upon . . . , and You should . . ."

While the lesser speeches caused Caron great consternation resulting in procrastination, the big one totally paralyzed her. When the assignment for the final had been made, she had decided right away upon her topic: animal experimentation. She launched immediately into her research, and when she didn't come home from school on the bus on non-therapy days, I soon learned that she was most probably at the city library gathering information for this persuasive speech. In a short period of time, she accumulated much data, but there the progress stopped. For weeks, she postponed tackling the job of tying it all together into a speech. Finally, Memorial Day weekend, I insisted that she assemble the thing. It should have been done weeks before, to allow memorization time. Now she was only days away from the target date for delivery, and she hadn't yet begun even to write the speech.

The first week in June, when Sheila Bradley should have been winding down at the end of the semester and readying for a long-planned summer trip to Italy, she was, instead, worrying overtime about Caron. She was in touch with me almost daily: Caron was to have delivered her animal experimentation speech that week but had only memorized one of the five pages . . . had I noticed any procrastination techniques at home?

!

And defense mechanisms: had she put those into play at home as well as in school? Oh yes, I "assured" her: we were both "suffering!" *Many* times in that past few weeks I'd been the object of Caron's verbal abuse: "You want me to be just like *you!* Well, I'm *not* going to be just like you! I *won't* study all the time! I have lots of other things I like to do!" Ironically, she always *had* been just like "the me" that she was describing. Certainly, she had never studied *continuously*, as she obviously must have felt she was now being expected to do, but she had always planned well for her studies first, occasionally even canceling social events when she knew that, otherwise, time wouldn't allow for homework completion. It was rare that she ever had to do this, as she planned and organized her time so well, *and* her studies were easier for her then. She remembered all of this but wouldn't concede that it was now more difficult for her to concentrate. She was caught between her memories and the present reality, and in conflict between her values and her wants. All of this was further compounded by a return to the infantile state of being wherein wants are all consuming. Embodied in her values were high academic standards for herself, including maintaining a 3.8 GPA and graduating summa cum laude. But at this time she was embracing only her wants, willing the difficulties to vanish: if she didn't address them maybe they'd just go away.

Yes, avoidance techniques were a regular part of Caron's behavioral repertoire: if it's hard, ignore it; maybe it'll go away. Sheila had sent a note to me via Caron the previous Friday. Caron hadn't liked the message. Had I received the note? No. This deceptiveness had never before been a problem for this child. Then again, perhaps this was the first time in her life that she'd ever been asked to deliver to her mother a note with content that wasn't appealing to her. Other children experience this dilemma in first or second grade, conveniently lose the note on the way home, get caught, suffer consequences, and learn not to do it again. But what consequences are grave enough to teach this lesson to a teenager whose time is all tied up in classes and therapies, and who has already had her driver's license revoked (pending six seizure-free months following a head injury, Michigan law)?

The first weekend in June, Caron still had that speech hanging over her head. So she tackled her spring cleaning. Nothing in her room was missed: closet, cupboards, shelves, drawers, walls, windows, under the bed, everything! Whenever I reminded her to work on the speech, she'd "spaz out," pick it up briefly, then revert to her housekeeping. It was infinitely easier to clean up her room than her mental processing.

Government became a synonym for avoidance technique. Despite having missed three months of it and with only six weeks left in the semester, Caron was determined to make up the entire semester's work. She could have all the time she needed for this: into the summer, even into the next fall. It wasn't realistic to try to do a semester's work in one-third of the time, we told her repeatedly, but it was her goal to do it—instead of work on that dreaded speech.

At least I didn't have to help her with her Government. Social studies wasn't my forté, but it was Larry's major, so when Caron had added Government to her schedule, he had agreed to be the mentor for this subject. Additionally, he was now picking her up from her TBI therapies two days a week, as I'd resumed my graduate work at Eastern Michigan University a couple of weeks after Caron was discharged from the hospital. One Thursday night when I returned home, Larry was especially frazzled. On the way home from therapies, Caron had appealed to him for help with Government. She was studying a chapter about the Supreme Court and wanted to know how many of the Supreme Court justices were elected.

"I'll bet it tells you that in the chapter," he challenged her.

"No, it doesn't," she argued. "I've read the whole thing, and it doesn't say."

"Look again. If it's a chapter about the Supreme Court, it surely gives that information."

"No," she persisted, "all it says here is that they're all appointed by presidents."

"Then how many are elected?"

"It doesn't say!" she thundered.

For the entire drive home, Larry tried every technique and analogy he could think of to try to help Caron arrive at the answer, but she could not make that small logical step between A and B: if all are in Group A (appointed), then none are in Group B (elected). Finally, when they got home, he acted out a scenario with her, placing objects in her right hand and closing her fist around them while saying, "Caron, if I give you some candy, and you put it all in your right hand, how much candy is in your left hand?" He lifted her left hand, palm up.

She looked into her left palm, which was empty, and answered, "None." Stupid. Dumb question. Obvious answer. Why did he ask me such a stupid question? "O-o-o-o-o-o-o-o-o-oh!" Finally she got it! The analogy had had to be concrete. She was back to a very concrete level of thinking and understanding. It's the stage at which my first graders are when they begin school in September, but many are moving out of it by the year's end. My daughter, almost seventeen, was there again. We had a long way to go to abstractions, logical processing, and common sense!

During the entire first weekend in June, Caron alternated studying Government with cleaning her room, avoiding "the speech" as much as possible. Whenever I reminded her, she begrudgingly picked it up for a bit, but it was interminably easier for her to put it back down again than any responsibility she had ever before in her life encountered. Finally, on Sunday night, she explained, "Oh, Mrs. Rose gave me an extension 'til Thursday—so I'll work on it Wednesday night."

Meanwhile, her goals for Government were to take a two-chapter makeup test on Tuesday of this week, so that she could be ready for her final makeup test on Friday, so that she could take the final exam with the third-hour class the Tuesday following.

At 7:00 a.m. Tuesday Caron was still poring over those two chapters in her Government textbook, looking very anxiety-stricken. It just wasn't coming together.

"So take it tomorrow," I casually suggested.

"*Really?!* I could *do* that?" She perked up instantly.

"Of course you can. There's no hurry. You have as long as you need to complete Government." (Why did these words sound so familiar to me? Why didn't they sound familiar to her?)

"Mrs. Bradley won't be upset?"

"Why would she be? She's there for you. She'll give you the test whenever you're ready." (Because she needed more time than other students, Caron took all of her tests, Government and French, with Mrs. Bradley first hour, instead of with her class. This reduced her distractibility, as well.)

"Will Mr. Sherman be upset?"

"No, Caron. He doesn't *expect* you to complete Government this semester."

"Okay, then I'll take it tomorrow." That was too easy, I thought. Then she continued, "I should still be ready to take the other one on Friday." Wednesday morning was a repeat performance of Tuesday morning, complete with "Really?!" and "Mrs. Bradley won't be upset?" and "I could probably still be ready for that one-chapter quiz by Friday." Hm-m-m-m-m, earlier this was a test, and now it was being downplayed to quiz status—but still on for Friday!

"Why not take it Monday?" "NO! I want to be *done!*"

Wednesday night, then, she tried to juggle government study with memorization of the final speech that was to be given the next day. Finally, the reality she'd been suppressing hit home: she couldn't do it in an evening.

She felt she did well on the two-chapter Government makeup test on Thursday, but she had to obtain another extension in Speech. Mrs. Rose put an end to the procrastination, however, in saying that it had to be given on Friday.

Fortunately for Caron, the only available appointment for installation of a much-needed new heating and cooling system at our house was Thursday, so I was unable to drive her to her TBI therapies. Now on a strict deadline for the speech, she abandoned Government and worked diligently all afternoon and all evening on the speech.

I was pleasantly surprised when Caron bounded into the car after classes on Friday, exclaiming, "Mrs. Rose was *speechless* for the *longest* time" [after the speech delivery that morning]. Then she emphasized, "It [the speech] was *fifteen minutes long*, and she said there was not a *single* deviation from the written speech in the first *thirteen!*" If this was true, and Mrs. Rose later confirmed that it was, then Caron's memory had indeed improved! Perhaps the very process of being forced to memorize had been significant in helping her internalize strategies for remembering details. Her animal experimentation speech had been power-packed with details, including many statistics.

She studied almost constantly that weekend. The monster speech was behind her now, and she could breathe easier. Her personality improved immensely! She was even able to laugh at my mockery of her previous month's verbal abusiveness toward her parents. Now she could study Government to meet her goals rather than to avoid other threatening responsibilities, and the relief enabled better concentration. She did well on the one-chapter quiz on Monday and then took an extra day to prepare for the final exam. (Because it worked perfectly into her mornings-only schedule, she had completed the year in Mr. Sherman's third-hour class, for which the exam was scheduled Tuesday; but her original government class had actually been fifth hour, and that exam wasn't until Wednesday. Relaxed now that the big, scary speech was over, she had no trouble deciding to allow herself the extra time to study for the Government final.) Her exam grade was a B-, but she had earned As for her third and fourth quarters, for an overall semester A—in Government.

Speech came in at an A, also, and Caron was ecstatic: "Wow! Three-semester As!"

"Four!" Yes, there was Mrs. Bradley's tutorial too.

Caron would be tutored in Precalculus/Analysis with Trigonometry during the summer. Mr. Steele lived just around the corner from us and could schedule flexibly, around therapies. Additionally, Caron would take the state of Michigan required health course through the Howell Community Schools during the summer. If all went well, she would enter her senior year as a senior in the fall, having undergone some revisions in her program, but not having lost any credits.

CHAPTER 23

MARCHING WITH BELLS ON

Concurrent with beginning classes at Brighton High School in April, Caron had also begun her therapies at the Joyce M. Massey Traumatic Brain Injury Day Treatment Service at St. Jo's in Ann Arbor. Outpatient therapy differed in more ways than daily transportation to and from the hospital. Parents weren't allowed to observe therapies in TBI. I couldn't very well follow through at home if I had no way of knowing what Caron was working on in therapy. I did voice this concern, and it was the new social worker's task to relay the message to me that the reason for the visitation policy was twofold:

1. It's distracting to the patient.
2. It's distracting to the therapist.

The time seemed opportune for me to return to graduate school classes. I had dropped the two I'd been taking at the time of Caron's accident, so I now enrolled in two spring semester classes. My chauffeuring job left me alone several hours each day in the hospital parking lot, so I decided I might as well share the time with a few textbooks. It kept me busy, and out of the way of the TBI personnel, who weren't receptive to visitors.

Jennifer, the speech and language therapist, had begun her work by reviewing Yvonne's recommendations and then had done some tests of her own. On Caron's third Monday of therapy (the first day in May) she invited me in to review the results. Yvonne had recommended work on sustained attention and attention to detail; simultaneous processing (two things at once, including improving recall of information and auditory processing speed simultaneously); memory skills, to maximize learning in the educational setting; higher order thinking skills (logic and problem solving); and reading and writing skills.

Jennifer found Caron's reading to be at a ninth-grade level, which she reported to be average for her age group but, at the thirty-seventh percentile, qualified as "extremely low for Caron, taking into account her academic record." Additionally, she was still showing severe deficits, eighth and first percentiles (and grade equivalents of 5.5 and 2.2) respectively, in expressive language and general knowledge (science, social studies, and humanities). General reasoning scores were in the fortieth percentiles, low for Caron. Math remained a strength. On Jennifer's tests Caron was also showing strength in written language, although (by observing Caron's struggles writing speeches at home for Mrs. Rose) I recognized language problems as causing difficulties even in her writing. This is where I saw parent input as necessary to a recovering TBI patient. Had I not said something, Jennifer may have dismissed Caron's writing as not needing attention, yet I could see that it was nowhere near her pre-accident writing capabilities. Writing was permitted to remain in the course of study.

Caron enjoyed the time spent with Jennifer, who treated her like a person, not like a patient. Jennifer helped her to feel normal again, and despite her overall resistance to outpatient therapies in general, Caron always had positive things to report about the day's events with Jennifer.

To put it mildly, Caron was not enchanted with the weekly TBI community re-entry outings. The first was bowling. She bowled a score of 30 and whined, "I don't want to go again. They all smoked." But she had to go again. These outings were part of her prescribed program of therapy, and until her doctor wrote them out of her program, not to go would have jeopardized even insurance benefits. After the next bowling trip she was more emphatic: "I hate these trips! I'm not going again!" A large part of the problem, surely, was that 90 percent of all head-injured patients are male. The day of the trip to a Detroit Tiger baseball game, she was, in fact, the only female in attendance. A couple of the fellows were rather reserved, but most were boisterous and crass. Only one was even close to Caron's age: a young man who had sustained his head injury a couple of years before, when he attempted skateboarding while holding on to a car. Upon her return that evening, Caron self-righteously reported the many naughty words the guys had said—every other word out of their mouths, she was sure—and complained about the smoke.

I did let her beg out of a trip to a dairy farm, as it really didn't make economical sense in terms of time: we'd have driven a half hour to get her to TBI, from which it was another seventy-five-minute drive south to the dairy farm for just a one-hour tour. Additionally, she'd have missed the last fifteen minutes of the tour to leave early for a previously scheduled doctor's appointment at 4:30 p.m. Somehow, a forty-five-minute tour didn't seem worth the travel time of over four times that much time.

The TBI team felt that community re-entry was important not only for Caron but also for them, affording them an opportunity to observe her in a social setting. How realistic was this social setting? I asked. If they wanted to observe her in a social setting, I'd be glad to arrange invitations to more natural gatherings of her friends. They assured me that community re-entry wasn't forever, but only until Caron met the team's goals: to initiate conversation with the general public, to get her needs met, to increase eye contact, to problem-solve in the community, and to participate fully in an outing. But for Caron it *could* go on "forever," as it wasn't natural for her to open up to people with whom she felt she had nothing in common.

At Caron's first TBI team meeting, to which she was invited, Dr. Seigerman granted her permission to bring a friend to the next outing, which would be at Kensington Park near us. He also entertained her complaints about community "re-ent" in general and promised to explore some other possibilities for her, including one-to-one or small group socialization in OT or RT, rather than the large-group Tuesday afternoon outings.

Jennifer shared her testing results, as she had with me the previous Monday, and again Caron was given a chance to input: how was she getting along in school? She stated that it was most helpful to her if people *show* her rather than just tell her how to do something. She was also concerned that she often didn't get things done on time or at the right time. I asked if it might be possible to increase Caron's speech therapy, as she was now only getting two hours per week and this seemed minimal given the difficulties that persisted. Dr. Seigerman stated that this was a valid point and that he'd look into it.

He projected that therapy would probably continue all summer and through the first semester of her senior year in high school. "If we err, it's better to do it on the conservative side—that is, to give her too much rather than too little," he explained. But he also stated that the major variable in determining the extent of therapies would be how she did in school when engaged on a full-time basis. For the time being, the team okayed government as "an opportunity in a non-grade situation, [for the purpose of] seeing where her strengths and weaknesses are." I didn't have the heart to tell them that Caron had already made up her mind to try to complete the class for credit. But as he had said before, it's the high school's business whether or not to extend credit; the hospital team makes recommendations based on its best judgments of the patient's capabilities.

The day of the Kensington Park outing was drizzly, and the trip was cancelled. Community re-ent outings were never again listed on Caron's weekly schedule of therapies. Nor did the structure of OT or RT ever change. In OT she was working primarily on a cross-stitch project, alone. In RT she reported playing Scrabble with her therapist to tedium and planting flowers outside, despite her protests that she hated gardening. While Caron objected often and loudly, at least at home, to the game of Scrabble, we supported its use as a means of attacking her rigid thinking. Rather than exploring all possibilities for a given set (of anything), she was still clutching at the first idea that entered her mind. In Scrabble, for instance, a common statement of hers would be one such as this: "I have an 'I,' a 'C,' an 'M,' and an 'S.' All I need to make 'music' is a 'U.'" And without guidance, she would continue to wait for a "U" to become available.

Caron was making her own social settings, so we didn't worry about community re-entry. She was determined to achieve this and was accomplishing it. While we understood the purpose of Scrabble, we questioned the value of stitchery and gardening. She'd be doing the former at home in her leisure time—indeed, if she *had* any leisure time after travel to and from the hospital for therapies four afternoons a week and studies in the evenings both for school and for speech therapy. Gardening had never been an interest of hers. Sometimes I felt that at least some of the team members found it easier to endeavor to change our daughter into someone she never was before, a stranger to herself and us, rather than to take the time to get to know who she had been and to try to help her get back to being that person.

Toward the end of May, there was another IEPC at the high school, for the purposes of reporting Caron's progress thus far and ascertaining her probable needs for summer and fall. None of the hospital therapists were in attendance; but all of Caron's teachers were, and some potential teachers, as well. Mr. K proudly gave a report about Caron's having marched the two-and-a-half-mile Tulip Festival Parade in Holland, Michigan, the previous Saturday. Caron had expressed a desire to do this way back in rehab, and Sue had started her on marching exercises and worked her up to marching while carrying a heavy object to simulate the bells she played in the marching band. When Caron was discharged, Sue had given her strict instructions to continue the marching, *with* the bells, at least three days per week until the parade, working up to two or three miles. So we had determined the length of Spencer Court, a dead-end road by us: it was one-third of a mile down and back, so she had to be able to do it six to nine times. She practiced faithfully, either before dawn or after dusk, for she surely didn't want to be seen marching all alone, with bells on! But she knew that we wouldn't let her participate otherwise.

On the actual day of the parade in Holland, Larry and I got two or three times the exercise that the band did because, not knowing if or when she might faint or have a seizure, we were determined to do the entire parade route too. Caron would have been humiliated if we marched along with the band, so we'd agreed to blend in with the crowd. For most of the route, however, the crowd was so thick as to be impassable, so after each corner we had to duck back down the street perpendicular to the parade route, parallel the parade route on the next street over, and turn at the following corner to get back to the parade route street. The band was marching at a fast clip, so we had to run fast around each block to arrive at the next corner in time to see Caron marching stalwartly by, and very serious about this endeavor. Other band members smiled when we snapped their pictures, but Caron was grim-faced. This trip was important business to her; she needed to prove that in yet one more way she was okay. In fact, when the parade was over, she would be one of the very few whose faces weren't flushed; a couple of band members even fainted before the finish.

Tulip Festival Parade, Holland, Michigan

Mr. K joked that he'd had a much rougher time of the route than Caron had; and I ribbed back, "Ah, you do okay for an old guy," to which Caron took offense and came to his rescue.

Caron must have tingled all over as she sat through this second IEPC. Sheila Bradley spoke next, reporting on how receptive to learning Caron was, how motivated, how . . . "Well, I *love* having her as a student!"

"We all did," interjected Eric Dahlberg, a teacher to whose class Caron did not return second semester. Others chimed in their agreement; and I assured Eric, who was sitting next to me, that Caron was planning on completing AP Biology second semester of her senior year.

Diana Rose had some nice things to say about Caron's progress in speech and language.

Max Sherman, Caron's Government teacher, stated that while she seemed to do okay with information from the text, he'd noticed her having more difficulty than before taking notes, processing lecture-type information, and performing on tests. *And he only thought her textual understanding was okay because he wasn't at our house when such topics as Supreme Court judges' election vs. appointment were being discussed!* But he was right on all other scores: her note taking was prolific, but she couldn't identify the main idea, so her notes were simply a string of as many words as she could remember—meaningless. Her ability to process auditory information was still severely impaired. And tests, never a strong point before, were even worse now due to problems of memory, attention to detail, logic, problem solving, distractibility, and so on. Despite the struggles he noted, he did say she was succeeding remarkably.

Marty Lindberg, Caron's counselor, was kind, thorough, and efficient, as always. He had prepared a letter stating that Caron would need a summer class and tutoring "to place her graduation possibilities back on track." Barbara Zukowski, our insurance liaison, was at the meeting; and Marty's letter expedited the summer arrangements. She spoke with Art Steele afterward regarding estimated hours to cover the Precalc/Analysis with Trig requirements and his fee. When he had volunteered to do this summer tutoring, he had had no intention of being paid, but tutoring fees were covered by Caron's auto insurance, and we had insisted that he accept payment.

Meanwhile, Diana Rose and Sheila Bradley had lingered behind to chat. They were being very complimentary, and I smiled. "Yes, she's a girl of many hats, isn't she?"

"Mom!" She was indignant. "You know I don't even wear hats!" Yes, she was still very rigid, very literal.

A new problem was hair loss. In May, she lost most of her eyebrows and eyelashes. Her face certainly looked naked before her morning application of makeup, and Caron was also worried because after every hair washing, "gobs of hair" would come out on her brush. She saw Dr. Perlman at the end of May, and he said that hair grows in cycles and that it's not uncommon for a TBI to cause a disruption in the cycle so that no more hair grows for a while. He expected that with the next cycle hair growth would resume. (It did, in fact, but for several more cycles, hair loss followed growth. It would be a couple of years before she would have facial hair— eyebrows being most important—that stayed.)

During the rest of his examination, Dr. Perlman seemed pleased. As he started into his informal memory and cognition test, he noted that her "affect" was still "rather flat": monotone speech, with little expression or inflection. But when he began his "Touch my [moving] finger" and "Touch your nose" exercises, she smiled and loosened up a bit, and he commented that he could see a little more affect then.

During the church social hour Sunday, May 28, we passed out cookies in sandwich bags tied with red ribbons and boasting stickers that read, "Happy 17th Birthday, Caron!" We surely were glad to be able to celebrate this birthday!

Caron never once suggested a party. In recent years, she had had picnics on pontoon boats at Whitmore Lake for her birthday, and all of her friends had gotten to ride in John's seaplane. Before that, there had been several years of pajama parties, always with Aebleskivers (spherical Danish pancakes) served for breakfast the next morning. When she was very young, there'd be cake and presents at Grandma and Grandpa Schreer's house following a day at the Detroit, Lansing, or Toledo Zoo, and then cake and presents at our house the next day, with young friends. Once, when her birthday fell on Memorial Day weekend, we made a weekend of it, camping and taking in the Cincinnati Zoo. And another time we did King's Island. Perhaps the birthday which stands out most vividly in my mind was her eighth, which she planned in detail—including guest list, games, prizes, type of cake, etc.—on the day after her seventh birthday party! Such an organizer! If she had asked for a party this year, she'd most certainly have gotten one, but all she requested was corned beef for dinner and Marv's Bakery white cake. She got both, of course.

On her twelfth birthday, I'd bought her a porcelain figurine of a pretty blond-haired girl holding a wide-brimmed hat with a gold 12 printed on it. The following year she received the next in the series, a slightly taller figurine of a maturing girl of 13. Each year came a new figurine of an older and more sophisticated young miss, but 16 was the last in the series. This year I bought the rest of the set. I set aside 8 and 9 for Christmas of '89 and reserved 1, 2, 3, 4, and 5 as symbolic of her preschool years, to be given to her upon her graduation. Now, for her birthday, I gave her 7 and 10, wrapped together with a note, "Remember, 10 + 7 = 17." She didn't understand. We walked her through the thought process until she seemed to grasp why I'd chosen to give her 10 and 7. Then she opened Larry's gift: 6 and 11. And she had no idea why he had given her those particular two. Instead, she could only say, "Well, this is great! Now I'm only missing 1, 2, 3, 4, 5, 8, and 9!"

Following exam week, Caron began taking the ACT, a test prerequisite for college admission. Because she was certified POHI, she qualified to take the test in a privately monitored situation, and untimed, rather than in a large group on a predetermined day, for a specified period of time. Counselors at the high school must work an extended year in posting grades after final exams, so Marty Lindberg had volunteered to monitor Caron's taking of this battery of tests.

Some weeks later, results arrived. Caron had achieved a composite score of 20 (fifty-seventh percentile overall). It was encouraging to us that she had regained sufficient concentration to perform this well on a national assessment test. Caron was very disappointed, however, for she had had her heart set on attending the University of Michigan, where a composite score of 25 to 29 was the norm for admission. The other colleges she was considering, Kalamazoo and Albion, were accepting students with ACT composites of 23 to 29 and a mean of 24, respectively. With her final grades in Speech, French, Government, and Tutorial, she had moved to the rank of fifth in her class of 381 students. This would be in her favor, of course, but the ACT composite of 20 could be enough in and of itself to justify a rejection from the colleges of her choice. While this was a setback of sorts to Caron, in another sense it spurred her on to better success in therapies and schoolwork during the summer. She was determined to retake the ACT in the fall and to do better.

CHAPTER 24

SUCCESS . . . AND FAILURE

Excepting that Matt made a decision to move to Arizona to live with his father, the summer passed uneventfully. Caron successfully completed her math course with Mr. Steele. And because summer school courses are primarily taken by students who have either previously failed the course or missed it by dropping out of school for one reason or another, Caron actually felt like a star in her Howell Community Schools health class. Unlike her descriptions of others in the class, she was motivated to take it and wanted to do well. And doing well really bolstered her self-confidence. She earned an A+ in this class and an A in trig, and she was eager to launch into her senior year. She wanted to be allowed to try the full load that had previously been planned for this year, and she reluctantly but nevertheless agreed to special education (POHI) support as needed.

With the beginning of her final year of public education came also the necessity for the six-month follow-up neuropsych tests. I was somewhat apprehensive about the results, as her recovery had not continued to be so rapid over the summer as it had been initially, and in the back of my mind I kept remembering Dr. Seigerman's words, "I know a problem is permanent when I do a neuropsych testing six months later and the results are the same." Realistically, I knew that Caron's results would not be the same as they'd been in early March. But I had also noticed a tapering off of improvement and hoped that the test results wouldn't be foreboding of a soon-to-arrive end to her progress. She still had so far to go.

In fact, the neuropsych results showed progress. In attention and concentration, she had progressed from the fiftieth to the sixtieth percentile. In March, her information processing speed had been severely impaired, at two full standard deviations below the mean. Now she was scoring within the mean at 0.5 standard deviations below on the written portion of this test and 0.3 standard deviations below on the oral portion of the test. (In other words, now slightly more than half of her age-mates could process information faster than she could, whereas in March she was in the lowest 2 percent of all age-mates in this area.)

With regard to memory, Caron now showed no retrograde amnesia: her memory for past personal information was unimpaired. Her anterograde memory (capability for encoding, storing, and retrieving new information [i.e., learning]) was assessed. Verbally, she was up from the fifteenth to the thirty-seventh percentile on immediate recall of structured, logically related prose passages. Delayed recall, which is the type of memory most used in real-life situations, was still impaired at the twenty-fourth percentile, but up from her March score of fifth percentile.

In the area of visual memory, recalling simple geometric figures, her immediate recall had improved from the thirty-ninth to the seventy-fourth percentile, and her delayed recall was up from the first to the thirty-second percentile.

Within the wide arena of executive functions, Caron had improved from severely impaired to mildly impaired in such areas as flexibility in attention (the capacity to shift attentional focus in response to changing situational demands) and simultaneous processing, including flexibility, speed, and efficiency in problem solving.

Double vision remained a problem through the
end of Caron's junior year of high school.

During the March neuropsych tests, Caron had still been seeing double and responding with slow fine motor speed and poor control, especially so on the right side, due to the damage to the left hemisphere of her brain. Now, in late August, she demonstrated no anomalies in her visual fields. Also, her fine motor control and speed were unimpaired on both left and right sides and simultaneously.

With the exception of reading comprehension, her academic skills had all shown improvement but were all except math still depressed from her premorbid (pre-accident) status. She was now at the ninety-eighth percentile in math, *timed!* But her reading comprehension had advanced only from the sixth-grade level to the seventh-grade level. Given a 1,000-word passage written at the eighth-grade level, she was able to obtain 100 percent comprehension while reading at a rate of 154 words per minute. At 182 words per minute, however, her comprehension dropped to 60 percent. The neuropsychologist stressed reading comprehension as "the big concern. We are very concerned about this in terms of her workload and going on in school."

Overall, Caron's full-scale IQ was up from 85 in March to 91 now, which placed her at the twenty-seventh percentile for her age, and still out of range for projected success at the college level the following year. But Caron often surprised us with what she could do with how little. We decided to let her try her wings with a full schedule at the high school. The TBI team eliminated OT and RT from her schedule and recommended continued speech pathology to work on impairments in verbal memory, reading comprehension, and problem solving skills. I would be returning to work, so Caron would be taking a taxi to Ann Arbor for this therapy three days each week following her full day at school.

At Brighton High School, Caron was scheduled for Advanced Placement English first hour, again with Mrs. Rose, and we'd spent countless hours during the summer searching through used-book stores in the Brighton and Ann Arbor area for the twenty-five books on the required reading list for the year. How was Caron ever going to succeed in this college-level course with her slow reading pace and her severe disability in reading comprehension? But there was no convincing her to back out of such a stringent course, and Mrs. Rose insisted that she'd be able to do it. Mrs.

Rose was still willing to offer all the one-to-one help that Caron needed, bless her.

Second hour would be World History, normally elected by freshmen, but Caron hadn't had room for it then, due to her electing band and a language. Now she was expressing interest in pursuing a college degree in international relations, so she definitely would benefit from an introductory course in world history, if she could retain the facts necessary.

She would take her required semester of Consumer Economics third hour, leaving this hour open to complete Advanced Placement Biology with Mr. Dahlberg during the second semester.

In the middle of the day, she would have her tutorial hour. If she needed help, or just a respite, she would be able to get it there. Otherwise, she would be given a pass to the media center to study during that hour. While the tutorial had replaced a class in the second semester of her junior year, it wasn't actually replacing one now. In her junior year she had completed the last French course offered at the high school, but because she intended to continue French in college, she had obtained permission to take an evening French course at the University of Michigan during her senior year, so as to stay fluent in her skills and the language. Therefore, she had only planned to take five courses at the high school in her senior year. Tutorial merely filled the empty hour, which she would otherwise have used as a study hour.

Fifth-hour physics was scheduled, and sixth hour: band. For the first marking period, this would be marching band in which she played the bells, as there are no oboes in marching bands. The results of her summer arteriogram had again precluded her playing the oboe, but Mr. K knew how much music meant to her and was willing to let her stay on in the band. A precedent had been set in May, when Caron had surprised him by appearing in the percussion section of the symphonic wind ensemble as they performed a number which had not been included on his program for the evening's concert: It was Mr. K's thirtieth year directing bands in Brighton; so Mr. Pethoud, one of the middle school band directors, had composed a piece in his honor; and for several Wednesday nights, the high school symphonic wind ensemble had assembled, unbeknownst to Mr. K, to practice it. Larry and I had been concerned that Caron might spill the beans, as poor as she was at keeping secrets.

One afternoon, she'd gone out to lunch with a male friend from church. When he had come to pick her up, I had teased him about her voracious appetite; and he'd responded, "Not to worry! I brought my whole bank account!"

Caron was hardly in the door before the words came tumbling out of her mouth, "John didn't have enough money to pay the bill. He told me not to tell you."

She had, however, kept the secret from Mr. K. He was genuinely surprised and flattered by the new piece in his honor, and he grinned upon seeing Caron in the percussion section. Her friends Karen Herbst and Frank Pavlovcik, percussionists, had appealed to Mr. Pethoud to write in a small bell part for Caron. So now she was a percussionist! Obviously, she couldn't step into any of the complicated drum parts that Karen and Frank had been practicing and perfecting for many years, but there were occasional bell parts which could justify her being a part of the band, and when she wasn't needed in percussion, Mr. K could put her to work filing or pulling music for him. Still depressed about not being able to play her beloved oboe, she was nevertheless ecstatic just to be back in the band. Most of her closest friends were here, and music was a special joy in her life.

As foretold by her reading comprehension scores, the amount of reading required in the AP English class was at first overwhelming to Caron, and I saw her slipping into those procrastination techniques again, which only compounded the problem. Also, due to her mild impairment in delayed memory, she had difficulty retaining factual information in World History. Consumer Economics held no meaning for her at first, but once she grasped what it was all about, she was able to build from there, piecing information together because it related; once it was proven to her to be logical, she could proceed methodically without having to rely too much on rote memory.

Physics was an impossibility for her. To solve a physics problem, one must understand the problem and then pull information from several-to-many sources in order to solve the problem. Caron was incapable of doing this. (She couldn't even understand the Sunday comics, because to understand a joke one must be able to see two possible meanings.) And neither Larry nor I had sufficient time or expertise to be of any significant amount of help in physics. Caron spent a lot of time on the phone with Leeann, who was saintly in her efforts to help; but because she understood everything so readily, she couldn't really begin to understand how much Caron *couldn't* understand, so in the end Caron almost always went to bed crying. She'd never forgive us if we insisted on her dropping this class; she needed to determine this for herself. She refused to give up; she had never been a quitter. But she couldn't succeed, either. By the time she was finally so distraught over her difficulties here as to admit defeat, it was too late to drop the course, and she had to stick it out until the end of the semester. She had come face to face with that opportunity to fall flat upon it, and she now was experiencing it.

Meanwhile, with all the reading involved in AP English, the memorization required in World History, and the anguish poured into physics, as well as significant time spent in travel to and from speech therapy, Caron could not cope with the evening French class at the University of Michigan. It wasn't the course content which defeated her. It was her emotional state, primarily due to the physics, and sheer exhaustion. By 7:00 p.m. she couldn't cope with anything, let alone yet another class. She dropped the class after three weeks and began worrying about how she'd be able to fit back into French in college after not hearing it for a year.

Caron retook the ACT and scored a composite of 24, four points better than her June testing. This put her within striking range for acceptance at the colleges of her choice.

She submitted applications to the University of Michigan, Kalamazoo College, and Albion College. Her teachers wrote some fine recommendations, and her grade point average was impressive enough to overcome the somewhat weak ACT scores. She was accepted into all three colleges. Now the dilemma would be "Which one?" She had until May 1 to make her choice. "Fortunately," decision-making was difficult for her, and she'd wait until the last minute to decide. It would give her more time to become better acquainted with each college, and it would give us more time to assess her strengths and gauge the probability of her success at each given college. At the present time, no one who knew or worked with Caron was supporting the large university as a wise choice for her; but maybe she would show improvement over the year such that everyone could again be so confident of her success there as we had been prior to her accident.

Seizure-free six months after her accident, Caron was eligible to renew her driver's license. Through TBI she was assigned an instructor to review driving skills and rules of the road with her. Once this instructor felt confident of her ability to resume driving, he notified Dr. Perlman, who then wrote a letter to the Michigan Department of State. She passed all testing with no difficulty and was reissued her driver's license. Despite this little plastic "permission slip" she proudly carried in her purse, Larry and I worried about her safety as well as pedestrians' safety when she was driving. She was still very rigid in her thinking, had difficulty problem solving, and was unable to cope with sudden changes. She literally displayed tunnel vision when driving, and we had no confidence about what might happen if a child were suddenly to dart out in front of the car she was driving. It was very important to her status as a senior in high school, she pleaded, to be able to drive to school, and after all, she argued, there was an "extra car" sitting in our driveway.

My '76 vintage car had literally died and been hauled away that year, and Larry's was on its last legs too, when we really needed dependable transportation. God was surely watching over us, for at this precise point in time, a welcome sum of money came to Larry that he had not been expecting to receive at this time. With this money we were able to purchase a reasonably priced compact car for each of us without assuming any additional loans. Larry's old car, a '79, while not reliable for daily trips to Novi anymore, was still functional for around the town; it was, in fact, the extra car to which Caron referred.

We agreed to allow her to drive to school and home daily, with many restrictions. To lessen the possibility of unforeseen circumstances, she had to take the same route *every day*—straight down Main Street from our house to the driveway into the high school parking lot. And she had to return home promptly after school let out. This assured us that she'd be well off the road before the elementary schools let out an hour later. No passengers were allowed, as this would be too distracting. This was the extent of our permission for her driving. She accepted the compromise well, as it was all she really wanted to do for the time being. Meanwhile, Larry took her out to practice driving often, especially once snow and ice conditions arrived. Sometimes I'd go along to the parking lot selected for the evening, and I'd cower in the backseat as he instructed her to accelerate, send the car into a deliberate skid, and pull out of it. By the end of the winter she was getting quite good at it, and I felt we could be more confident about her driving the following winter. For the meantime, she had at least earned our confidence as regarded her using the car for spring senior class activities.

With the onset of winter, Caron still needed a winter coat, and she continued to whine about her favorite-ever coat, which had been cut off her on January 28. On a whim, I drove north one day to an outlet mall whose prices are sometimes low due to selling last year's styles; and sure enough, there was the herringbone coat she wanted! I invested in a red scarf and red gloves for color and brought everything home to one delighted little gal who, I then discovered, didn't know the difference between gloves and mittens. Funny how little things would crop up now and again to show that we might never realize what she had lost and not yet regained. She had a terrible time retaining the mitten-glove concept that winter. Subsequently, I bought her a pair of red mittens; and every time she dressed to go outside, we addressed the issue of whether she was wearing her gloves or her mittens. For the duration of that winter, she never was quite sure.

Other misunderstandings became evident in conversations at home, where we could then talk them through, helping Caron derive meanings other than the mistaken one at which she had arrived. Sometimes, afterward, she was able to get a good chuckle out of the whole thing, but during the misconception, she was frequently confused and sometimes even irate. One Saturday, when Larry had gone fishing for the weekend, Caron and I decided to eat dinner out. I made her choose the restaurant and make the reservation, but I suggested seven fifteen as a good time. Within seconds, she was back to report, "That was strange. I told the lady we wanted a reservation for two at seven fifteen, and she said they only take on-the-hour and on-the-half-hour reservations. So I told her I'd call back at six."

Eventually, after many emotional evenings, the horrible semester was over. Caron was upset to have to see the reality of a head injury in bold black print on her semester progress report. In her mind, she had failed at physics: she'd never before in her life gotten a C. The three Bs she had accumulated since she'd been in high school had been unsettling enough to her (and two of them had even been B+'s)! Now she was faced with Bs and Cs on four of her exams, as well as a B and a C as two of her final grades. It was still a report card most kids would have been proud of, with the other four final grades being As and A-'s. We were awfully proud of her. But she was extremely distraught. She had always set her goals high. Back in middle school, she had decided she would be the high school valedictorian. After meeting her friend Leeann and also getting her first B+ (in physical education, where she couldn't master a somersault or a cartwheel—let alone jump rope), she revised her goal to that of graduating in the top ten. Now she was about as down as I'd ever seen her, positive that even her revised goal wasn't achievable.

Coming off the results of her progress report, Caron had to spend a full day at the hospital for her one-year post-injury neuropsych evaluation. She hated the hospital. She hated these "stupid tests." She hated the people who gave them to her and especially today because she hated being so "dumb!" She must have done an about-face when she entered into the testing situation (Aha! She was developing "the capacity to shift attentional focus in response to changing situational demands!"), for the report reads, "The patient's mood was pleasant . . . the patient was friendly and cooperative . . . the patient was willing to be tested and appeared highly motivated and concerned with the quality of her performance. Overall, this appears to have been a valid assessment of the patient's current cognitive functioning."

Attention and concentration were now up to the seventy-fifth percentile. Information processing speed had moved from below the mean to 0.2 and 1.5 standard deviations *above* the mean on the written and oral portions, respectively. (We were sure that it was all that yakkety-yakking on the telephone that had so boosted her oral information processing speed!) By contrast, she tested less well on verbal anterograde memory (capacity for learning) this time: thirtieth percentile on immediate recall (down from the thirty-seventh) and the same score as in August, twenty-fourth percentile, for delayed recall of the prose passages. (The implications of the discrepancy between information processing speed and memory were that she could now carry on a conversation quite well, such that anyone speaking with her would assume she understood most everything—but while she may well have *understood* most everything, she was still not consistent in *remembering* it at some later time. This was particularly not a good sign for a student bound for college, where lectures are the predominant teaching method. In college, it wasn't likely that she would find teachers like Mrs. Rose, who would spend extra time with her or who would be willing to use the teaching method by which Caron had stated she learned best: to be *shown* rather than *told*.) Recall of visually presented stimuli, on the other hand, was up to the eighty-third percentile for immediate recall and the sixty-ninth percentile for delayed recall. If Caron were to succeed in college, she would have to capitalize on her relative strength in retaining visual stimuli.

In executive functions, Caron was, indeed, showing improvement. While recognizing perseverative errors, the examiner deduced that, overall, Caron now had developed some capacity to develop, maintain, and shift strategy in response to changing situational demands. (Yes, she could use the car more frequently now!) The neuropsychologist stated that she was now "at the low end of the average range."

All academic skills were on the rise. She had resumed premorbid status in math. In other areas, while performance was good, she had not yet gained back everything lost. Reading comprehension was up, but speed was not: she could now read a one-thousand-word passage written at a tenth-grade level, with 100 percent comprehension, but only at 159 words per minute. General knowledge too had improved only to a tenth-grade level.

Full-scale IQ was now at 102, up another nine points from five months before. This put her at the fifty-fifth percentile for her age.

Following this evaluation, team recommendations were fivefold:

1.   That she utilize compensatory strategies such as repetition, association techniques, and mnemonics to facilitate her memory of information, because of lingering impairments in her memory for structured information.
2.   That she take advantage of a learning center to increase her performance to a competitive college level. Suggested treatment focus was recall of general information.
3.   That she make contact with a speech and language pathologist in proximity to her college so as to be able to seek assistance if she experienced problems.
4.   That due to residual problems in her verbal memory for new information, she not work while in school as she'd require extra time devoted to applying memory strategies in order to facilitate successful performance.
5.   That she return for another neuropsychological reevaluation in January of her freshman college year to assess any cognitive changes and for further recommendations at that time.

In speech therapy, Jennifer too found Caron to be weak in general knowledge. She gave her exercises to help her learn general types of information, especially in the social studies area, and she showed her how to put association techniques and mnemonics to work for her. But she also recognized that Caron's growing resistance to having to return to the hospital several times a week was beginning to defeat the purposes of her being there. Caron was in need of much more help, and I can't believe anyone could have provided it so well as Jennifer, but as the old adage goes, "You can lead a horse to water, but you can't make it drink." I had long been aware that, in my own profession, if the student didn't *learn*, then I hadn't *taught*, for effective teaching necessitates a learner who benefits. Jennifer was aware of this also and couldn't effectively combat the negativism of her patient, so she began looking for alternate forms of help. She appealed to Sheila Bradley at the high school, and Sheila arranged for Caron to work during her tutorial hour with the high school's career placement coordinator on a computer inventory of basic skills, which would strengthen her vocabulary development and enhance her general knowledge. Additionally, Jennifer was the impetus for Caron's enrollment at the Sylvan Learning Center.

Sylvan did its own diagnostic testing, deriving similar scores to previous tests Caron had taken: her vocabulary was low (forty-seventh percentile); she was poor at sequencing, drawing conclusions, and locating answers; and reading at 214 words per minute, she could only achieve 20 percent comprehension. The Sylvan Learning Center scheduled Caron for a program concentrated on listening strategies and reading and study strategies. Caron was comfortable in this program, especially because it was just a couple of miles from home, and she could drive there herself and not be humiliated by a taxi picking her up at school. Jennifer physically released her to Sylvan but stayed in frequent touch both with Caron and with all concerned with Caron's progress: Larry and me, teachers at the high school, and teachers at Sylvan. In effect, she moved into a consulting and overseeing role. It was a good feeling to know that Caron hadn't simply been turned loose, but that someone was keeping tabs on her and that if she floundered, help was available.

During the five months that Caron studied at Sylvan, she increased her vocabulary, sharpened her listening strategies, and improved her reading rate considerably: by mid-July, 1990, she was reading at a rate of 215 words per minute with 90 percent comprehension. Upon completion of her course of study at Sylvan, she still needed work on sequencing ideas, drawing conclusions, and skimming quickly and accurately; but she had learned much to help her move forward toward her goals.

While Caron was progressing mentally, physical problems continued to need attention also. Following the emergency surgery on her left ear on January 28, 1989, the ear had been monitored closely; and the ear did survive but required further reconstruction in two steps. Now a year later, the scar tissue was sufficiently healed to withstand another trauma, so the first reconstruction of the outer rim was scheduled and took place during Brighton's midwinter long weekend. The second surgery would be early in the summer, right after graduation. It occurred to me that the poor kid hadn't had a vacation in well over a year. So that she wouldn't have to miss any school, every school break had been heavily scheduled with the necessary doctors' appointments, neuropsych evaluations, surgery, and so on.

A new problem surfaced in March. The ravenous appetite initiated in the hospital (once "real food" had been reinstituted) had not dwindled.

Caron continued to eat more food, and more often, than she needed and was never satiated. She was putting on quite a bit of weight: twenty-five to thirty pounds. We had tried several diets at home that had previously worked for Larry and me, but Caron couldn't stick to them, yet denied that she was cheating. She'd claim to have been dieting diligently, but we'd find McDonald's bags stuffed under the seat of her car, as well as plastic takeout containers from ice cream and yogurt shops. Her bedroom wastebasket yielded many a candy bar wrapper on garbage collection day. And some items, although nutritious enough in moderation, we simply had to stop buying in quantity because she couldn't put the brakes on once she started eating them: bagels with cream cheese, granola bars, breads and rolls of any kind, ice cream, and so on. She tried keeping a food diary as a means of alerting herself to her own overeating, but this didn't work either because she denied the truth even to the pages of the book: "I'd do something wrong, and I wouldn't want to write it down," she finally admitted.

Dr. Perlman diagnosed the overeating problem as hyperphagia secondary to traumatic brain injury. Weight gain is not uncommon among brain-injured patients; for a person's appetite control center is, of course, located in the brain and is as vulnerable as any other control center to blows to the head. Caron was referred to a medically supervised behavioral modification program to effect and maintain weight loss.

Because the program was high in cost, the auto insurance company requested a second opinion and designated a psychologist whom they wanted Caron to see before they would agree to pay the cost of this weight loss and weight management program. The psychologist, who had had extensive experience with TBI patients, interviewed both Caron and me and administered to Caron a personality inventory. Her responses on this latter indicated a significant degree of denial, possibly due to a strong need to feel normal, and resulted in her minimizing problems, or "faking good." The psychologist, on the basis of her responses both on the test and in his interview, could not concur with the diagnosis of organic hyperphagia. He felt that her weight gain was, instead, due to lack of follow-through, decreased exercise and activity levels, and a tendency to eat more when emotionally upset. Nevertheless, he recognized these variations as related to her head injury and was, therefore, supportive of the behavioral modification program, as she would need structure and supervision in order to achieve weight loss and maintenance. She entered into the program in April, six weeks before her high school graduation.

Academically, Caron felt much more successful in the second semester of her senior year. In AP English, she was converting Bs (that she had had to struggle for) to As with increasing confidence in herself due to the compensatory strategies that she had learned with Jennifer and the study skills she had learned at Sylvan, in addition to Mrs. Rose's 1:1 help whenever needed. And in lieu of second semester physics, she had decided upon an independent study in music history, with Mrs. Rose. World history dropped from As to Bs, primarily due to increased quizzes and tests; but Caron's confidence would be restored somewhat by a B+ on the exam, as contrasted with first semester's exam C. She'd finished first semester AP biology with an A-, but that had been a full year before (the junior year semester before her accident), so she wasn't too hard on herself for the Bs she was earning now, and she decided not even to try the exam that might have awarded her college credit for this course. She did take the AP exam in English but was not awarded college credit.

As her senior year drew to a close, it became clear that while Caron would not, in fact, achieve her goal of graduating in the top ten of her class, she may not have lost the opportunity to achieve the impetus for that goal: the desire to graduate summa cum laude.

For several weeks in May and June, the *Detroit Free Press* ran a weekly column called They Made the Grade to recognize students who had beat the odds to graduate. Caron received in the mail a copy of this letter, which had been sent to the *Free Press* by the president and chief executive officer of McPherson Hospital in Howell:

May 11, 1990

Dear Free Press,
    I am writing to nominate Caron Schreer, a senior at Brighton High School (Brighton, MI) as

someone who has overcome a significant hurdle to earn her high school diploma this year.

On January 28, 1989, Caron was brought to our emergency room in critical condition after a serious car accident. Our staff stabilized her and she was airlifted to St. Joseph Mercy Hospital in Ann Arbor for further treatment.

Caron sustained a traumatic brain injury and was in a coma for over a week. No one knew if she would survive or if she did, what mental capacities she would regain. But Caron surprised everybody. After . . . 3 months of intensive care and rehabilitation, Caron was discharged from the hospital in mid-April.

Even though others didn't think she was ready, Caron wanted to go back to school. She started back slowly, with the help of tutors, summer school and more therapies . . .

And Caron has triumphed. She will graduate summa cum laude from Brighton High School, on schedule, on June 10th and she will continue her education this fall at Albion College.

Caron has not just "made the grade," she has surpassed it.

Sincerely yours,
Peter J. Schonfeld

Caron was not one of those featured in this column, but the nomination itself was a tremendous boost to her self-confidence: Not everybody saw her as someone who needed to be "fixed"! There were people, people she didn't even know, who recognized her achievements!

CHAPTER 25

RAIN AS A POSSIBILITY

June 10, 1990: As we started off across town toward the high school, I glanced hopefully up at the sky. It had been bright and sunny earlier, but the weather forecast had included rain as a possibility. The sky was still blue, but now—forerunners of an impending storm—large gusts of wind were chasing away the wispy little puffs of soft white clouds. Commencement was scheduled for two o'clock in the open-air stadium where, dozens of times, Caron had marched "with bells on," with *her* band. I prayed that the rain would hold off for just a few more hours.

In the large gymnasium, the prospective graduates were taking their places in seating arranged to simulate the seating on the football field. From here, they would march in orderly fashion out onto the field—unless it rained, in which case the ceremony would take place here; and three-fifths of the spectators, who didn't have tickets for inside seating, would have to return home. I wouldn't be one of those, as I was garbed in black commencement robe and cap in preparation to lead the processional, along with other teachers who'd volunteered to support these students' public education experience to its conclusion today.

I found Caron in the first seat of the second row, chatting with friends surrounding her; and I joined them for a few minutes, took some pictures, hugged Caron, shared a private moment with her, then took my place among my colleagues.

The teaching staff, leading the procession, marched to the seats left of the podium, facing the students' seating. It afforded an excellent vantage point from which to view the excitement of the graduates as they marched first around the entire track and then up the center aisle onto the field, the young ladies in white and the gentlemen in black. Strange, I mused: Even as they now prepared to launch into their lives as adults, they appeared still as girls and boys—marching two by two as they had been required throughout their school years to do whenever they took a field trip away from the school. Now they prepared to embark on a new and very important journey, one that would take them through all of the rest of their lives; and when they left here today, they wouldn't leave in twos, with all of the protection that their parents and teachers had always provided. Today, they would leave independently, each exploring in his or her own way the future. Hopefully, each would find a comfortable combination of success and happiness. I felt assured that Caron would. I had witnessed a powerful will in this young lady; and I knew with certainty that she would achieve the quality life in adulthood that she was determined, and deserved, to have. As did all other parents present, I also knew that the road wouldn't always be smooth. But I was confident now that Caron would be able to make it over the rough spots, for the most part independently. She had made outstanding progress in her eighteen years. She had come a tremendous distance in the past year and a half!

The wind forced its way through the microphone as the student master of ceremonies tried to welcome everyone to this commencement ceremony, but when another student stepped to the lectern to deliver the invocation, the wind calmed just as surely as the students quieted their own restlessness. A reverence fell over the entire stadium as these words floated into the stilled air: "We came into this world blessed with gifts and talents, and as we have grown, You have protected, nurtured, and guided us. You have blessed our families and given them insights to direct us. You have blessed us with teachers who have instilled within us the desire to learn. On this day of celebration, we thank Thee and ask that You continue to bless us. Amen."

I became lost in my own thankfulness. God had indeed held Caron in the palm of His hand. A year and a half before, no one had been able to offer any guarantee that she would be here today and doing so well. But God had worked His own miracles—sustaining her, healing her, and delivering her to family and teachers who could continue His work with her until she was ready once again to take command of her own life.

When I snapped out of my own reverie, the symphonic wind ensemble was already into the bold refrain of "The Stars and Stripes Forever." The wind, as if on cue, rumbled through the microphones, adding a new dimension to this day. One could almost imagine oneself on the prisoner exchange boat with Francis Scott Key during the nightlong British bombardment of Fort McHenry in 1814. The next morning, joyful at seeing that our flag was still there, he was inspired to scrawl on the back side of an unfinished letter the words which would become "The Star-Spangled Banner." Years later, John Philip Sousa would compose this equally inspiring march, "The Stars and Stripes Forever," winning him the title of the March King. And today, as families of students of the class of 1990 gathered to celebrate this occasion, we could enjoy music from moments in our history and look toward these young loved ones of ours making tomorrow's history.

The sky had darkened, and I thought back to not so long before when Dr. Farhat had spoken to me about "the sun passing behind the clouds and then back out again: there'll be bad days as well as good ones—but in the total picture, the good days become progressively more plentiful and the bad ones less frequent." Yes, it was true: I could look back on many bad days for Caron but knew now that the good days had become the victors. Even if it rained on this day, it couldn't dampen our spirits. Caron was basking in a renewed sunshine that warmed and inspired her from within.

"It's a tradition at Brighton High School to recognize the students who have achieved an overall 3.8 grade point average during their high school career," the principal of the high school was now saying. "I recently had the privilege of spending a few minutes with these young people as a group. And I was truly impressed with their warmth, humility, and wisdom—by the fact that they're not only very bright and high achieving but have been contributing members of our school community during the four years that they have been here . . . : Leeann Fu, Lisa Phillips, Matthew Jones, Kevin Bohnsack, Adam Wittman, Beth Baillargeon, Timothy Chang, Lisa Darby, Michelle Hargrave, Connie Krayer, Jennifer Churgin, Timothy Laughton, Sarah Holmes, Caron Schreer." Despite the tragedy of the year before, Caron had triumphed: she had dropped only to fourteenth in her class, maintaining summa cum laude status with a 3.8 GPA—graduating in the top 2 1/2 percent of her class.

Leeann's valedictory address was spunky but insightful, as Leeann is, and we enjoyed it as we have always enjoyed her: "We have been given all kinds of opportunities to learn valuable lessons that we will now be able to apply to our lives. In our classrooms, we were taught the important lesson of *how* to learn. Through preparing for all those tests and doing all those assignments, we learned how to go about learning. We often asked, '*When* will I ever *use* this?' But even if we don't use the specific things or the specific skills that we were taught, we will be able to use the *approaches* and apply them to what each of us will find important to our own individual lives. Through our classes, we have been taught how to learn."

Yes, and Caron had had more classes than most of her peers. She had had extensive therapies and tutoring and study skills classes. Her one-to-one work with doctors and nurses, therapists, neuropsychologists, teachers, and parents had taught her approaches she'd never before have dreamed she would need to use but which were now *her* approaches, her "*how* to learn" techniques. Because of her relative weakness in memory for verbal messages, she needed to take extensive notes in lecture classes. (Taking a tape recorder to class had been suggested, but she refused to do this for fear of being labeled as "different.") Fortunately, Caron had always been a conscientious note taker. Now equipped with new techniques, she was more efficient than ever at note taking. Her anterograde memory—or ability to learn new things—was not so good as it had once been. This is common among head-injured people: learning is harder to do and takes longer. But Caron had learned to utilize such techniques as mnemonics and just plain old-fashioned repetition. She had gotten into the habit of using a computer to retype her lecture notes, thereby combining a visual and tactile-kinesthetic repetition of the lessons, even before the concentrated study of the hard copy. With the money friends and family had given her for graduation, she planned to purchase a computer so as to continue this practice in college.

The sky had darkened increasingly, and as Britt Caldwell stepped onto the podium to present the class gifts, a few isolated drops of rain brushed the cheeks of random participants. Because the class gifts, outdoor benches and tables, were made from recycled plastics and Styrofoam, Britt's speech centered on renewed awareness to the environment. She mentioned the senior float's theme of concern for the destruction of the waterways; and as she did, a drop of rain fell upon her hand, and she smirked appropriately as she looked skyward and gave a little harrumph.

It appeared as though the heavenly theatrics were Britt's doing to accentuate her speech, for when she had finished, the gray began to lift, and soon the sun was shining once again upon this ceremony—just as Dr. Farhat had predicted!

When Caron stepped up onto the podium to receive her diploma, the board member who had been distributing these stepped aside; and I presented my daughter's diploma to her, as parents who are educators in the Brighton Area Schools are entitled to do. What a glorious moment this was! We shared a hug, and then she turned and walked away, ready to make her own place in the world.

Mr. K continues to be a positive role model for Caron
and one of her favorite people, a most important father
figure in her life.

Seniors' Final Act: Caron is in the front, on your left, behind the first of the empty chairs in the front row. Note: She's in her dress flats! No more high-topped turquoise and yellow tennis shoes!

In mid-May, Caron and Larry and I had spent a weekend at Albion College, becoming acquainted with the programs and facilities and getting Caron registered for fall classes. Late in April, she had finally made a decision to attend Albion. We hadn't told her she *couldn't* choose Michigan, but we had reminded her pretty consistently that Michigan offered great graduate school opportunities, whereas her other two choices were only available as undergrad schools. Albion had impressed us as a warm environment where professors were willing to give extra support to students when they encountered difficulties in their studies, and I secretly hoped she'd select this college. It was a difficult choice for her. Each of the schools was known for excellence in international relations, in which she planned to major, in combination with a major in French. In the end, she wistfully put U of M on hold until grad school and selected Albion over Kalamazoo because "it's closer to home." While this reason may have seemed relatively inconsequential at the time, it turned out to be fortunate for us the following fall, when she refused to miss any of the Brighton High School home football games—or at least the half-time shows!

Here's the coveted herringbone wool coat! With Caron is Laurence ('Laurie'), an exchange student from France who lived with us during Caron's freshman year at Albion.

CHAPTER 26

"MY TWO NOTES ARE IMPORTANT!"

Concurrent with her first semester at Albion, Caron took yet another reading and study skills course, which was offered at the college through a private learning skills organization. In this course, she showed a marked increase in her rate of reading textual material, and she improved her reading of light material to 292 words per minute with "very good" comprehension.

Despite Caron's hesitancy, due to her counselor's warnings not to do so, we insisted that she take advantage of the college policy that one course per semester could be taken as a credit / no credit class. At the outset of each of her freshman semesters, she took note of the instructor's outline for the course, including graded weights of attendance, participation, daily and long-range assignments, and tests and exams. By this time, Caron had effectively woven compensatory strategies into her studying methods and was always confident that she was prepared for class. In testing situations, however, she was consistently not doing well and, additionally, usually "clutched" when taking a test, so she'd do even more poorly than she might have. We encouraged her each semester to use the credit / no credit option for the course that would weight tests and exams most heavily. I really do believe that doing so enabled her to worry less about these testing situations, such that she was able to go into them with less stress and was, therefore, better able to concentrate on the task at hand and thereby improve upon her test-taking techniques, as well as her self-confidence and her comprehension. She finished her freshman year with a 3.4 GPA, a full 0.5 grade point above the expected freshman GPA at Albion.

During spring break, she had taken her final neuropsychological tests at St. Joseph Mercy Hospital in Ann Arbor. Because all healing from head injuries is expected to take place within the first eighteen months to two years, the two-year assessment is considered the final analysis as it relates to the head injury. In this analysis, Caron had ceilinged at a full-scale IQ exactly the same as that of the year before. In some areas, she showed some improvement; and in others, scores were depressed from the previous year's scores. The aggregate score of 102 reflected a marked intratest scatter, which meant that she was able to obtain points for some items deemed difficult while missing relatively easy ones. This scoring pattern is indicative of a person with a decrease in cerebral efficiency.

The tests, while indicating overall excellent cognitive recovery, also recognized that she had not achieved premorbid levels, especially in verbal abilities and overall IQ. Additionally, she demonstrated difficulty understanding social situations and practicing problem solving.

Indeed, Caron had gone through two roommates (one at a time) in her first year at college and had finished the year in a single room—where she reported being much less distractible and much better able to focus on her studies. The resident advisor on the floor, having counseled the girls separately and together, reported that Caron had tried harder than either of the other girls to resolve differences; and later, one of the girls' mothers even apologized to me for her own daughter's "despicable behavior." Nevertheless, we did recognize Caron's difficulties in social situations; and Caron, for all that she wanted to believe that such problems were nonexistent, admitted being uncomfortable talking to people, feeling like people were against her, being left out by friends, feeling different from everyone else, feeling anxious, feeling depressed, getting too emotional.

As regards problem solving, Caron was assuredly doing much better; but occasionally, relatively easy tasks would stump her. One weekend, when we returned her to her dormitory, she discovered that she hadn't brought her key with her; so we couldn't unload immediately from the parking lot near the back door, for all doors except the main entrance were always locked to people on the outside. Consequently, we drove up the single-lane half-circular front drive and dropped Caron off at the front door with instructions to go open the back door for us. We proceeded to the parking lot, unloaded the car, carried everything around the back of the building to the west wing back door, and waited and waited . . . and waited. Finally, someone else came along with a key, and we slipped in too. Halfway up the back stairs, we were met by a breathless Caron coming down the stairs. Because she only used the back door when we were picking her up or returning her on the weekends and otherwise always proceeded directly to and from her room and the front door, it hadn't occurred to her that she could have reached the back door from the front door by any other route than to climb the stairs to her top-floor room, pass the room, go on to the back staircase, and descend to the back door!

Occasionally, we'd discover lapses in her general knowledge too, which had gone unnoticed because the topic had not come up since the accident. In Caron's sophomore year at Albion, my husband was discussing world affairs with a friend of hers, who began to answer one of Larry's statements by saying, "Yes, ever since Charles de Gaulle died . . ."

Caron interrupted midsentence. "Oh? Did he die?"

And her brain has not yet found all of the words from her past vocabulary either—only those which she has had occasion to use. Anytime she experienced something for the first time since the accident, she was likely to have to grope for at least one word. Her confidence was by this time so high, however, that she seldom caught these mistakes herself; for she was no longer expecting herself to make mistakes in word choice. For instance, after attending a wedding and observing the bridal garb and traditions, she talked at length about what her wedding would be like. Of course, there were so many positive male role models in her life that she had difficulty finding important positions for each of them in this wedding of her dreams! Dissuaded from designating all of them to accompany her down the aisle, she finally settled upon a special job for Mr. K: "Mr. K will carry my trail." Sometimes everyone around her would smile, and she had no idea why!

One other remnant of her closed head injury lingered: she still slept uncannily soundly. In her freshman year at Albion, she got into trouble for sleeping through the confusion of middle-of-the-night dormitory fire drills! After that, she alerted the RA on her floor of her "problem" (Oh, how I wish I had such a problem!), and they would rouse her—despite the risk of getting a blackened eye for their efforts. She'd get somewhat violent when her sleep was disrupted!

In college, Caron used her computer extensively. This tool became an integral part of her learning technique. She did double-major in French and international relations, raising her GPA every semester and being named regularly to the dean's list. Within a couple of years, she no longer had need for credit / no credit courses.

Caron had been unhappy much of her college freshman year due to roommate problems, difficulty with some of her studies, and homesickness—most of it normal, but perhaps a little attributable to her having been tied to our apron strings in her final year and a half at home, as she had never been before. She applied to the University of Michigan after her first year at Albion, but was rejected. As a rule, U of M doesn't accept sophomore transfers. She could have made application again at the close of the following academic year, for U of M does accept junior transfers, but she didn't. She had become very comfortable at Albion. She had acquired many friends; and once again, they were, in large part, members of musical groups to which she belonged. She played the bells (glockenspiel) in the Albion marching band, the British Eighth, and she was a percussionist in the Albion Wind Ensemble. Also, she played handbells in a church handbell choir. It was in this group that she especially learned the importance of teamwork and cooperation and from where her idea that one person can make a difference blossomed. In Caron's words:

> Perhaps my best example of the contribution one person can make in society is the example of my participation in a church hand bell choir: I hold but two bells, two notes. By themselves, two notes don't make a very interesting melody, and there isn't much room for diversification! So my part becomes a small part of a much larger contribution that is very interesting! Together, my fellow hand bell friends and I can play virtually anything. But I can't do it without them. And they can't do it without me. My two notes are important!

Caron is third from the left.

Caron studied two of her college semesters in France and graduated magna cum laude from Albion College, with majors both in international relations and in French. She has since then completed her MBA at Eastern Michigan University with a 4.0 GPA. She has relearned everything she had lost and now has no problems with common sense and learning new things. Caron has been happily married for fourteen years and lives with her husband, John, and their yellow Labrador, Mataya, in Howell, Michigan. It was in Howell, just eleven miles northwest of her hometown, Brighton, where she lifted off on her first helicopter ride. Ann Arbor, seventeen miles south of Brighton, is where that helicopter landed—and where Caron now works. She is employed by a business firm for which, among other things, she handles all of its French accounts.

Caron's very life has been an inspiration to many within our circles of family, friends, and acquaintances. We look forward to many more years of observing her contributions to this world. She truly has made it a better place already, but she'll never stop trying to make an even larger dent in the hearts of mankind. She's special in this way and is living proof that a head injury needn't mark the end of a person's productivity. She and I hope that this book will be an inspiration to you and that its messages enrich your life.

We do wake up from nightmares. This family did. Most importantly, Caron did.

Laurie, Matt, Caron, and Judd, Christmas of
Caron's freshman year at Albion College

AFTERWORD

"Two roads diverged in a wood, and I— I took the one less traveled by, And that has made all the difference."

Robert Frost

O ur family, our daughter especially, can look back and say honestly that we do not regret the divergent path Caron chose to recovery. At the same time, I must say that I would not recommend this type of journey for most people who sustain a head injury. In brain injury rehabilitation facilities, you will find the professionals best trained to ensure that each TBI client reach maximum potential.

While inherently driven to succeed, our pre-accident daughter was compliant with authority, always respectful to her teachers. The insult to her brain seemed to manifest itself in a new headstrong quality that proved counterproductive to all of the best intentions of her most qualified therapists. Her focus on a return to school stunted her desire to please these people she had come to love at the hospital. She was extremely blessed that she was so loved by her teachers at Brighton High School that they were, without exception, willing to learn about head injuries, adapt their teaching styles to meet her needs, and make sacrifices to accommodate her in any way.

INDEX

While all numbers reference the indicated indexed topics, highlighted numbers signal definitions and/or explanations.

A

attended the afternoon sessions of, 207
mood swing after, 234
most challenging were the exercises
in, 214
playing lots of games in, 205
visual tests in, 133
otorhinolaryngologist, 270
overeating. *See* hyperphagia

P

paralysis, 23, 24, 80, 249
paramedic, 24
paranoia, 263
PCA (patient-care assistant), 135, 229,
269
penicillin, 33
percentages, 221
percentile, 220, 221, 222, 252, 255, 294,
303, 305, 307, 314, 316, 317
Perlman, Owen Z., MD, 91, 92, 93, 128,
130, 133, 151-154, 174, 175-176,
183, 189, 191, 194, 195, 216, 219,
251, 253, 255, 270, 301, 311, 319
perseverance, 183, 244, 286
perseveration, 158, 200, 245
personality changes, 118, 264
phonetics, 137
physiatrist, 91, 174, 270
plastic surgeon, 36, 270
Pleur-evac, 39
pneumonia, 77
Pneumovax, 152
POHI (physically or otherwise
health impaired), 128, 254, 304-
305
post-traumatic memory. *See* PTA
(post-traumatic amnesia)
Precious Moments doll, 61, 69, 78, 85,
148

stopped to admire the, 61
premorbid, 307, 315, 332
pressure sores, 77
problems
behavioral, 263, 264, 274
age-inappropriate behaviors, 264
agitation, 42, 95, 168, 170, 263
apathy and indifference, 263
belligerence, 263
impulsivity and disinhibition,
263
irritability and decreased
frustration tolerance, 263
lability, 263
paranoia, 263
rigidity and inflexibility, 222, 231,
263,
self-centeredness and
egocentrism, 264
psychosocial, 264
problem solving, 231, 256, 307
difficulties with, 154, 233
specifically working on, 231
prophecy, self-fulfilling, 51
psychological/psychiatric problems
aggression. 263
anxiety, 26-27, 66, 148, 263, 290
depression, 263, 265, 275
flat affect, 263
psychologist, 319, 326
psychosocial problems, 264
PT (physical therapy), 133, 135, 178,
225, 243, 267
attended the afternoon sessions of,
207
cancellation of morning, 144
fabulous experience in, 235
PTA (post-traumatic amnesia), 153, 167,
176, 194,
pyloric sphincter, 71

CPSIA information can be obtained
at www.ICGtesting.com
Printed in the USA
BVHW051045160623
666053BV00003B/260

9 798887 750415